PARADISE

ONLY HALFWAY TO PARADISE

Women in Postwar Britain 1945 – 1968

Elizabeth Wilson

TAVISTOCK PUBLICATIONS
LONDON AND NEW YORK

I'm only halfway to paradise
So near yet so far away.

BILLY FURY

First published in 1980 by
Tavistock Publications Ltd
11 New Fetter Lane, London EC4P 4EE
Published in the USA by
Tavistock Publications
in association with Methuen, Inc.
733 Third Avenue, New York, NY 10017
© 1980 Elizabeth Wilson
Typeset by Inforum Ltd, Portsmouth
Printed in Great Britain by
J.W. Arrowsmith Ltd, Bristol

British Library Cataloguing in Publication Data

Wilson, Elizabeth, *b. 1936*
Only halfway to paradise.
1. Women – Great Britain – Social conditions
2. Women – Great Britain – History – 20th century
301.41'2'0941   HQ1593

ISBN 0-422-76870-7
ISBN 0-422-76880-4 Pbk

Contents

Acknowledgements

I am grateful to Melanie Stiassny and Angela Weir for their extensive help and support during the writing of this project. Amongst many individuals who discussed particular aspects of the period with me, and for whose help I am also grateful are: Michèle Barrett, Marie³ Betteridge, the Birmingham Feminist History Group, Aileen and Colin Boatman, Zelda Curtis, Richard Hill, Mrs Hazel Hunkins Hallinan, Mary McIntosh, Meg Stacey, and Cicely Turner.

CHAPTER ONE

Introduction: the woman on the pillion

The starting point of these reflections was usually a feeling of impatience at the sight of the 'naturalism' with which news-papers, art and common sense constantly dress up a reality which, even though it is the one we live in, is undoubtedly determined by history. In short, in the account given of our contemporary circumstances, I resented seeing Nature and History confused at every turn, and I wanted to track down, in the decorative display of what-goes-without-saying, *the ideological abuse which, in my view, is hidden there.*
(Roland Bartheş: *Mythologies*)

To look back from the embers of the seventies to Britain as it existed twenty or twenty-five years ago is to look back at what now seems like an oasis of plenty in a desert of crisis and insecurity. There was the period of the late 1940s when the Labour government was thought to be building a socialist Britain: there was the consensus of the 'classless' fifties; there was the hedonistic Britain of the 1960s. True, the optimism was always ambiguous. It was ambiguous in proclaiming leisure and affluence at home while using the doom language of the Cold War abroad. There was always an undertow of uncertainty – about Britain's economic performance, and about the moral condition of the people. And although affluence may be recalled as a past reality, to sift through the collective memory stored in stale newsprint and old photographs is to wonder whether the oasis was not always a mirage, receding as the traveller in time approaches it. For examined more closely, the remembered certainties of the period dissolve into a series of contradictions. There was more than one 'society' and many moods in Britain between 1945 and 1968.

There was, all the same, a real attempt to build consensus, to bring the whole nation within the wide circle of citizenship (with the exception of a residual dross of deviants, who were needed to mark the boundaries). And women were central to this scheme. Women's traditional role as a stabilizing and civilizing force – the ideology of the Victorians – was made a lynchpin of consensus now that women too were citizens. If women had become equal citizens, then the need for feminism – or so at least the argument might run – had gone, and there certainly was a widespread belief that feminism was dead: 'a spent force', 'today, the spirit of the old pioneers is so dead it seems a miracle that it ever existed', 'here are the mass of women still preoccupied with their love-life, clothes, children and homes . . . (their) dreams of power . . . the femme fatale rather than the admin. grade of the civil service', 'a freedom relatively few women seem to want'.

Yet uneasiness continued to surround the topic of the 'position of women' in postwar Britain, and although I had originally set out to discover why there was no feminism between 1945 and 1968 – had believed the myth, in fact – it always seemed improbable that a powerful social movement and political crusade, an expression of the aspirations of (potentially) half the population, should suddenly have withered away, only to reappear as suddenly, and – as it seemed – as if out of nowhere, around 1970. Yet so pervasive was this myth that it has become the 'facts' for the women's liberation movement too.

In my attempt to account for this 'demise' of feminism I found instead that I was studying the creation of myth and ideology. There was a continuing uneasiness surrounding the subject of the position of women after the war, a feeling, only dimly acknowledged, or not acknowledged at all, that really women were *Only Halfway To Paradise*. There was, somewhere, still a knowledge and an understanding that women remained in many ways subordinate and oppressed. But myth and ideology operated to create a counter-belief that feminists had achieved their goals and that women had gained entry to Paradise. Brigid Brophy (1966) spoke of women as resembling the animals in a modern zoo; the old cage bars of legal disability had simply been replaced by 'zones of fierce social disapproval' through which it might be as hard to step, but which confused because they were invisible. Ideologies constructed a confusion in which it became difficult to know how to voice these feelings of oppression – they became Betty Friedan's 'sickness without a name' (Friedan 1963). I have tried to reconstruct these ideologies and recreate the atmopshere in which they flourished, rather than simply describing, discussing, and analysing them from the vantage point and with the hindsight of 1980.

Only Halfway To Paradise is then a study of the construction, in the postwar period before the emergence of the contemporary women's liberation movement, of a discourse or discourses that created the ways in which a category 'women' was understood. While it is neither a study of postwar political and feminist movements, nor of sociology, social policy, literature, or the media, I discuss separately a number of these disparate areas in trying to show how they operated together and all contributed to the making of a received wisdom about the position of women. In the end the attempt failed, and something broke through that was called women's liberation. This burst the whole parameter of the previous debate. Yet it is itself equally complex, contradictory, and many-faceted.

The orchestration of consensus on the position of women in postwar Britain was the achievement of a deceptive harmony out of a variety of noisy voices; and perhaps that false harmony says something about what ideology might partly be. The orchestration was harmonious – in a peculiar way – in covering up what was really a silence; what was not said: the absence of women battered, of women raped, of women sexually attracted to women, of women in revolt, of women despised, of women despairing. And the most significant political lesson, perhaps, to be learnt from this exercise in harmony was the role played by progressives. In the creation of what was objectively a conservative consensus, reactionary ideologies took over the progressive ground.

In the process some of these progressive forces were themselves transmuted. If I started by asking the question: where did feminism *go to*? I was left at the end almost asking: what *is* feminism? For after 1945 women who thought of themselves as feminists were, in the name of something they still called feminism, tending to discredit the feminism of an older generation, so that they as well as anti-feminists must be held responsible for the situation in the sixties when to many young women like Sheila Rowbotham: 'Feminism . . . meant shadowy figures in long old-fashioned clothes who were somehow connected with headmistresses who said you shouldn't wear high heels and make-up. It was all very prim and stiff and mainly concerned with keeping you away from boys' (Rowbotham 1973:12).

Political and social movements do change and regenerate themselves, and this is sometimes done by jettisoning the very beliefs that originally formed the core and heart of the movement. Look at the changes in what 'socialism' has meant and does mean, for example. Look at how, after 1945, conservatism as expressed by the Tory party rejuvenated itself precisely by getting rid of many of its more centrally 'conservative' beliefs (Gamble 1974) (which are now of course coming back into fashion), and at how in the early 1960s progressive Church of England leaders paradoxically more or less abandoned the idea of a deity in their attempt to retain belief.

What happened to feminism after the war and the ways that then developed of discussing and defining 'women' has therefore a significance beyond the position of women. For the lessons of that situation might be applied to other movements, situations, and groups. Although, too, it is written about Britain, myths and ideologies and discourses of persuasion operate everywhere.

OVERVIEW – 1

Britain has changed enormously – fundamentally – since 1945. So have other countries. The British have been unusual, perhaps, only in their failure politically and culturally to recognize and adapt to change.

Britain's stand in the Second World War, the moral victories of Dunkirk and the Battle of Britain especially, shielded her from recognition of an economic decline in relation to other industrial countries that had set in long before, and has since accelerated. Psychologically we did not assimiliate – and perhaps the existence of the National Front shows that we still have not assimiliated – a precipitate loss of wealth and power and the vanishing of an empire. True, the moment of euphoria that marked the ending of the war and the Labour Party's landslide victory in 1945 was shortlived. Hopes of a new and just society were quickly followed by economic crisis and we became a poor relation of the United States, dependent on her largesse. But in the fifties we swung into the boom, and at the time of the Suez crisis in 1956 the *Daily Express* headline, 'It's GREAT Britain again' seemed to voice the feelings of the nation.

Postwar Britain seemed, paradoxically, culturally most conservative during the years of Clement Attlee's Labour governments (1945 to 1951). Many intellectuals then completed their flight from prewar socialism into a new Bloomsbury of the private life, while John Betjeman spoke for all conservatives when he described the horrors of the socialist utopia:

> I have a vision of the Future, chums,
> The workers' flats in fields of soya beans
> Tower up like silver pencils, score on score;
> And surging millions hear the Challenge come
> From microphones in communal canteens
> 'No Right! No Wrong! All's perfect, evermore'.

> (Betjeman 1958:128)

This was a potent fear, inherited at some removes from Kafka, and popularized by Aldous Huxley and George Orwell. Individualism was precious in this 'socialist' society, in which the vision of socialism had become a nightmare. Once, socialism had meant the glorious Soviet Union, and for many the Soviet Union had represented the utopia on this earth. Now it meant Siberian labour camps, it meant torture and liquidation, it meant the mass purges of the Stalin era to which so many individuals, victims and survivors, testified painfully in the late forties. And if Stalinism was used in the construction of a negative case against socialism (Anderson 1964), the 'affluent society' destroyed the positive arguments for socialism which had seemed so compelling in the thirties.

Yet in the fifties Britain was a conservative society described in the rhetoric of a radical ideology. This held out in one hand the image of social revolution achieved, a political achievement, while with the other it demolished politics as a valid activity. Anthony Crosland of the Labour Party (in imitation of the American prophet of permanent affluence, John Kenneth Galbraith) hymned the glories of the post-capitalist society that had achieved social justice without socialist dogma, repression, or violence. This was a society in which simultaneously socialism had been achieved and the need for it negated. Socialism was vilified, yet somehow, simultaneously, Britain *was* socialist.

In fact, this socialism was the socialism at which Marx and Engels had sneered long ago. It was not the socialism achieved by a working-class seizure of power, but an illusion of socialism achieved by contriving to make all classes *appear* 'middle class' – 'a bourgeoisie without a proletariat'. Alternatively, the working class was seen as preserving its essential attitudes and culture while having been drawn within the magic circle of citizenship. Either way, the result was a consensus society, and the idea of consensus was built round the absent centre of socialism. This was a society in which the old battles were no longer relevant. Affluence made class war unnecessary. With the emancipation of women achieved, the sex war became meaningless too. With politics redundant, there came an opportunity for private life to flower.

Full employment did transform the lives of many whose parents' lives had been pinched and drab. The proliferation of tempting consumer goods held out the promise of a new kind of life, one in which the old puritanical virtues of restraint and of thrift rewarded ceased to seem relevant. The old ways of the classes began to crumble, and the conventions governing personal life came under prolonged and continuous reassessment too.

And, while economic rifts were pronounced healed, cultural rifts seemed to widen. The materialism of the affluent society began to give cause for alarm, for while it was said that there had been a social revolution, no-one ever suggested that there had been a cultural revolution. While it had been no surprise if in the twenties and thirties the working man with his low wage or his miserable dole had seldom raised his sights (according to the stereotype at least) above pub or dog track, in the fifties more was expected of him. Fat wage packets and universal free education would, it was hoped, produce a new universal culture. This failed to appear, and the regeneration of progressive politics in the sixties came partly out of the search for a progressive culture that would include the working class, and out of an attempt to understand what many felt to be the cultural wasteland of affluence. As the *New Statesman* (2.1.60) put it:

> 'Few tears will be shed for the fifties. Cynical, meretricious, selfish, the decade made the rich richer, the poor poorer. To the advanced countries of the West it brought unprecedented prosperity, achieved largely at the expense of the vast and growing proletariats of Africa and Asia. . . .
>
> The Tories imprisoned homosexuals and prostitutes – and pacifists. But they allowed the striptease joint and the drinking club to multiply. . . . They made Britain into a windfall state, a national casino with loaded dice; and when violence and dishonesty increased they clamoured for the birch.'

It is customary to contrast the 1950s with the 1960s, the former as a period of right-wing traditionalism and cultural stagnation, the latter as a period of 'permissiveness' and innovation. Such stereotypes contain some truth, but the contrast is also misleading. For one thing, change is never simultaneous nor uniform, and 'swinging London' might always be a far cry from Wigan or Ipswich (not to mention the American mid-west or southern Italy). There was in any case considerable continuity between the 1950s and 1960s. The further penetration of capital into areas such as clothing, pop music, and leisure and entertainment generally was an extension of what had been happening in the fifties, as were changes (for example) in the use of birth control. To measure time in decades is after all simply a convenience, and there is no material reason why the flavour and atmosphere of 1957 should be radically different from 1964. Yet on the other hand certain moral barriers had to crash before the exploits of the Rolling Stones and of David Hockney could be dramatized in the mass media. There had been hedonistic life styles in the fifties too, but at least Sir Bernard and Lady Docker, with their gold-plated Daimler, were a *family*.

But however the morality of the sixties is judged, the economic froth was not the healthy froth of a new fermentation but the sinister bubbles breaking on a stagnant canal to hint at what might be rotting under the water. And that carcass was British imperialism. John Lehmann might describe as a good joke in the early fifties the suggestion made by a dinner party guest who 'developed fantastic theories . . . about the coming invasion of Britain by coloured peoples from former colonies culminating in a negro prime minister in 1984' (Lehmann 1966). But the arrival in Britain of immigrants, at first mainly West Indian, was never welcome. After the Notting Hill (London) race riots of 1958 (and there were disturbances in Nottingham as well) the sixties saw the beginnings of immigration regulations. I am not suggesting that one was the direct result of the other; but it was only in the 1960s that governments (regardless of party) began to react in an organized way to the last irony of empire when 'bringing it all back home' meant West Indian and Asian communities in our old metropolitan and industrial centres. Racial prejudice on the other hand had always lain beneath the surface. Oswald Mosley polled more votes in North Kensington in 1960 than either John Tyndall or Martin Webster was able to command in the East End of London in 1979. There was a long build up to Enoch Powell's 'rivers of blood' speech in 1968.

Immigrants were only one minority amongst others. Because most or many sections of society had by now achieved new standards of comfort, there was a sharpening of resentment amongst the more marginal groups still left beyond the wide circle of consensus. As the gap between the classes appeared to close – however false this appearance was – that between the generations gaped more widely, and later 'youth' were joined by immigrants, homosexuals, prisoners, and the mentally ill – all the stigmatized. For reasons that it will be one purpose of this book to explore, women did not appear as a distinct group until the very end of the period.

The 1950s were characterized by the organization or further development of a number of pressure groups around particular issues (Weeks 1977), often not political in the traditional sense, though they were good liberal causes. Kingsley Amis was attacked by radicals such as Dennis Potter for having described the attachment of the middle-class radical to 'good causes' as political romanticism. Amis was not, though, altogether out of line in sensing a gap between traditional working-class politics and the new issues:

> 'The issues which will attract our contemporary romantic are non political ones, or ones that are not in the first place political; the colour bar, horror comics, juvenile delinquency, the abolition of capital punishment, the reform of the laws relating to divorce and homosexuality.' (Amis 1957:13)

Initially the reformists used traditional pressure-group tactics, and their work achieved a measure of change in the sixties. It was only after changes in the laws relating to abortion, to divorce, and to homosexuality that these issues were, right at the end of the sixties, to be made dramatically political by groups who despised absolutely the polite methods of their predecessors. These had, all the same, created the preconditions necessary for the emergence of more militant sexual liberation groups and of the women's liberation movement.

CULTURAL CONTRASTS

To underline the continuity between 1945 and 1968, the economic logic of decline, and the persistence of underlying inequalities, is not to deny the subjectively felt and real changes in custom, manners, and culture. The whole atmosphere, for example, of the years immediately after the war was caught in the Festival of Britain, which took place in 1951, right at the end of the first period of postwar Labour government. The Festival summed up the achievements of the Labour Party in office in terms of the universal provision of health and educational facilities and the benefits to the employment structure of the nationalization of certain key

industries. Yet its vision was also inward-looking, an embodiment
of a romantic, non-expansionist nationalism – not Empire but
Commonwealth, an illusory community of equals (Banham and
Hillier 1976). The Festival promoted a particular style, a superficial, spindly modernism that could be superimposed on highly
traditional structures. There were the same dining and bedroom
suites for the traditional family; but their shapes were
'scandinavian' or 'contemporary'; there were the same suburban
houses revamped with abstract wallpapers and pastel paints. The
Festival was also obsessed with monarchy. And Coventry
Cathedral, built at the same period, epitomized the importance of
the conventional Anglicanism which was still lurking behind the
pseudo-modernity. In being only superficially modern and much
more deeply traditional, the Festival accurately reflected the
'socialism' of postwar Britain, and also prefigured the 'materialism' of the 1950s. It managed to reflect both the cautiousness of the
outgoing Labour government, its depoliticized, cosy family
version of socialism, and the 'you've never had it so good' of the
Tories who were about to be returned to power, and who would
soon be masterminding the Coronation even as they continued to
dismantle the empire.

In 1967 and 1968 two cultural events took place which marked
the distance Britain had come since the Festival. Neither the
Dialectics of Liberation Congress, nor The Obsessive Image, the
opening exhibition at the expanded Institute of Contemporary
Arts, was comparable to the Festival in scope or aims. The
Dialectics of Liberation was organized at the Round House by
radical psychiatrists and the new left; the Obsessive Image was
consciously *avant garde* and was intended to encourage the
experimental arts in Britain. But both events expressed a spirit that
had not existed in the Britain of 1951.

At the Dialectics of Liberation in July 1967 an attempt was made
to link explorations of individual disintegration and family violence with the madness of genocide, the war in Vietnam, and the
racism of the West. Liberation was liberation from the destructiveness of modern civilization, and this required the linking of mass
revolution with the personal liberation of the individual. The
attempt to reassure and domesticate, so clear in 1951, and so

weakening, had completely broken down. Now, even the individual self seemed in danger of disintegration, but that had to be faced and even accepted before any kind of new self or new world could be built.

The Obsessive Image ran from 11 April to 30 May, 1968. The exhibition made clear how far we had come from the romanticism of John Piper and the whimsy of Emmett the cartoonist, the artists of the Festival of Britain. Their work was superseded by an art of cruelty, of madness, of the absurd. Obsessions with commonwealth abroad were pilloried in the painting 'I'm Dreaming of a White Christmas' by Richard Hamilton, which made a sick joke out of a fleeting resemblance between Ian Smith and Bing Crosby; obsessions with family and stability at home were parodied in a kitsch collection of soft dolls modelled on Mae West, Shirley Temple, and W.C. Fields, bizarre and slightly sinister.

In 1953, the year of the Coronation, the young Queen Elizabeth had offered a reassuring symbol of family which had drawn the nation into consensus (Shils and Young 1953). In the same year the tragic Rosenbergs went to the electric chair for having allegedly betrayed the secret of the atom bomb to the Russians. They were represented as a family in which the natural sexual hierarchy was disturbed, since Ethel Rosenberg was popularly portrayed as the more dominant and fanatical partner, and in which 'unnatural' parents indoctrinated their children into the Communist creed. So out of the cruelty of their ordeal, McCarthyism created a powerful ideological image of the dark side of family.

In the Obsessive Image the themes of nuclear family and of family of nations were replaced by themes of sexuality and madness, and the imagery of mass communications. The exhibition emphasized the disintegration of the official culture in the face of challenges to the status quo and the onslaught of pop imagery – and this was an imagery to which all classes had access.

WOMEN IN POSTWAR BRITAIN

There was no mention of women as oppressed at the Dialectics of Liberation. On the contrary, Stokeley Carmichael, who was present, displayed contempt for white women, and for many black militants the white woman was simply the property of the white man – which made her rape a political act. Such attitudes aroused guilt as well as anger in white women.

The new left was trying to develop a genuinely working-class culture, which Raymond Williams (1961), for example, believed should be built on the characteristic social institutions of the working class, the trades unions and other organizations of the labour movement. But again, what place was there for women in this working-class culture?

And yet women were persistently perceived as the touchstone for the social revolution, their situation as *the* paradigm of Britain's successful experiment in non-revolutionary democracy and the gradualist approach to equality – of class as well as sex. The revolution in the production of small-scale consumer durable goods affected women first and foremost in creating or expanding opportunities for their employment *and* in – supposedly – easing their lot in the home. Somehow the installation of hoovers, refrigerators, electric mixers, and washing machines was held to have given housewives *equality*. Quite apart from the fact that only a minority of women had access to these aids, while many still laboured at home without even hot water, there was an awful complacency about this myth. Yet it was a widely accepted myth, and even Edward Thompson, whose immense and scholarly account, *The Making of the English Working Class*, gave full weight to the contradictory effects of the industrial revolution on the position of women and discussed at some length both the subordination of women and the struggles for women's rights, apparently believed it: 'It was to be a full hundred years before (industrial) differentiation was to bring returns, in the form of labour-saving devices, back into the working woman's home' (Thompson 1968:455). In any case, even where electricity did replace muscle power, most of the burdens and responsibilities of domesticity remained untouched. But this was just one example of how myths and stereotypes proliferated so that the woman wielding the hoover could become the symbol of the social revolution that had obliterated inequality; for women were above all *classless*. The commentary of one journalist-economist summed up the prevailing view perfectly:

'The refrigerator and washing machine revolution accompanied by the concurrent disappearance of servants from middle-class homes has had one other social effect. . . . Up to the late 1930s the gap in enjoyment and opportunity for tolerable living between middle-class and working-class women was the great inequality in our society. The former had human maids, the latter not even mechanical ones. Nowadays it is quite literally true that the solicitor's wife with three children and no mother's help in Wimbledon has a life which, so far as claims upon her time are concerned, is no different from that enjoyed by a steel-worker's wife with the same size of family in Middlesborough. Each has the same modern equipment in her kitchen and vacuum-cleaner cupboard. Part of this equalization of living standards . . . has come about because of a fall in the solicitor's wife's standard; no amount of mechanical slaves quite makes up for the disappearance of the housemaid and nanny. But a very great deal of it has taken the form of a rise in the standard of living of the steel-worker's wife. . . . This deproletarianization of the working-class woman (is) the most remarkable social change in Britain in recent years.' (Macrae 1963:992-93)

It would be more accurate to call this process the 'proletarianization' of the middle-class wife. (And the women she lost as servants were lost to her husband in the shape of secretaries, waitresses, and clerks.) It is hard at this distance in time to understand how an equalization of drudgery ever came to be misunderstood as emancipation. Yet for Macrae and many others it was. And women were to be more equal too in acting as symbol for the nation's pleasure:

'What I cannot understand is how the rich man in his Jaguar or professor in his Austin can look out upon the housewives' tight trousers on motorbike pillions and family side cars on a summer Saturday morning rolling along the road to Brighton and fail to feel a great and surging sense of poetry welling up within him at the sight of them.' (Macrae 1963:98)

In an appropriately sexist way the housewife's sexy bottom clad for leisure symbolized Britain's postwar new deal. A simple, even a vulgar image you might think, and patronizingly cast in the language of the common man. But it was a complicated matter to create the imagery of womanhood on which this writer drew. *Only Halfway To Paradise* explores the construction of this archetypal postwar 'woman' and also her disintegration.

CHAPTER TWO

A new ideal for women

The girl's mother was . . . an uncultivated woman and above all a foolish one, who had concentrated all her interests upon domestic affairs. She presented the picture, in fact, of what might be called the 'housewife's psychosis'. She . . . was occupied all day long in cleaning the house with its furniture and utensils and in keeping them clean – to such an extent as to make it almost impossible to use or enjoy them. This condition, traces of which are to be found often enough in normal housewives, inevitably reminds one of forms of obsessional washing and other kinds of obsessional cleanliness. But such women . . . are entirely without insight into their illness. (Sigmund Freud: *Fragment of an Analysis of a Case of Hysteria* – *'Dora'*.)

When Harold Wilson in the sixties called for a return to the 'Dunkirk Spirit' we all knew what he meant. One Nation! All pull together! Dunkirk – a defeat – is recalled as our finest hour, for Britain at the lowest ebb of the war had been – at last – one nation. In the early postwar years it was hoped to retain that sense of national community.

The Second World War had total domestic impact *because* it was global. Its effect, in emphasizing at once Britain's world imperial role in defence of democracy, and the breakdown of class divisions at home, was contradictory. We were able to congratulate our-selves on our strength and status as a world power; at the same time we had a vision of ourselves as unsolemnly egalitarian.

The British housewife with her ration books, gamely carrying on through the queues and bombing so that family, community, and nation should hold together, symbolized our national spirit. Princess Elizabeth became an ATS girl and was photographed underneath a lorry; even the Queen had to 'make do and mend'. The housewife was *the* heroic figure of the Second World War, and additionally so because she was often a worker as well. The 'glamour band' twisted round her hair served both to protect it as she bent over an industrial war machine, and, as its name suggested, glamorized the utilitarian. She flashed sexy legs beneath short skirts, yet her square shoulders suggested a military purpose. She kept the Home Front going and the Home Front was what the boys were fighting for, for that and for the welfare state that was promised when war was over. This wartime housewife was lapped round with state solicitude and with honeyed praise from the press; a striking contrast with her neglect in prewar years.

That women became more emancipated during the Second World War has become a cliché of the popular literature on that war. Set against this are feminist suspicions of a drive to reverse this emancipation and get women back into the home when hostilities ended; by closing the nurseries, by dismissing them from their jobs.

But there was compromise and confusion rather than a con-spiracy (Riley 1979). Few doubted that full employment (for men) and better social services (for women and children) should be priorities; and there *was* anxiety about the family. The welfare state was certainly perceived as supportive of family life, and was intended both to ease the lot of the breadwinner and to improve the situation of his dependants. Yet it supported this particular form of family life – a breadwinner and dependants – simply because no-one thought of any other way of doing things. The return of the soldier from the battle front was the return of the Father to hearth and home, but – whatever else could it have been? In any case, hopes for a better world for men, women, and children masked, to some extent, the conflict, uncertainty, and division over women's place.

THE NEW COMMUNITY

A complex act of reconciliation between the classes was being attempted after the war. It was hoped to preserve the sense of one nation that war had created, by building a new and democratic community, of which Commonwealth was the expression overseas and the welfare state at home. If full employment was to end the class war, the other side of this coin was to be the community in which family life would find its full expression.

The ideal of community that was promoted had a history. Hatred of the teeming cities it had created was a curious feature of the ideology of industrialism throughout the nineteenth century (Petersen 1968; Platt 1969). The Romantics expressed it. So did the Pre-Raphaelites and William Morris, Ruskin, and Charles Kingsley. The Christian Socialists created a Settlement movement to bring back the qualities of the medieval community to the slums. The founders of Guild Socialism took their alternative into the Labour Party. Writers and reformers compared the stress and vice of urban life unfavourably with the solid, enduring, humanistic values of the medieval village community and the rural social order as they imagined it to have been. City life was associated with breakdown, 'anomie', and absence of solidarity, with the loneliness of the individual lost in a crowd of fellow beings who were yet strangers and alien to him, a nightmarish situation explored by Kafka, by the Chicago sociologists, and in the novels of Raymond Chandler and Mickey Spillane.

As early as 1909 the Town Planning Act had provided for suburbanization as the answer to the problems of the city slums; in 1898 Ebenezer Howard published a book setting out the idea of the garden city' (Howard 1946). But although a number of the Fabian and social democratic planners whose ideas found expression in the Welfare State after 1945 favoured the garden city as an ideal, it was only in a very watered-down form that this ideal influenced postwar planning or the new towns. Council housing and postwar council estates became a major project (pursued by Labour and Conservative governments alike) but in their planning and as they actually exist represent for the most part the negative idea of a hatred of cities rather than the 'positive' (although equally questionable) vision of the garden city.

The postwar experiment of the New Towns was a conscious attempt at community building. Architects before the Second World War had admired Soviet (and also Mussolini's) planning and had been interested generally in total concepts of planning and in the 'total environment' – of which an ocean liner might provide the perfect example. In this tradition was the building of Keele University after the war. Built on a campus away from any town, Keele quickly came to be known as the 'red' university, not on account of its students' politics, but because the whole concept of planning that had gone into its making was perceived as Russian – Communist.

However, this sort of 'totalitarian' architecture soon became unfashionable. Instead, the idea of the working-class street with small, cottage-type houses became an ideal. It was perceived as a kind of spontaneous development that faithfully reflected the cosy solidarity of working-class life in the urban 'village'; it was truly 'English' because it seemed so unideological – when of course in fact the narrow streets of Bethnal Green and Bermondsey had been created by Victorian jerry builders, as had the back-to-backs of Leeds and Manchester. But like some of the descriptive sociology of working class life after the war, this view expressed a reassuring and rather sentimental view of working-class life.

Postwar environmental planning, which attempted to combine these two ideals, was not particularly successful. The high hopes of the new towns – today they are called simply 'overspill' – foundered partly on shortages, partly on the conservatism of their planners. Also, while they were officially held to express the ideals of the garden city, in practice they became massive outlets for the giant retail chain stores that were thrusting out their tentacles in all directions. The pedestrians-only shopping precincts were meant to make life easier for the housewife. They also brought an amazing uniformity to the centres of huge conurbations, to old market towns and to new towns alike.

New towns were criticized for their preservation of class-segregated housing and for their absence of fun and entertainments. Even William Beveridge, who was one of their most ardent supporters, chairman of Newton Aycliffe New Town Development Corporation, and author of a short pamphlet defending the New Town concept, admitted that they lacked that very 'sense of community' they had been built to provide, while claiming that they would end urban blight and the wrong use of land.

To create the sense of community Beveridge looked to voluntary action and therefore, implicitly, to women. Within the framework of the welfare state, rising standards of living and more leisure for all, voluntary action would flesh out the community and create the mutual services that went to the making of community feeling. Ideals of community and ideals of voluntary service were related to a conception of women's place in the postwar world.

THE NEW IDEAL FOR HOUSEWIVES

Beveridge expressed much sympathy for the 'tired housewife'. He certainly sincerely believed that his Report, with its special insurance provision for the housewife as part of a 'team' with her husband, replaced and *resolved* her former condition of dependence. But he also felt that these insurance principles should be supported by a range of services in kind, and that *no* housewife should be expected to slave away without domestic help:

> 'The housewife's job with a large family is frankly impossible, and will remain so, unless some of what has now to be done separately in every home – washing all clothes, cooking every meal, being in charge of every child for every moment when it is not in school – can be done communally outside the home. This is part of the general change in the direction of reforming effort which is long overdue, from improving conditions and giving more leisure to the paid worker in the factory, to improving conditions and giving more leisure to the unpaid worker in the home.' (Beveridge 1948:264)

Domestic work was very widely seen after the war as a problem for which interventionist solutions were needed. In the first days of the Attlee administration, when for a brief period there was an euphoric – or horrified – belief that socialism had arrived, it was hoped that the State would intervene with schemes to help the housewife, schemes that would be as much a part of the welfare state as the education or health services. But economic crisis and the atmosphere of the cold war were rapidly operating against all 'socialist' ideas, and the social services remained a service for times of crisis. But for a time there was talk of domestic help for all wives, and of nurseries, not to enable women to seek paid work, but to make it possible for them to shop in peace, or simply to have a rest, or an evening out with their husbands.

Beveridge's main interest, in fact, was in the gaps in the welfare state that still created problems *for* women, rather than in the contribution women could make to the filling of those gaps with voluntary work. Arguing for voluntary action in a society of increased leisure, he seemed uncertain whether the housewife *would* have more leisure in the 'social service state'. She had benefitted from improvements in the home environment – piped water, electricity, modern kitchens; and through the decline in family size. At the same time her work had been increased, because she had become 'an auxiliary labour force for the distribution of consumer goods'. Domestic labour was recognized to be a mammoth task. In November 1945 a general practitioner wrote to the *Daily Telegraph* to comment on the physical strain housewives had suffered as a result of the war: 'Many are strained to breaking point by long hours of work without assistance and standing in queues in all weathers to serve food of sorts for those dependent upon their patient exertions.'

The problem of the tired housewife could, though, become the problem of the inadequate (working-class) housewife, especially in the wake of the wartime and immediately postwar revelations and anxieties about evacuees, neglected children, and 'problem families'. The work of Brentwood, a home in Lancashire for neglectful mothers, showed this ambivalence towards such women – were they simply exhausted, or were they inadequate? 'A housewife and mother may at times be as much in need of rehabilitation to do her job as a crash-shocked airman or injured workman.'

The harsh conditions under which almost all women now laboured in the home were *noticed* because of the plight of the middle-class housewife bereft of nanny, cook, and housemaid. As

Naomi Mitchison (1979) remembers, the inter-war years had been unique for at least some women in offering them the opportunity to take up a career, for which they were freed by the still plentiful supply of servants. It was a transition period in this respect. Suddenly and drastically this situation was changed. As one middle-class housewife said:

> 'It's very hard when women have at last come into their own and realize they have got a brain and there are things they can do other than domestic work, if they never have time to sit down and read a book. I don't want sherry parties or to play bridge, but your brain just becomes stagnant when you do nothing but housework.' (*The Listener* 11.4.46.)

It became clear, too, that housewives were discriminated against in quite specific ways. During the war there had been fury because women were compensated for war injuries at a lower level than men. Now, because they were classed as sedentary workers, housewives received fewer clothing coupons than many workers, and fared badly over rations.

Beveridge was typical of a whole ideology when he used the imagery of factory work and fighting men in his descriptions of the housewife. This was a general imagery used by social democrats to give dignity to women's labour. In 1946, at the Labour Party Conference, the Fabian Group announced that 'housewives are rapidly becoming the oppressed proletariat of the modern world'. Margaret Cole demanded a Housewives' Charter. Ian Mikardo on the other hand:

> 'wanted to take the drudgery out of housework with kitchen floors designed to obviate dirt and dust, like those in modern factories. He suggested communal central kitchens with a hot meals delivery service, properly staffed nurseries and central play rooms, district heating centres and even communal sewing centres.'

That housework was drudgery to be taken out of the home and that home-making was a career were *not* two contradictory themes, as might superficially appear, but were both part of the same argument, that in order for it to be a worthy career for all

(including middle-class) women, the *drudgery* must be removed so
that the more stimulating and rewarding aspects of child care and
beautification of the home could have a higher priority; the theme
of 'the housewife's home is her factory' was *part* of the broader
theme of 'homemaking as a career' so popular after the war. In
November 1945 both Margaret Bondfield, pioneer woman trade
unionist, and Eva Hubback, a feminist who had followed Eleanor
Rathbone into the family endowment society and then became
caught up in the postwar panic about the declining population,
were writing in the *Sunday Times* on this theme, both arguing that
'domestic work in a modern home will be a career for educated
women' – a short-lived attempt to make it a career for *all* women.

The housewife's role *as housewife* was a source of anxiety because
universal free secondary education and the labour shortage might
tempt women into paid work at a time when the fears of a declining population reached panic proportions. By the year 2035, it was
predicted, there would be only four million Britons. The extinction
of the race might be the price of women's independence.

Women in a Man's World, a pamphlet written by Ruth Bowley and
produced by the Bureau of Current Affairs (a body supported by
the Carnegie Trust), summed up these fears and the ideological
solution being offered. Ruth Bowley's solution – but she was only
reiterating what was being said on all sides – was a 'new ideal' for
women. The drudgery was being taken out of housework, and this
was to free women to become the 'friends and companions' of their
husbands. 'This is what mothers must learn.' There were new jobs
in the community that women as mothers could and should do, for
example, in planning and helping run, in a voluntary capacity,
schools, clinics, and leisure facilities:

> 'Above all the housewife – the wife and mother – should be
> acknowledged as a full and responsible member of the com-
> munity. . . . Her home is her factory, her husband and children
> a worthwhile job. . . . Let women make the most of their hard
> won freedom, not to build an independent women's world, not
> to escape from their family responsibilities, but to aim at build-
> ing a *family* world in which men and women act together for the
> sake of the children . . . a world built . . . on *partnership*.'
> (Bowley 1949:13)

Yet there was a dilemma, as the evidence presented to the Royal Commission on Population, which reported in 1949, makes clear. Many women and women's groups gave evidence to this committee, and amongst all classes of women there seemed to be a recognition that a large family meant endless drudgery for mothers. The evidence of the Standing Joint Committee of Working Women's Organizations defended women for the ways they had found of dealing with their plight (p. 148):

> 'In a period when nearly every section of workers was enjoying improved conditions through trades union and Parliamentary action those who were engaged in the biggest single occupation in the country – that of housewife and mother – began to buy a little leisure with the tin opener and birth control. If this has led to unfortunate results for the community, the community must bear the blame for its neglect of the worker in the home.'

This expressed a kind of trades union consciousness about women working in the home. The sexual division of labour was not questioned, but it was recognized that women's domestic work *was* work and it implied social democratic measures to bring women in their domestic role – as paid workers had been – within the wide consensual circle of full citizenship.

DOMESTIC SERVICE – A SKILLED CRAFT

The second way in which the government attempted to assist women in their domestic role was in trying to restore the popularity of domestic service as a job. The Labour Government tried to introduce proper training, wages, and conditions of service. Violet Markham undertook an enquiry into domestic service as a field of work, and in 1947 an Institute of Houseworkers was opened. Ernest Bevin persuaded Dorothy Elliot, Chief Woman Officer of the National Union of General and Municipal Workers, to run it; and it continued to be almost ritually discussed at the women's TUC for years, although the number of domestic workers dwindled steadily. Even after the huge falling off during the war there were in 1951 still 750,000 women in domestic service, but by

1961 this number had fallen again to a mere 200,000.

In the spring of 1946 Violet Markham chaired a radio discussion on the subject of domestic work. She herself expressed the official view. She spoke of domestic work as an appropriate training for (working class) married life, of housework as a 'skilled craft', and the need therefore for training in it, and she insisted that it was women's work and not men's. She summed up the discussion with a little homily: 'Above all we want family life with its loyalties and affections to be made safe, and *home* – not an apartment house or a residential hotel – the centre of it.'

Yet the women who participated in the discussion, working-class domestic workers and middle-class housewife-employers alike, somehow raised a dissentient note. They did not entirely agree amongst themselves, as this exchange about clothes makes clear:

> 'I don't see why we shouldn't say "would you please wear something dark and plain?" In the average factory you are told what to wear – either dungarees or a white overall. If a girl is going out and she's dressed up to the nines with her hair full of little flowers, she's doing it for a purpose. I want my baby taken to the park, not to the barracks.'
>
> 'It isn't right to keep another woman deliberately in the background by making her dress in dark colours.' (*The Listener* 11.4.46)

The women *did* agree that the relationship was a personal and delicate one, with the domestic worker possibly at the mercy of her employer's whims. But when Violet Markham wondered if it were possible for one woman to employ another, they united against officialdom to speak of women co-operating and offering mutual help – invoking the kind of sisterhood or at least neighbourliness that had been so much valued during the war.

It seemed clear that none of the women wanted the sorts of schemes the Government was proposing. The middle-class mothers expressed suspicion of servants who were too highly trained – it would no longer be possible to tell them what to do – and the working-class women knew they could not afford them and anyway would have preferred the help of their menfolk to the (means tested) assistance of state-paid domestics. This was not surprising, given that in general the working-class wife and mother had never taken kindly to the prewar schemes, such as they were, for assisting her in times of difficulty. It was considered unnatural and even dangerous to have a strange woman to replace you if you were in hospital or lying in, and many women had felt criticized or undermined even by the feeding of school children, which like all such schemes had historically been associated with charity and/or the Poor Law.

Alison Settle's women's column in the *Observer* in the years 1945, 1946, and 1947 returned repeatedly to the problem of the absence of servants, and to the variety of schemes that were floated to deal with the problem. Towards the end of the war the ministries concerned had privately discussed the idea of a new corps of domestic workers, but the internal correspondence was mainly obsessed with what uniform these women should wear and whether the now redundant women fire-fighters' uniforms could somehow be pressed into service in this new context (Public Records Office 1941-1946). Then there was a scheme for foreign girls to be allowed into the country to provide a more properly regulated scheme than the 'au pair' system that later grew up. But it all came to nothing.

If the plans for better domestic organization came to nothing so too did the hopes many women had that the wartime British Restaurants should stay open in peacetime in order to give women a break. In this case it was the men who put the boot in. In May 1947, when there was a 'housewives debate' in the House of Commons, Jim Callaghan said: 'Ought we not to reverse the principle of public feeding now and put more emphasis on private feeding?' And in general men seemed opposed to the whole idea of giving up their home-cooked meals. Herbert Hodge in a radio broadcast said:

> 'I am the chap who has to eat the grub. When I was going to work (before the war) the wife would give me some sandwiches, and she would say: 'here you are, you know what you've got.' You do not know what you get in some of these restaurants.' (*The Listener*, 5.11.46)

while another speaker on the subject cherished the special personal service that only a wife can give:

> 'I am looking forward to eating all the meals I can at home. That is the only place I really enjoy a meal. You know how a woman can cook when she is cooking just for two or three people; you can't compare it with all this mass produced belly fodder.' (*The Listener*, 18.4.46)

And on this issue the men certainly won the day.

THE BIOLOGICAL URGE

The population debate, and the tenor of the Report of the Royal Commission on Population, show clearly how difficult it would have been, even had there not been a strong demand for women's labour, to legislate for women's return to the home. The Report did not, and could not, result in legislation, but does demonstrate the delicate balance social democracy at this period maintained between conceptions of freedom of choice and an orientation towards rational planning. On the one hand, it was in the spirit of the Labour Government to emphasize women's right to work. On the other, there was a strong concept operating then of responsible citizenship, and eugenicist arguments could still at this period be used, provided they were clearly distinguished from any taint of Fascism – which could partly be done precisely by the emphasis on free choice rather than compulsion.

The Mass Observation survey *Britain and Her Birthrate* (1945) sums up the progressive dilemma. Its authors were haunted by what now read as rather racist fears: 'Only those who want the white part of the human race to decrease and eventually to disappear can legitimately claim that the survey is partisan.' They *were* partisan in fervently advocating larger families. Apart from the obvious economic arguments in favour of raising the birthrate and thus avoiding an aging and therefore less productive population, they used other moral and eugenicist arguments. It was suggested, for example, that the lowered birthrate was due to a 'devitalization' of the race. They quoted the Peckham experiment, a pioneer health centre in South London. Workers there claimed to have found a high percentage of infertility, of non-consummation of marriage, and of 'rarity of connection'. These families, they concluded, were inadequate: 'Just as this type is work shy because of relative incapacity, so they are sex shy for the same reason'.

The moral arguments centred round the idea of the 'selfishness' of not having a large family. The authors of the survey, furthermore, believed that this 'selfishness' could be reduced to one main factor; that the modern woman found the continual routine involved in rearing children 'boring and limiting', and that in refusing multiple maternity women were expressing their (irresponsible) wish for a good time and for independence.

Even the Standing Joint Committee of Working Women's Organizations, which took an emancipationist attitude towards the position of women, betrayed a suspicion of feminism as having encouraged the idea that paid work was preferable to the role of wife and mother:

'The bearing and rearing of children is peculiarly women's work, and it has never had adequate recognition. Some of the earlier feminist propaganda with its emphasis on equality in fields of work previously closed to women merely on grounds of sex, tended to perpetuate the idea that the work of a home and children is of less importance than work outside the home, and a less eligible career than most others, and may have helped to influence some women against motherhood. This attitude was found chiefly in middle-class and professional groups and is probably less usual today than it was twenty five years ago. Our working women's organizations have never accepted it, and while insisting on the right of women to follow the work of their choice they have worked for many years for a better status for the work of the wife and mother in the home.' (Oral Evidence:12)

This group also, in their oral evidence, expressed a fear of the *biological* effect on women of improved education and opportunities:

'Q: You say it is possible that the development of intellectual and other interests as a result of the greater educational opportunities and wider spheres of work open to women may have led to a weakening of the biological urge and the desire for children. . . .

A: People say: 'The desire to have a family can be satisfied with one or two children instead of five or six'. . . . Professional women and middle-class women who were the spearhead of the feminist movement before and during the last war . . . tended, instead of lifting the status of women in the home doing work in which there was no competition with men, rather to think that . . . being a mother of children was something beneath the intellectual woman . . . as if the work of a home is so menial as to be beneath the dignity of an intelligent human being. . . . This prejudice still exists, but I think it is not so prevalent as it was among the teachers who instructed me in my youth and who were very keen feminists. . . .

Q: The people who expressed that point of view were people who never had a biological urge at all?

A: That is just about it.'

(Oral Evidence:16)

Yet just as Mass Observation had no concrete suggestions as to how the birthrate was to be raised, so the Report itself and those who gave evidence to it were hampered by their complex, contradictory ideology. Compulsion never seemed feasible. A number of witnesses did suggest that contraceptives might be banned, and in the context of statements which make it clear that in the late forties the idea of marriage as including sexual fulfilment had not become received wisdom as it did in the fifties. But to ban contraceptives would not only have smacked of Nazism, it would also have offended eugenicist assumptions, for eugenicists had always *supported* contraception so that the reproduction of the race could take place in a planned fashion and the overbreeding of the unfit be prevented.

Although, too, the Report mentioned the changing status of women in nineteenth-century Britain as a cause of the declining birthrate, a simplistic assumption that has since been questioned (Banks and Banks 1964), those who wrote the Report felt it necessary to reject explicitly any attempt to limit the role of women in modern society: 'We think that a deliberate effort should be made to devise adjustments that would render it easier for women to combine motherhood and the care of a home without outside activities.' So the Report resembled a number of later social policy documents, most of which showed an essential ambivalence and inhibition in the face of the economic and demographic changes that were taking place. Response and adaptation to changes that had already occurred never transformed themselves into strong policies that could have changed the future course of events.

WOMEN AND THE WELFARE STATE

In 1950 the *Manchester Guardian* published the report of a questionnaire Eva Hubback had sent out to housewives. Some of the women's groups who had given evidence to the Royal Commission on Population, the Association of Midwives, for example, had sent out questionnaires to their members, or to groups of women with whom they came in contact in their work. Some of these women's groups expressed in strong terms the view that women had a right to work if they wished; but the evidence they gleaned from their researches suggested that poverty in the form of poor housing and low wages were more likely than a desire for paid work to deter them from producing a large family. The British Federation of University Women found from a questionnaire sent to 227 women that only 10 per cent desired more career opportunities for married women, although 46 per cent of those who answered were in fact engaged in paid work after marriage.

Eva Hubback too found that the women who replied to her questionnaire wanted changes in the direction of more domestic help rather than paid work; 40 per cent said they did *not* want a job, although 50 per cent said they felt unduly bored. Only 20 per cent had help in the house from husbands, even at weekends, and one women commented: 'I don't think it is realized to what extent the generally higher standard of living involving better care of children, more elaborate meals etc. has increased the strain on housewives.'

Richard Titmuss, speaking in 1952, was aware of this problem

(Titmuss 1963): 'We have extended the number of years that a child spends at school and added to the psychological and social responsibilities of motherhood by raising the cultural norms of child upbringing.' These writers, however, led the debate off into a different direction.

The Labour Government was unable to solve the problems raised by the whole question of domestic work. In the fifties the consumer boom led to an emphasis on the ways in which small electrical gadgets had solved the problem – the myth became that housework hardly was housework any more. This was, supposedly, the alternative to increased state services, and the trend was of a piece with the general tendency of Conservative governments not to make a direct attack on the welfare state, but rather to let welfare services imperceptibly run down while wages pushed upwards meant immediate rewards for work which perhaps seemed more attractive. Nevertheless the full implementation of a welfare state after the war in some ways foundered on the inability of the state to make provision for domestic work. As a *Daily Telegraph* journalist put in it 1956: 'The welfare state is based on the drudgery of women'.

THE HOUSEWIFE'S INCOME

If the housewife's role was to be dignified as labour, how was it to be remunerated? This was another problem impossible to resolve. For years feminists in Parliament, notably Edith Summerskill, campaigned unsuccessfully for ways to ensure that the non-working wife received her just portion of her husband's income (and this aspect of income maintenance proved a knotty problem in the discussion of divorce as well). The investigative sociologist, Ferdynand Zweig, suggested in the fifties that the 'housekeeping money' was *the* dark secret of the British family, and that it was as much neglected by researchers as it was the subject of coy equivocation on the part of both husbands and wives. He also discovered that, amongst the older generation at least, the housekeeping allowance was still often referred to as 'wages for the missus' – a significant phrase.

In 1952 Michael Young published one of the very few pieces of work in this neglected area. He made three important points, although little notice was taken of them. He suggested that men did not pass on to their wives as large a proportion of their income as it was supposed they did. To support this suggestion he referred to a wartime survey. This had shown that poverty was usually measured in terms of the incomes of whole families, but that if you measured it in terms of the actual sums of money wives received from husbands for themselves and their children, there was a proportionately greater amount of poverty. He also looked at the work of Charles Madge, of Mass Observation, who had carried out a survey of *Wartime Patterns of Saving and Spending* (1943). Madge had detected signs of a 'full scale revolt' against the whole system of housekeeping allowances. Michael Young argued that the financial burden of having an extra child fell not, as was always assumed, on the family as a whole, but on the mother and the previous children: 'Some husbands behaved like employers. They did not increase their wives' "wages" as the size of the family increased.'

In this context the fierce debate in the House of Commons over the question of which marriage-partner should receive the children's allowance was important. Eleanor Rathbone carried the day in arguing that men would not deduct money from the house-keeping allowance to offset the gain to their wives of the family allowance, but no-one troubled to find out what actually happened.

Michael Young then turned to the question of inflation and the welfare state. He argued that a period of full employment and inflation would lead to a loss of real income for wives, who, like others with no union strength and like those on fixed incomes, had no protection against rising prices. Housewives – the familiar theme – were 'unorganized workers'. However Michael Young did also argue that the welfare state had provided an important hedge against inflation for mothers of families – food subsidies, family allowances, school meals, and the NHS had all reduced their financial burden, and had been in part financed by husbands who were being heavily taxed on their consumption of drink and tobacco.

Michael Young's third point was one that had already been made by Richard Titmuss. Writing in *The Listener* on Family Problems in the Welfare State (15.3.51) he expressed his astonishment that in the period of 'the so-called welfare state' there should have been an increase of possibly 200 to 300 per cent in the numbers of women working.

There was some recognition at this time that wives were going out to work because an independent income was more satisfactory than waiting on a husband's generosity. Willoughby suggested:

'Her husband gives her a housekeeping allowance but it is rare in this country for the woman's share in running the common enterprise of home and family to be recognized by a personal allotment from her husband's income. Her personal expenditure has to come out of the housekeeping or she has to ask her husband for the amount she requires for a new dress or hat. The higher the economic and social status of a woman before marriage the more she may resent this situation. She continues to work, in part, for the psychological satisfaction of remaining independent.' (Willoughby 1951)

This went further towards recognizing the position of the married woman without an income than did the popular explanations of the mid fifties, when it was usual to say that a wife worked for luxuries or to avoid loneliness.

The wife's income *was* an issue when changes in the law of divorce were proposed. In the later fifties and the sixties the question of maintenance was a vexed one. Frederick Le Gros Clark, speaking at the Eleanor Rathbone Memorial Lecture in 1963, even questioned the whole popular concept of marriage as a partnership, since that implied some legal sanction and agreement around the economics of the situation whereas, as he pointed out, a woman's marriage contract said nothing about this. He felt that surprisingly few wives minded about their precarious financial situation. But objectively it was an unstable area in family life.

EDUCATION

Since it was impossible to increase family size or improve family life by legislation or coercion, planners and ideologues placed their faith above all in education. Universal free education for the young adolescent created an opportunity to educate girls for their future roles as wives and mothers. John Newsom became famous – and has been anathematized by the women's movement – for his views on this subject. Yet his fullest statement of them, in *The Education of Girls* (1948), merely elaborated on what feminists such as Eva Hubback were saying after the war.

Newsom accepted an academic education as suitable for a few really gifted girls. His plan reflected the view found also in the 1946 Equal Pay Report that at the top of the intelligence scale male and female intellects and abilities converged, and that they diverged more and more towards the bottom end of the scale.

The very limited vocational training he outlined for the girl of 'average ability' was intended to train not just a new generation of working class mothers and wives but, hopefully, a new generation of the domestic workers then in such regrettably short supply. As in Aldous Huxley's *Brave New World*, there had to be a helotry of Gammas and Epsilons to service the Alpha brains. As also in Huxley's fantasy of the future, some at least of the Alpha women were to be a sexless élite, or honorary men.

For despite Newsom's snide, smooth assumption that equality for women had arrived, he actually believed that the biological differences between men and women were of such importance that those women who minimized these differences came into some sort of eunuch category – or something even more sinister, as his paranoid invectives against lesbian schoolmistresses made clear. The brave new world he looked for was a return to pre-suffrage days: 'The future of women's education lies not in attempting to iron out their differences from men, to reduce them to neuters, but to teach girls how to grow into women and to relearn the graces which so many have forgotten in the last thirty years' (Newsom 1948:109). In the general postwar discussion about education the special problems of girls were lost in the general problems of the tripartite system, and also because at that time Newsom was voicing a view with which many, even, who had fought for the emancipation of women, agreed.

In the fifties the number of schools expanded, the idea of the comprehensive school was being fought for by progressive educationalists, and Newsom's position remained unchallenged, although there was occasional uneasiness. An article in the *Economist* (22.6.57) described a large new secondary modern school for girls in South London, and asked: 'Is there too ready a flight in the new schools from academic subjects into pottery, cookery and dress-making?' And the writer concluded: 'The familiar argument about its being better to be a happy craftsman than a struggling professional worker can be carried too far, and Britain's new schools must guard against using this argument to justify the malnutrition of minds.'

Government reports on education proliferated in the late fifties and the sixties and the Crowther Report (1959), which dealt with the education of those between fifteen and eighteen years of age, caused the subject of the education of girls to surface once more. This was in the context of the 'brain drain' and the general failure of Britain to compete successfully with other countries. If the most highly trained doctors and scientists were setting out for greener pastures, usually in the United States, who was to replace them? Immigrant doctors from the Commonwealth could not entirely solve this problem since their command of English was sometimes poor; and their presence in any case raised the whole question of British ambivalence (or outright hostility) to immigrants. It began to seem as if only an élite of women could fill this gap.

An explosion of discussion in the correspondence columns of *The Times* and the *Guardian* showed how much bitterness and prejudice still surrounded the whole issue. Professor Marisfield Cooper, Vice Chancellor of the University of Manchester, criticized the Crowther Report for its conclusions on the education of girls. He argued for more resources to be spent on the education of women, and for a greater value to be placed on the special qualities and gifts which the 'able' woman could bring to society. On the other side M.J. Jacks, former Director of the Oxford University Department of Education, saw a 'radical' approach to the education of girls as being one that would train them for their role as mothers and for the 'leisure' that always seemed to be just around the corner in the fifties. It was for women, he argued, to prevent the decay of family life.

Many 'career' women wrote to *The Times* in indignation to argue against this view, and although some merely suggested that a degree is not wasted on a married woman since it enhances her upbringing of her children, there were others who recalled the fight women had had to get the right to education at all, and who restated this right in the face of what seemed like a backlash. As Elizabeth Pakenham put it: 'The battle has not been won. The pendulum shows signs of swinging back to pre-emancipation days.'

Out of this debate came a pamphlet, *The Education and Training of Girls*, prepared by the Women's Group on Public Welfare, and published by the National Council of Social Service in 1962. Its authors worried less about the academic girl than about the mass of young women in the permissive society. Education was seen as a barrier against the degeneration of moral standards of which there was evidence in the increase in veneral disease amongst the young, and in the commercial exploitation of sex. This was a liberal document and stressed the need for more women scientists and engineers as well as more women nurses and teachers. Yet it did not question women's 'dual role' and it also clung to the idea of women as moral saviours in the face of declining standards of behaviour. Implicitly this invoked a double standard, in which men had natural sexual urges which it was for women to control.

In 1964 Nancy Seear and others published a book, *A Career for Women in Industry*? which again attempted to find ways of attracting more girls into the scientific and industrial fields. Yet in the schizophrenic way so characteristic of the whole period, this could go alongside the Newsom Report (1963), in which John Newsom, as chairman of the Committee reporting on the education of the 'less able' half of secondary school children, could continue to impose his views on a new generation of schoolgirls. By this time his views on the doubtful value of an academic education for girls were out of fashion, and met with highly vocal disagreement when in September 1964 he published an article in the *Observer* in which he suggested that girls should concentrate on flower arranging and other 'feminine' skills. Yet liberal indignation was largely focused on the effect such proposals would have on middle-class women – or grammar-school girls might be a more accurate way of putting it – and Newsom's views on 'vocational' – by which he meant domestic – education for the average girl (or rather the working-class girl), whose vocation was still seen as marriage and family, were not only still widely accepted, but even became more popular as sex education was introduced into schools after 1956 under the rubric of 'preparation for parenthood' – in theory for boys as well as girls, but in practice aimed primarily at the female half of the school population.

As early as 1948, Newsom wanted to promote women's role also as consumers – which could still in the forties be linked with notions of Britain's imperial commercial role. He included a whole chapter on 'woman as purchaser' in his book, and envisaged education as guiding working-class girls towards middle-class standards of taste. His list of what he disliked in interior decoration reads like a compendium of kitsch, ranging from imitation crocodile to teapots in the shape of cottages, and he connected good taste to our continued supremacy as a trading nation. His standards of taste were in the functionalist 'true to materials' tradition that had originated in the Bauhaus and were to form one important element in fashions in design in the fifties, but the intensity with which Newsom spoke of the threat to British standards suggests an underlying fear of the Americanization so dreaded as well as the old fear of a flooding of the market with cheap goods from the third world:

> 'Our standards of design, and therefore our very continuance as a great commercial nation, will depend on our education of the consumer to the point where she rejects the functionally futile and aesthetically inept and demands what is fitting and beautiful. . . . Woman as purchaser holds the future standard of living of this country in her hands. . . . If she buys in ignorance then our national standards will degenerate.' (Newsom 1948:103)

THE CONSUMER SOCIETY = THE NEW COMMUNITY

In 1960 the girls who had been fifteen in 1945, and who had been encouraged to think of marriage as their future career, were women of thirty. A generation had grown up in the postwar world for women. And the idea of women's special role as homemaker had been given a different twist when it was seen that not an improvement in family life, but a 'feminine mystique' with a highly acquisitive slant was the result.

The affluent society was criticized as a materialistic society, and one sign of its materialism was the growth and orientation of the women's magazines. During the war, magazines such as *Housewife* had taken a progressive stance on a variety of issues. Women's magazines had been used both to help the wartime housewife 'make do and mend' and use her rations wisely, and to explain the reforms that would come once fighting was over. For example *Housewife* ran two articles by John Newsom in 1945, not on women's rightful place in the home, but on the 1944 Education Act, explaining the advantages of free 'unstreamed' primary schooling for all, and of the tripartite system of secondary education. *Everywoman* published an article on birth control that aroused the wrath of the Archbishop of Canterbury because it was so enthusiastic about this delicate topic. *Housewife* eulogized the Russian housewife, and the Soviet way of life for promoting women's equal place in society.

Not long after the end of the war, however, all this changed (White 1978). Soon the domestic market, where women, as John Newsom was aware, were the crucial spenders, became the key site of the increased spending and consumption necessary for Britain's economic recovery once the period of acute shortage and crisis had passed. The commercial advertisers on whom the magazine publishers depended for their revenue, knew this, and there was pressure on editors, even quite soon after the war, to return to a narrow domestic formula.

Advances in the technology of printing and the greatly increased use of colour also tempted advertisers and editors alike to a greater emphasis on pictorial material to the detriment of 'think pieces' and general interest features. In the fifties this formula succeeded and a huge readership was established. This was partly because of a convergence of interests among women *of all classes*. Mary Grieve, editor of *Woman* from before the war to the early sixties, recognized this:

'When the restrictions began to lift and money once again created differences, it was not so much differences of class as of personality. The professional man's wife struggling to manage her money so that her children could get a better education was just as glad of the practical recipes, the well-designed clothes, the hints on value for money, as was the welder's wife who now found that she too could benefit from that kind of service and information in her weekly magazine.' (Grieve 1964)

And although Mary Grieve was well aware of the criticisms levelled at the women's magazines, even at the period of their highest propularity, she was prepared to defend them on the grounds that they constituted a 'trade paper' for housewives. They did not, she argued, attempt to cater for 'woman in her whole humanity', but simply for her in her special nurturant and con-sumer role.

Mary Grieve saw herself as a feminist, and, before the war at least, as 'left of centre'. In the thirties, before joining *Woman*, her ambition had been to write for *Time and Tide*, founded and owned by Lady Rhonnda, and under her leadership a platform for the feminist writers of the thirties: Rebecca West, Vera Brittain, Winifred Holtby, and others. So it is sad that she must be judged, in retrospect, as having, perhaps unintentionally, contributed towards that over emphasis on the domestic that women by the sixties were finding so constricting.

Even in 1964 she wrote that 'sad though it is, there are fewer women strongly drawn to subjects like equal pay and racial problems than to practical skills, personal relationships and increased self-confidence'. Yet in the sixties the sales of women's magazines began to slide. The convergence of class interests had been more temporary than anyone had predicted. Not only did inflation make the magazines more expensive to buy, but it was thought that their content had not kept pace with women's 'wide-ning horizons'. IPC already dominated the market, but they con-tinued to try to differentiate their products and introduced several new and more 'swinging' journals, notably *Woman's Mirror* and *Nova*. The 'failure' – in commercial terms – of these magazines was held to prove that women were not in fact as emancipated as had been believed. It may also be, though, that the kind of emancipation represented, in *Nova* especially, was of so 'trendy' and metropolitan a kind that it was both too sophisticated for most readers and too frivolous for the new feminists of the late sixties and early seventies. (It folded in 1975.) True, in its early issues Alma Birk, later a Labour peeress, spoke directly of women's unequal position, and there were articles on (for example) racism in Britain and on ex-revolutionaries living in the West. But it was designed for a type of woman who was perhaps herself more of a media creation than a reality: 'for the new kind of woman . . . for women who make up their own minds' – but the new woman seemed to spend most of her time making up her mind about sexual permissiveness and the new morality. Although most of the aspects of women's position that later claimed the attention of the women's movement were discussed – with the single and significant exception of lesbianism – it was within a glamorized and consumerist presentation that stressed the lives of female 'personalities'. Its fashion pictures, which *were* on occasion suggestive of lesbianism, betrayed the limits of its emancipation, with groovy black girls, punk fashions, and ethnic chic – the whole paraphernalia of the media fantasy of women's liberation in the sixties and early seventies. It was still wholly consumer-orientated, and in an even more alienated way since this was glossed over with a superficial coating of serious comment.

The women's magazines of the fifties had concentrated on child-centred mothering as well as on the importance of domestic skills and, of course, the necessity for women to 'make the best of themselves' so as to appear desirable to boyfriends and husbands. Women could see, though, that these were separate and separable roles and came to resent the way in which husbands as much as women's magazines rolled them into one.

Several years before the women's movement Suzanne Gail, a married graduate student, was writing in the *New Left Review* of the horrors of domesticity. Hers was a biting and perceptive description of the psychology of subservience welded into the domestic relationship by the arrival of a child, who shatters the illusion of freedom possible for a childless couple to sustain. 'It was never a burden to me to be a woman before I had (my baby). Feminists had seemed to me to be tilting at windmills; women who allowed men to rule them did so from their own free choice.' The arrival of her son changed all that.

She wrote with delight of her child, yet with exasperation of the way in which her job of looking after and stimulating him as a toddler conflicted directly with her other job of keeping the house clean – the toddler makes everything messy, the housewife must keep everything clean. And her role as mother was in conflict with her third role – as lover – for the mother must get dirty, wear old clothes, lose her figure, smell of sweat and shit, while the sexual object must look serenely beautiful and smell lovely. No wonder women rifled the pages of *Woman* and *Woman's Own* to find a way out of these contradictions.

CONCLUSION

The welfare state failed to create a network of social services that could support and legitimate the homemaking role of women. The theme of homemaking as an honourable career today seems reactionary to many women. Yet perhaps when the discussions died away, as they did, this represented an even lower level of consciousness, for at least the discussion of the validity and value of domestic work was a recognition that it was work.

Later, women were presented instead with the even falser image of the 'dual role' and as attempts were made ideologically to mesh their new role in the workforce with their continuing responsibilities as mothers and housewives, it was suggested that they were in the fortunate position of having a free 'choice' whether to work or not. There was however no choice when it came to domestic chores. These were women's 'biological' destiny.

CHAPTER THREE

Right to work?

There are women as well as men today, who enjoy their hours in mill or laundry. The skilled worker takes pleasure in his job. The clean modern buildings, the sense of comradeship, the respite from bickering, overcrowding and discomfort which are too frequently the dominating experiences of the 'home' – the sense of earning money, the independence, the chance of promotion – all these have made some women relish with gusto even monotonous factory labour. . . . In the modern factories of Bournville, York, Welwyn and other centres of improved equipment and modernized methods, there are many . . . women employees who really find satisfaction in their work comparable to the satisfaction of the professional and business woman. (Winifred Holtby: *Women and a Changing Civilization*.)

Today, virtually all single women work – which was not always the case – while it is well known that married women have also increasingly sought paid work since the end of the Second World War. Survey figures show that the proportion of all married women working has risen sharply. From 9 per cent in 1921 and 10 percent in 1931, numbers rose to 21 per cent in 1951, 32 per cent in 1961 and 47 per cent in 1972 (Westergaard and Resler 1975:98). About half these women work part time, and the age group in

which the greatest increase in taking paid employment has occurred is the 35 to 44 age group. John Westergaard and Henrietta
Resler have pointed out that until the mid-1960s there were factors
working in the opposite direction. These factors – later entry into
work, earlier retirement, earlier marriage, more marriage, and a
changing age structure – meant that only since then has the
number of married women working risen to over two out of every
five. Although, that is, more women have married and have
married earlier, so that they would almost inevitably appear in
larger numbers in the statistics of women at work, there has also
been an *absolute* growth in their numbers. Numerous surveys (for
example Hunt 1968) have shown too that far larger numbers of
married women would like to take paid jobs were these available
or were they able to find alternative care for their children.

As Westergaard and Resler argue, working-class women have
always had to work, and the most important feature of the entry of
married women into paid work since the war has been the
abandonment by middle- and upper-class women of the ideal of
'marriage as a career'. Popular myth has made much of the unique
experience of work for women in wartime, but what was unique
about this was not that women were then working, but rather that
they took on what was traditionally thought of as *men's* work. On
the other hand the ideal of the non-working wife was an ideal for
the working class too in the earlier years of this century, whilst
there was always a vocal group of middle-class and professional
women who demanded the right to work – and they were not all
unmarried. The picture drawn by Margery Spring Rice (Spring
Rice 1939) was of working-class wives who faced utter boredom
and futility once their children had grown up, but who were
physically so exhausted and unfit that they hardly could have
taken on paid work. In this respect, while the welfare state may be
said to have been 'founded on the drudgery of women' it did also
go a long way to improve the health of working-class women.
After the war they were for the first time well fed and fit enough to
enjoy the prospect of a paid job in addition to their domestic role.

POSTWAR RECONSTRUCTION

I have suggested that an attempt was made in the early postwar years to impart the ideal of 'homemaking as a career' to *all* classes of women and that this was a part of the general ideological enterprise which was to unite the classes and to identify the interests of the working class with the national interest. But from the beginning, the Attlee government was attempting a weird juggling feat, trying to promote ideals of family life while simultaneously desperately in need of labour for the work of peacetime reconstruction. Women as well as men were released from the armed forces as well as from munitions work from 1945 onwards in order to take up this reconstruction work, and, for instance on 16 August 1945, the Prime Minister told the House of Commons that there was: 'a vast demand for labour for the urgent tasks of reconstruction at home'.

In September 1946 an ILO study, far from arguing for women's ejection from the labour force, was seeking to assess the probable effects of the wartime mobilization of women as workers on the future status of women. The conclusion drawn was that:

> 'experience has reinforced the continued development of public policy that recognizes the economic and social value of utilizing and rewarding labour in accordance with individual capacity and job performance regardless of sex. A sound and scientific basis for the employment of women is being increasingly advocated as serving the cause of democracy and as promoting the general welfare.' (ILO 1946)

At the same time, estimates of manpower trends in Britain in the later 1940s foresaw a considerable substitution of men for women in a number of industries, and also foresaw that a percentage of women would withdraw from the labour force owing to 'family responsibilities'. Yet the Economic Survey for 1947 (Cmd 7047) initiated a campaign for the recruitment of women to the labour force since women: 'now form the only large reserve of labour left, and to them the Government are accordingly making a special appeal.'

The terms of this appeal really set the limits within which the employment of women was perceived and understood at this time, and for many years afterwards. Indeed right up until the present time this view prevails amongst the powerful, and has only begun to be challenged by the women's movement and to some extent by sections of the trades union movement. The terms of the 1947 appeal were these:

> 'Women are urgently needed in many factories, in many services and in agriculture. . . . (The Government) was not asking women to do jobs usually done by men, as had been the case during the war. Second, the labour shortage was temporary, and women were being asked to take a job only for whatever length of time they could spare, whether full time or part time. Third, (they) were not appealing to women with very young children, although for those who wanted to volunteer, or who had children a little older there were in many places nurseries and creches.'

(And in fact nurseries were actually opened adjacent to industries and factors that were considered especially vital to the export drive that would earn us the dollars to plug the dollar gap and save the country from bankruptcy.) The Survey gave a list of the industries and services where labour was most urgently required. The boot and shoe industry, clothing, textiles, iron and steel, all required female workers, as did hospitals, domestic service, transport, and the women's land army. There was also a shortage of shorthand typists, and a dire shortage of nurses and midwives. This last group was fervently and repeatedly urged to come back to work, or to train, in the immediate postwar years.

All the same, in welcoming women into the labour force in this circumscribed way – as temporary workers at a period of crisis, as part-time workers, and as not disturbing the traditional division of labour in industry along sex lines – the Survey reflected the view, which was still dominant, that married women would not naturally wish to work.

THE EQUAL PAY REPORT

The Royal Commission on Equal Pay reported in 1946 and it too gave at best a guarded welcome to even the idea of married women at work. The Report assumed that the number of women at work would show little change, for, after all, 'even at the height of the war half the women of this country remained unavailable even for part time employment'.

Work and marriage were still understood as *alternatives*. The Report assumed in fact that there were two *kinds* of women. You could either be a wife and mother or a single career woman. To a certain extent this division corresponded to a (perceived) class division among women in relation to their work. It was assumed that the majority of those who chose to work belonged in the more interesting fields of work; in the professions, in the Civil Service, or in teaching. The rest were, as workers, transient, less highly skilled, inferior in class and status.

The Report implied that the first group should receive equal pay, partly because it was from these women that the pressure for equal pay had come; but it was argued that women in manual employment did not make a contribution equal to that of men. This was because of their lesser strength, greater absenteeism, and 'a certain relative lack of flexibility in response to rapidly changing or abnormal situations'. But the three women members of the Committee, Annie Loughlin, Janet Vaughan, and Mrs. P.L. Nettlefold, all disagreed with these assumptions.

What were the real obstacles to the implementation of equal pay? The evidence presented by the trades unions in various forms overwhelmingly supported the principle, yet there were suggestions that fears still lurked that whatever official policy, the rank and file of male workers did not support it. Straight prejudice was never far from the surface. For example, in March 1945 Arthur Woodburn, a Labour MP, and Irene Ward, a Conservative MP (and a feminist) both wrote in the *Sunday Times* on the related question of 'Should Marriage Bar Women's Employment?'. Irene Ward was for the ending of the marriage bar, but Woodburn, the Labour Party spokesman, argued for the retention of the bar on the grounds that 'homemaking comes first' and that state intervention of all kinds would make it unnecessary for women to work. He also attacked the 'vicious propaganda' (presumably of feminists?) for equal employment opportunities, for after all: 'Nature itself made the first and greatest division of labour and no arguments by super intellectual women can cancel that out.' The correspondence that followed these articles showed a sharp disagreement on the subject amongst women themselves. It was not always women who supported equal opportunities for women, nor men who always opposed them.

Perhaps even more significantly, the suggestion was made in the Report that in certain types of work, in the lower grades of the Civil Service, for example, it was *desirable* to have a rapid turnover of women workers who were neither highly trained nor highly motivated, but who would do the boring routine work offered at that level for a limited period of time, since they had no longer term career aspirations. A question was hinted at but the Report avoided answering it or even considering its implications. This question was: what would happen if these women were better trained and more highly motivated – who would then do the boring but necessary routine jobs? The Report seemed covertly to see women as not exactly a reserve army of labour in the classic sense but as a desirably unskilled, transitory labour force and an ever self-replacing one.

The questions that were to be posed by the Royal Commission on Population also surfaced in the Report on Equal Pay. There was, particularly, the important question: how was motherhood to be made more attractive to women? Not, it was argued, by the provisions of equal pay. Indeed, Roy Harrod the economist (and biographer of Keynes) really let the cat out of the bag when he argued against the principle of equal pay on the grounds that (p. 119):

> 'The . . . situation has proved tolerable and stable because it has been found to further certain deeper social purposes, namely i) to secure that the proportion of the national income flowing to parents is not unduly restricted; and ii) to secure that motherhood as a vocation is not too unattractive compared with work in the professions, industry or trade.'

This was of course the great fear – that independence, 'selfishness', and economic incentives were enticing women from their rightful occupation of producing children. Men seemed to believe that, given a free choice, *no* woman would want to reproduce. But since women were not paid for being mothers the attraction of marriage for women was held to turn partly on the adequacy of the man's 'family wage'. The Committee therefore discussed at length with the individuals and groups who gave evidence to it the relationship between the wage and the needs of the dependent family. Here the question of the housewife's 'income' surfaced once more. And the arguments here were between those who, like Eleanor Rathbone and the Family Endowment Society, believed that family allowances must meet the gap between the wage of a single person and the requirements of a family man; and those who like the National Association of Schoolmasters, argued that *all* men had greater responsibilities in terms of dependants than *any* woman.

WHAT WOMEN WANT

What no one in power seemed to understand was that many women no longer wanted to be presented with an 'either – or' 'choice' *between* work on the one hand and a family on the other. As Margaret Stacey puts it (letter to author):

> 'The point for me – and I can't have been the only feminist to have this view although we had no movement when I graduated – was that the women older than me chose *either* a career *or* marriage. You couldn't have both we were told. . . . (But) *we* said, I and my friends, we would be mothers *and* women in our own right.'

But there never were sufficient welfare provisions to make this easily achieved.

Men seem to have a propensity to divide women into two opposed categories. Once, women might be madonnas or whores. Then in the years between the wars they could be mothers or career women. As soon as this division began to be challenged, by the choices women began to make after World War Two, as soon, too, as class divisions were said to be narrowing, women began to be divided, for work purposes at least, along generational lines.

In the previous chapter the work of Richard Titmuss and Eva Hubback was mentioned briefly. Both suggested that intensified standards of child care and home management might have added to women's work in the home. At the same time both also discussed the way in which women's fertility had been compressed. That is, whereas once women had produced a large number of children and had started having their children later in life, now they started young and completed their families very early. Once, women had had only a few years of life left to them after the last child had left the nest; now many women had completed child-rearing by about the age of forty and could look forward to twenty or thirty more years of life. They were therefore more and more looking for work to fill those years. Richard Titmuss recognized what was happening. Subsequently 'women's dual role' was virtually elevated into a principle. Henceforward there was to be a generational drive, with the younger women in the wife-and-mother category, and the older in the returning-to-work role. These older women workers would often be both part-time and unskilled, to fit in with their diminished but not extinguished domestic responsibilities; to fit in, too, with a shortage of unskilled labour. As Eva Hubback summed up her 1950 survey findings (*The Manchester Guardian* 21.9.50):

> 'The cause of reasonable feminism has been virtually won. These developments have had the effect of glossing over the differences between the sexes. For biological reasons there is sexual division of labour; but culturally women have the same needs and desires as men. The new advance must be in the direction of so organizing home life and the education of girls that women are competent to bring up families without *so much* sacrifice of health and personality *that they are unable* to return to a broader life in middle age when they will not only contribute to the community through their work but find life worth living outside the immediate family.' (My italics.)

Laura Balbo (1979) has argued that this ordering of women's

lives into three sequential stages – full-time work before and after marriage; full-time role as wife and mother while her children are of pre-school age; and then part-time work at home and part-time work in the labour force – is quite rigid. It is not the case, she suggests, as a number of researchers have argued, that we live in a pluralistic society in which there are a number of alternative, tolerated ways of being in families and of organizing family life – a view that imagines there is an equality of status and opportunity for the remarried and for one-parent families as well as for the traditional nuclear family. On the contrary the sequence described above is seen as the only truly appropriate one. The male experience of the balance of work and home remains largely unchanged, but women now have a 'dual role'.

Laura Balbo makes another very important point about women's dual role. It shuts women off from the enjoyment of leisure:

'Just as important, in describing the status of the adult woman, is a third aspect: her absence – which follows from the previously described 'dual life' pattern – from any sphere of activity other than those of unpaid domestic labour plus paid labour. Study, leisure, creative rest, political participation, active membership in trade unions or other associations, are experiences unknown to the great majority of adult women.' (Balbo 1979:5)

INDUSTRIAL WORK, THE FAMILY AND WOMEN

Given that the entry of married women into paid work was accelerating, it aroused relatively little interest among sociologists in the fifties and sixties. Those who did interest themselves in this trend were primarily interested in the effect the entry of married women into the work force had on *family* life.

Ferdynand Zweig was one of these. Ferdynand Zweig became best known, amongst other sociologists at least, for his thesis that the working class was becoming not only 'affluent' but 'middle class'. His was the theory of 'embourgeoisement'. The interesting questions he raised about family life in relation to working women remained comparatively neglected.

In spite of his belief that: 'working class life finds itself on the move towards new middle class values and middle class existence . . . a deep transformation of values' (Zweig 1961), Zweig described the stringent limitations on this change, because the new and relatively high standard of living being enjoyed by working people during the fifties resulted only from long hours of overtime, and shift work, and/or by the presence of a second wage-earner in the household. The workers interviewed by Zweig were very conscious of home comforts and much attached to their homes, on which most of their spare money was spent. Home 'assumed a possibly romanticized image of refuge' and even the most highly politicized workers were, or seemed to be, affected by this domestication. Yet Zweig understood well the limits to this happy picture and was especially struck by the lack of culture and education amongst the workers he interviewed. For this he did not blame them. He realized that economic prosperity could not be matched with cultural advance when the prosperity was based on such long hours of work.

Zweig devoted a whole book to his researches into the experience of working women. In his study of affluent workers, he noted that the ideal image of marriage was the partnership model. Both childlessness *and* large families were looked at askance. This confirms Laura Balbo's view, which is indeed supported by other research, that the norm of a small family imposed itself fairly rigidly on the consciousness of the British in the postwar period. Disapproval was also expressed of the father who took no interest in his children. 'Absolute or "near" equality' was claimed by 75 per cent of the couples to whom Zweig spoke, although what this meant in precise terms was less clear. Only 25 per cent of those questioned claimed absolutely superiority for the man, amongst the others were women who simply stated that their husbands 'shared equally' in household tasks, and those who defined their own position as that of 'junior partner'.

There was a reluctance to discuss housekeeping money. Zweig commented that the amount of money that husbands gave wives was one of the least researched areas, and would be one of the most difficult to research. What is clear from his work, though, is the way in which postwar affluence eventually solved the problem of the housewife's income, which I discussed in the previous chapter. The 'general revolt' against the housekeeping allowance to which Charles Madge had alluded during the war died down. This was because full employment made things easier for both husband *and* wife. The wives who went out to work had their own source of independent income. So did husbands, who often regarded their overtime money as extra money for themselves rather than their family.

Zweig's optimistic view was not entirely supported by a small study carried out by the Christian Economic and Social Research Foundation in 1957, *Young Mothers At Work*. This showed that married women with children were often driven into paid work by dire poverty. Of fifty-nine women interviewed only three spent any of their earnings on clothes or make-up for themselves, for example. Most of these women had also been trained to a higher level of skill than that required by the jobs they were doing after marriage.

Zweig, however, found that the women who were working were much happier than if they had been staying at home, felt more independent, and led a more varied life:

'Working women fell into a special category, their outside contacts with each other being much more frequent than among
men. They go out shopping together, to cinemas, dance clubs
and so on. They find great pleasure in companionship at work
and they do not mind keeping it up outside.' (Zweig 1961:118)

Zweig speculated on the effect of working on fertility statistics, thinking it might be connected with a lower birthrate, and while he was clear that work for women led to greater independence, he was also aware of the limitations on their 'equality'. He observed that their earnings were only 53 per cent of men's, and that they formed a docile section of the work force. Such comments, com-
monplace today, were less often made in 1952, when his book was published.

Zweig also found a double standard operating. (This too is still with us today.) There was disapproval in many quarters of mothers who worked, unless they undertook only part-time work which fitted in with the child's hours at school. But if the mother were left unsupported, then her duty was not first and foremost to children, but rather to avoid being a burden on the state.

Zweig was under no illusion that women had achieved equality. Not only were they an underpaid, exploited section of the work-force, ignored by the unions and facing derogatory attitudes from employers, but he found evidence from the women themselves and from others he interviewed, such as trades union officials and personnel officers, that both men and women perceived women as inferior.

Pearl Jephcott and others (Jephcott, Seear, and Smith 1962), who undertook a much more localized study (of the Peek Frean factory in Bermondsey) came up with findings similar to those of Ferdynand Zweig. The Peek Frean factory had rearranged its shifts especially to fit in with the family needs of its locally based female workforce – women who could themselves count on the assistance of neighbours and relations in what was still a close-knit working-class community. Pearl Jephcott was just as insistent as Zweig on the positive aspects of work for married women. Her study was undertaken as a response to the fears in the fifties of 'latch key children' turning into juvenile delinquents, and made it clear that in a sense the fuss about working mothers missed the central point that the majority of working wives were doing part time work and 'this new role was in every sense subsidiary to the traditional one of wife and mother'. She seemed almost disappointed to find that:

> 'these working-class wives rode no feminist band wagon. They seldom mentioned frustration over wasted talent, while few would think of claiming that their job was of any particular value to society. Nor did they reject domesticity. Too hard headed to see this as "drudgerie divine", they appeared to be less in revolt against pots and pans, than not quite sure how to fill in their day.' (Jephcott 1962:106)

Here was an implied comparison with the mood of the educated wife, and Pearl Jephcott, like the investigators of the Equal Pay Report and the women giving evidence to the Royal Commission on Population, seemed to take it as absolutely evident that feminism was attractive – or had ever been attractive – only to middle-class women. As we saw, the right of those women to an education was challenged during the fifties, and while the debate that centred around the employment of working-class wives had to do with whether their children could be properly cared for in their absence or not, the demand for equality coming from middle-class women seemed to arouse perhaps even more profound anxieties, which ultimately had to do with its being a challenge to the manhood of men. Working-class women had after all always been exploited workers, but for a middle-class wife to work called many conventions into question.

WOMEN'S DUAL ROLE

Viola Klein made the study of women's position her major work, and her books are as interesting for their insights as for their omissions. *Women's Two Roles*, written with Alva Myrdal and published in 1956, was reissued in 1968 with the claim that its analysis was still valid. Yet 1968 was the year in which it was finally becoming too obvious to deny that women's problems were still not solved after fifty years of the vote; that more was required than Mrydal and Klein could suggest.

Their position was that women's two roles, caused by the division between workplace and home resulting from the industrial revolution, were now a permanent feature of society. Every effort should be made to facilitate the return of married women to the workforce after they had raised their families, but the basic division of labour between men and women was not to be modified. Myrdal and Klein aimed to influence policy and planners, but could suggest only a few minor adjustments to make it easier for women to combine work and motherhood, and acknowledged that these might be of little use to professional women who interrupted their careers in order to have a family.

Nine years later Viola Klein restated and advanced her theoretical analysis, in *Britain's Married Women Workers*. She agreed with those sociologists who had suggested that the family, far from losing its functions and being in decline, was an ever more important focus for 'togetherness'. She recognized DIY and home maintenance as important features of the family life of the sixties. Nonetheless, she was now more aware of the puzzle at the heart of housework – what was its relationship to the structure of the economy as a whole? It was outside the market economy. It might save money, but could not create wealth:

'The notion of "productivity" has no relevance to domestic labour; nor does the eight hour day or the five day week apply to it.'

'While in pre-industrial times the household was an integral part of and the mainstay of the economy in general (the very term "economy" originally meant household management) it has remained almost stationary as an island in the stream of economic growth. The anachronism between the economics of the household and those of society at large is to a considerable extent responsible for the sense of frustration and futility which fills so many housewives today when going about their daily task.' (Klein 1965:3)

This passage harks back to Josephine Butler, who wrote something very similar – even down to the imagery of women being 'high and dry' as the tide of history washed past them – and also anticipates some of the debates about the nature of housework in the Women's Movement of the 1970s.

In *Britain's Married Women Workers* the negative effects on women's employment of the gap in their working lives, and the problems that came with part-time work were more fully explored than in the earlier work. Viola Klein found – like the Christian Economic and Social Research Foundation – that women 'paid' for their return to work 'by a loss of occupational status'. While one third of unmarried women workers were engaged in office work, domestic work ranked first amongst the married women, and factory work second. Married women working full time were most likely to be employed in a factory, but 45 per cent of married women working part time were doing domestic work of one kind or another. Viola Klein commented that secretarial work and shorthand typing, for which vast numbers of girls were trained, offered little scope for part-time work; and she also observed:

'Sons of middle class families will as a rule adopt middle class occupations. This is not generally so among the daughters of the upper and middle classes, who can quite frequently be found doing the same type of work as girls of humbler background . . . the result of a widespread attitude among girls who regard their gainful employment as a temporary phase.' (Klein, 1965:49)

So before as well as after marriage, middle-class women in post-war Britain became 'proletarianized'.

Unlike some of the sociologists who explored family life after the war and came, as we shall see, to some very optimistic conclusions, Viola Klein's findings on the relationship of women's working role to their household responsibilities were far from rosy. She found that not only were 99 per cent of the married women in her sample caring for someone or some others than themselves, but 54 per cent of widowed and divorced women and 21 per cent even of single women were responsible for the domestic care of another or others. But:

'Seeing that there must be numerous women who are not very keen to do domestic work, particularly after a full day in a factory, office or shop, the percentage of *husbands* referring to the additional domestic burden seems extraordinarily small.' (Klein, 1965:74-5)

GRADUATE WOMEN AND WORK

In *Wives Who Went To College* (1957), Judith Hubback posed herself the question: how great a contribution to society can a highly educated and married woman make? Such a question immediately took on a whole set of assumptions carried over from before the Second World War, and revealed a continued embarrassment at the idea of having to weld the two 'roles' of 'career woman' and 'wife and mother' into one person.

Judith Hubback found that the graduate wives in her study were more, not less, fertile than the national average, thus allaying the fear, referred to in the previous chapter, that the development of a woman's intellect would somehow interfere with her biological instincts. The professional classes, Judith Hubback found, were in favour of having 'a family, rather than just one or two children' (sic).

She observed that 'many of the correspondents were obviously being very careful not to complain'. This was understandable, since they had made a total emotional investment in marriage and children and had in most cases sacrificed career advancement to family. In any case, it was not their relationships as wives and mothers that gave rise to dissatisfaction, but the difficulty of combining these with 'a life of one's own' for women. They had presumably in most cases no wish to be disloyal to a husband who was doing his best to make the situation easier, and indeed, 'the general tone of their letters, time after time, was: "Of course I'm very lucky to be happily married, but. . . ." '. Yet this was just the mechanism whereby the grievances of women were ultimately excluded from discourse, so that, as Betty Friedan was to describe it, their formless, vague unhappiness became a sickness without a name.

Wives Who Went To College offered the familiar solutions to a familiar, although perceptive, restatement of the problem as it was seen at that time. New demands were being made on married, highly educated women; to enjoy sexual relations and to be prepared to do the household dirty work no middle-class woman would have had to do unaided before 1939. Motherhood was still a primary function for a woman, as fatherhood was not for a man. The solutions were part-time work, domestic training in school, the pursuit only of those academic subjects not requiring too much specialization, so that women could return to teaching, social work, and other semi-professions, which would not make the same demands on them in terms of continuous employment as did the top professions.

These solutions were solutions for the period after the children had left behind their first period of dependency. They therefore did not answer the immediate problem of the women questioned, which was precisely their dissatisfactions during those years when they were most closely tied to domesticity. Although some of these women revelled in their domestic role and had no desire for outside work, most were 'fatalistic, rueful or even bitter'. Only 5 per cent said they regarded marriage as a career and many expressed their dislike for the drudgery of housework. More than half the sample suffered from a considerable degree of overtiredness, and even those who claimed that their university training was not in conflict with their current domestic life made ambiguous comments about it:

'I would not have been without my years at the University for anything in the world and I do not believe I could do the work I do now, which requires organizing ability, adaptability and imagination, if I had not a trained mind. . . . All the same I do not find it really satisfactory, mainly because I get tired of having very few personal contacts outside my family in which I am anything more than my husband's shadow. He does not realize this, fortunately, and one day, when the children are bigger, I may be able to escape.' (Hubback 1957:75)

The themes of escape and imprisonment were in fact the dominant metaphors used by these women to describe their condition.

Judith Hubback understood the importance of the problem discussed in the previous chapter – the disappearance of domestic help after the war. She made it clear that the wives she interviewed were not simply 'moaning about the servant problem', but that the absence of domestic help was objectively one major factor in preventing educated women from going out to work once they had had children. In the fifties, when working-class married women were being drawn willy-nilly into employment, the problem of 'family' versus career was discussed as the problem of the middle-class woman, and although few would have gone to the lengths of John Newsom in suggesting that it might be better not to educate women at all, the graduate wife seemed an embarrassment rather than a welcomed addition to society, even when there was an acute shortage of teachers and nurses.

In 1969, Pat Williams wrote a study of wives who were working part time, *Working Wonders*. This book came out of what had originally been a BBC initiative, a course and guide on career openings for women who were returning to work after a period spent in raising a family. It appeared in an atmosphere very different from that of 1957: 'Recently there was a rash of articles and TV programmes whose chief theme – marking fifty years of women's suffrage – was the frustration and complaint of housebound women. From their tone it would seem that a new feminist revival was in the air.' The women Pat Williams interviewed did not mind complaining, and they were more cynical than Judith Hubback's sample about the attitude of husbands. It seemed that the typical attitude of a husband was patronizing and fairly selfish. He approved of his wife working provided it did not interfere with his own comfort, because it 'gave her an interest', and – significantly – so long as she was not regarded as a breadwinner. Although a number of husbands were more constructive and helpful, the overriding impression was that the wife's work should be ideally 'a hobby that pays for itself'.

CONCLUSION

Throughout the period under discussion there were acute shortages of labour in Britain, and married women were more and more drawn into waged work. Despite this, their presence in the labour force was seen as a problem. Paid work could only be combined with their continued domestic responsibilities by the solution of part-time work. Domestic responsibilities were discussed mainly in terms of the needs of children, particularly small children. Yet it seems clear from the responses of husbands themselves (to Pat Williams' questionnaire) or as reported by their wives, that on the whole they were not keen to sacrifice their own comfort, nor to make more than a fairly marginal contribution to the running of the household.

Viola Klein, like Pearl Jephcott, found that the women she talked to were not motivated by anything that could be called feminism, and that they gave their work a secondary role in their lives. This was true also of the women investigated by Pat Williams, although they tended to deny that a problem even existed – despite their lukewarm husbands – by claiming that they *chose* to work part time and that this gave them the best of all worlds. (This could only be the case so long as their income was an addition to a husband's, and did not have to be a living, still less a family wage. They did not, therefore, challenge the principle of the financial dependency of the wife on her husband.)

Yet the questions that these researchers were asking structured the kind of picture that *could* be built up. Since Pearl Jephcott, for example, had as her aim the defence of working mothers she was unlikely to emphasize conflict or challenge to the *status quo*. Women themselves would also be likely to stress the positive aspects of their situation. An overall question about the wellbeing of children was rather unlikely to reveal a well of latent feminism. None of these researchers questioned the underlying Bowlby assumption that children under five needed the constant presence and attention of their mothers. For all, part-time work seemed the ideal solution.

CHAPTER FOUR

The chief means of fulfilment in life

It was difficult to recognize the slim, lively Natasha of former days in this robust motherly woman. . . .

There were then, as there are now, conversations and discussions about women's rights, the relations of husband and wife, and their freedoms and rights, though these themes were not yet termed questions as they are now. . . . Those questions then as now, existed only for those who see nothing in marriage but the pleasure married people get from one another, that is, only the beginnings of marriage and not its whole significance, which lies in the family. . . .

After seven years of marriage Pierre had the joyous and firm consciousness that he was not a bad man, and he felt this because he saw himself reflected in his wife. He felt the good and bad within himself inextricably mingled and overlapping. But only what was really good in him was reflected in his wife, all that was not quite good was rejected. (Leo Tolstoy: *War and Peace*.)

Attempts to create societies on a basis other than the family have failed dismally. . . . The chief means of fulfilment in life is to be a member of, and reproduce a family. (Peter Townsend: *A Society for People*.)

When married women entered the labour force this was widely discussed in terms of its effects on family life. I hope this was demonstrated in the previous chapter, but perhaps it needs to be said again that wives and mothers were granted entry into paid work only so long as this did not harm the family.

The condition of women is a seamless web; it is difficult even to unpick the different threads so that they may be examined separately. Whether or not women are held to be oppressed, one quality of their lives is the interdependence of their varying roles and spheres. That work and child-rearing, marriage and sexuality, family and social life should be so interdependent, need not lead to subordination or inequality. Indeed it may be that men suffer from the radical separation some of them experience between their work and their family, or for that matter between the sensuality of their sexual encounters outside marriage and the emotional tenderness of conjugal life. In our society however this may be experienced and described as a form of freedom, while the meshing together of the various aspects of the female condition may seem like an imprisoning net from which women struggle to escape.

For women especially the different elements of life are knotted together by marriage. Yet while it could be tirelessly repeated in the fifties and sixties that women's 'primary sphere' was marriage-and-the-family – that, for example, as we saw, she should be educated more adequately to fulfil her functions in 'her' reproductive sphere – theoreticians, popularizing sociologists, doctors, vicars, schoolmasters, and journalists engaged in prolonged and heated debates about the state of the family without ever seriously discussing the position of women at all.

OPTIMISTS AND PESSIMISTS

Moralists of every stripe set out to explore the condition of the nation, for when political questions appeared to be resolved their place was taken by moral questions. That these essentially moral debates were disguised as objective fact-finding excursions and often cast in the form of empirical investigation does not alter their ideological nature.

The boundaries of these debates were liberalism and conservative paternalism. That women had achieved equality was an unquestioned assumption built in to them. So Michael Young and Peter Wilmott could speak of the changed status of women as 'one of the great transformations of our time' and Ronald Fletcher, who wrote a standard textbook, *The Family and Marriage in Britain* (1966), could affirm that: 'In the modern marriage, both partners choose each other freely as persons. Both are of equal status and expect to have an equal share in taking decisions and in pursuing their sometimes mutual sometimes separate and diverse, tastes and interests' (p. 139). Ronald Fletcher was one of the liberal optimists, and his book was written as an answer to the con- servative pessimists – who were sometimes sociologists, but might also be drawn from the ranks of Church, Police, and Tory Party – whose gloomy predictions of national decay were blown up into moral whirlwinds by the mass media. Fletcher set out to answer both his fellow sociologists who claimed to be charting the objective *functional decline* of the family, and the public moralizers who preached on the theme of the *moral decay* of the family. He commented on the widespread and taken-for-granted nature of such views, which also encompassed assumptions about the crim- inality and viciousness of youth and the breakdown of law and order, all attributed to the attenuation and weakness of family life. Many of the pessimists, he also noted, related moral decay to the emancipation of women. They, that is, just as much as the liberals, never doubted that women's emancipation had been achieved. What was questioned was whether it was desirable or not.

WORKING-CLASS FAMILIES

Many British sociologists of the fifties and sixties were interested above all in class, in working-class life and working-class culture. The most influential works in this field were intended as cel- ebrations of working-class values, yet, progressive in intention, led to profoundly conservative conclusions and were ultimately ambivalent in their attitude to the working class as well. What working-class families did or believed might fit uneasily with the researcher's moral or intellectual commitment to the welfare state or child centred methods of child rearing, yet there was a reluctance to criticize what was seen as distinctively working class, and certainly no wish to attack or patronize, although the end result was sometimes patronizing. Embedded inevitably within such an ambiguous body of work were untheorized and imprecise understandings of women.

The Institute of Community Studies (Platt 1971) was set up in Bethnal Green in 1954 and concentrated its research work, initially at least, on London's East End. The workers followed the advice of Richard Titmuss to study the relationship between social policies and the working-class family, partly because it was felt that the study of family relationships in industrial society had been neglected. Yet their findings, presented as in some cases 'unexpected' discoveries, were pieces of special pleading, whose authors were committed to a particular point of view. The first book to come out of the Institute, *Family and Kinship in East London* (1957) by Peter Young and Michael Willmott, was meant, like Fletcher's book, to take issue both with the contemporary moralists who were agitated about rising divorce and juvenile delinquency rates, and with existing pessimistic accounts of working-class life in postwar Britain.

Their stated intention in this book was to discover the effect of housing policies on family life, and the book compared the lively social and family life of Bethnal Green with the bleaker, more introverted life on the new large estates on the outskirts of London where many of the Bethnal Green families were rehoused. Yet other witnesses remember the new flats as a source of pride, and later investigators, such as Coates and Silburn (1968) who studied an inner city area of Nottingham in the sixties, have also found that at least some working-class men and women are more than anxious to get away from the cosy warmth of their 'genuine' old slums.

The work of Young and Willmott, and of Peter Townsend, who wrote *The Family Life of Old People* (1957), also about Bethnal Green, was not accepted without criticism even when it was first published. Margaret Stacey (Stacey 1960) for example questioned the validity of using such small numbers of interviewees on which to base such large conclusions, and also questioned why the Institute workers had studied only kinship relationships, and ignored friendship and neighbourhood networks and she rectified this in her own study of life in Banbury. Yet the Bethnal Green studies became classics, and managed to impose their myths on the national consciousness. This myth was of the warmth, charm, and humanity of working-class family life, and the work accomplished was designed to show that the old myths of the brutality of the working class were now at least no longer relevant.

Since it had in the past been working-class women and children particularly who had suffered from the brutality of the working-class male as well as bearing the brunt of working-class poverty, it was important for the Bethnal Green researchers to show that women's lot had improved. Few would disagree that contraception had by the fifties freed women from multiple pregnancies and that far better wages had brought co-operation instead of conflict between husbands and wives. What does not seem to have occurred to Young and Willmott was that 'affluence' and birth control might have sweetened the lot of women while leaving underlying forms of male female dominance and submission relatively untouched. So, where they found a husband who refused to let his wife use contraceptives, this was described as a 'survival' and not 'a still dominant form of behaviour'. They used help with the washing up as an adequate index of male household responsibilities. And, perhaps most significant of all, and relevant to my earlier discussion of the housewife's income, they attempted to explain away the continuing practice whereby most of the men concealed the amount of their wages from their wives.

Young and Willmott managed to negate the significance of this by stressing the extent to which husband and wife engaged in the joint planning of important purchases. An impression was created that however many men were still secretive about their earnings, this was unimportant by comparison with the new practices of sharing expenditure. They did not ask the question: *why* do men conceal the amount they earn from their wives? Peter Townsend in his study of old people did try to account for this. He suggested that in many marriages there were pre-existing loyalties to others outside the marriage. The husband had loyalties to his workmates, the wife to her kin group. Concealment of the wage 'may be a particularly effective way of avoiding or reducing conflict' where there is competition as to whether some of it should be spent on the wife's 'loyalties' or on the husband's.

This seems an extraordinarily contorted argument, but it is necessarily contorted because it will not confront the fact that concealment is 'effective' overwhelmingly for the husband. The use of the word 'loyalty' here conceals the real differences in the situation of man and wife – it is his recreation that competes with what certainly were historically, family necessities such as food and rent. It would be more logical to argue not that the concealment of the wage was the result of pre-existing loyalties, but rather that the loyalties developed in an antagonistic way because of the conflict within the family arising from the dependence of wife and child upon the wage of the breadwinner. This had been the argument put forward in a much grimmer account of working-class life, *Coal is Our Life* (1956), which was the study of a Yorkshire mining community. The authors of this book, Norman Dennis, Fernando Henriques, and Clifford Slaughter, noted, even amongst couples where much of the expenditure was jointly planned, 'an undercurrent of rivalry between the demands of the family's well being and the demands of the husband's pleasure'. And they noted too that the prevailing currency of jokes and assumptions supported the notion of conflict, cheating, and secrecy between spouses.

Perhaps the most famous discovery made by Young and Willmott was of the Bethnal Green Mum. As the *New Scientist* (11.7.57) put it: 'The most significant thing that emerges . . . is the importance of Mum – the Mother Goddess of Bethnal Green. Mum is the oracle whose word is law in everything from babies' dummies to dockers' dinners.' Again, Margaret Stacey disputed the invariant importance of this and other kinship ties and in her own study found tremendous variety. But the Bethnal Green Mum, taken up in this way by serious reviewers and popularizing journalists alike, became a widely recognized stereotype and therefore, however partial her relationship to what actually went on in Bethnal Green, developed a life and a reality of her own.

Young and Willmott suggested that married women in Bethnal Green needed their mothers' help in child-minding and sometimes in the preparation of meals if they were to take paid work, and although these researchers believed that the economic dimension of the relationship was of diminishing importance, they ended by making an emotional plea for the continuance of this relationship to which they evidently had a strong commitment. Margaret Stacey, however, pointed out that provision for a deserted wife or widow was so beggarly that she would desperately need the economic support of her family if she lost her husband.

This being the case, the findings of Peter Marris in his study *Widows and Their Families* (1958), also based on Bethnal Green families, seemed inconsistent with the Bethnal Green 'myth', for as Young and Willmott themselves commented:

> 'From the strong attachment of married women to their mothers which the previous studies had brought out, we had expected that widows would tend to be drawn even more closely into the circle of their kin. In fact, widows showed a slight but consistent tendency to withdraw from their family relationships'. (Young and Willmott 1961:206)

This unexpected discovery was said to be a reflection of 'an emotional reaction to bereavement', also of a wish on the part of widows to retain their independence. It might also reveal the limits of the mother-daughter tie.

Material conditions were making possible a higher standard of living within the context of the nuclear family. If certain conditions were fulfilled, considerable comfort and some leisure could be expected. For this, however, there must be a reasonable 'family wage' brought in by the man, if possible supplemented by the wife's wage; there must not be too many children, but above all there must be employment. The unemployment, or worse, the death of the breadwinner, transformed the picture, which at once became one of reliance on inadequate social security, hardship, the stigma of poverty. A working married woman drawing her own wage, however small it was, might experience a subjective sense of independence. Her dependence on her own mother for help with children and housework could be reciprocated with material help as well as companionship and the sense of the older woman's usefulness. Even if the daughter herself were not working, her husband's wage would run to some 'little luxuries' for her mother. The destruction of the family unit by death revealed the illusory nature of the wife's independence and in these circumstances she might well fear a new dependence on her mother and not wish to be a burden to her. Michael Anderson in a recent study of kinship structures in nineteenth-century Lancashire (Anderson 1971) stressed the importance of *reciprocal* services in maintaining these bonds. Widows had little to give.

Michael Anderson emphasized the possibilities of choice now open to working-class families, and also suggested that perhaps, in contrast, kinship ties have retained and increased their importance for middle-class families where gifts of capital, large or small, continue to cement the bonds between generations. Colin Bell (Bell 1968) also implied that this might be the case. So maybe the middle-class academics who researched the working-class community projected onto that community kinship bonds that may more truthfully have reflected the middle-class experience.

In this context it is of interest to study another influential piece of sociological writing, *Family and Social Network* (1957) by Elizabeth Bott. An intensive, small-scale study of twenty couples with young children, its findings were also over-generalized into a myth of the growth of a pattern of 'joint conjugal roles' held to be a response to social mobility which broke up close knit kinship networks. Sometimes this type of relationship was said to be associated with a 'middle-class' way of life, at others with equality between the sexes. Elizabeth Bott has herself since commented on the lack of evidence to support such a generalization (Bott 1971). At the time she did not seem to feel that the basic sexual division of labour that was absolutely taken for granted by the husbands and wives in any way modified the idea of a 'joint conjugal role' with its implications of equality. It seemed to be taken for granted that 'equality in difference' was a realistic goal even for companionate marriage. Yet because her study ignored the economic dependence of wives on their husbands, and further masked it with discussions of the subjective and psychological aspects of marital relationships, the wives' unformulated, vague feelings of disturbance remained a puzzle.

'[They] seemed to feel that their position was rather difficult.

They had certainly wanted children . . . and were getting a great deal of satisfaction from their maternal role. But at the same time, they felt tied down by their children and they did not like the inevitable drudgery associated with child care. . . . Most complained of isolation, boredom and fatigue. They wanted a career or some special interest that would make them feel they were something more than children's nurses and housemaids. They wanted more joint entertainments with their husbands, and more contacts with friends. These complaints were not levelled specifically at their husbands – in most cases they felt their husbands were trying to make the situation easier – but against the social situation and the conflict in which they found themselves. One wife summed it up by saying, "Society seems to be against married women. I don't know, it's all very difficult." ' (Bott 1971:83–4)

THE SOCIOLOGY OF THE FAMILY

The main role of sociology in the fifties, and in the sixties as well, was to give a reassuring view of 'ordinary life', reaffirming a core of British normality beneath the alarming surface appearances of crime, vice, and disintegration. Whatever normality was, the families studied by the writers I have mentioned represented it. Researchers wanted to find out what 'real families' actually did. Yet they also wanted to reassure their audience that affluence was not in the process of destroying working class family life. As John and Elizabeth Newson put it 'At a time when he has more money in his pocket, and more leisure on which to spend it, than ever before, the head of the household chooses to sit at his own fireside, a baby on his knee and a feeding bottle in his hand' (Newson and Newson 1963:145).

So the perpetuation of traditional yet improved patterns of working-class family life gave emotional sustenance to a liberal middle-class readership. In order to be able to give this emotional comfort the Newsons, like other researchers, had to ignore the continuing inequalities within the family. What matter if half the husbands in their study never changed a nappy? 'The family' was always discussed as a global and indivisible whole. Conflicts within it therefore conveniently disappeared.

Both the questions asked and the methodology used ensured that no really disturbing features of women's lives would be brought to light. Young and Willmott *created* a vision of the life of the working-class woman by a consistently subjective presentation of their findings. By focusing on child care, kinship networks, the consequences of 'affluence', and, above all, class, most of these writers avoided confronting the problems still facing women. To study this body of literature is above all to study how ideology operates by *excluding* whole areas of debate from the very consciousness of readers and authors alike. Where were the battered women? Where was the cultural wasteland? Where was the sexual misery hinted at in the problem pages of the women's magazines? Where was mental illness? – Young and Willmott banished it to a footnote. Invisibility cloaked these problems. The sexual division of labour, because it was taken for granted, was an *absence* in these works. The most significant things about women were not said at all, but were represented by a silence.

There are many valuable aspects to family life. It would seem that men – of all classes – were discovering the pleasures of domesticity during this period and were therefore exalting family life, especially working-class life, in a way that left no space for women's unfulfilled desires. Women were wanting to escape the nest just as men were climbing back into it. About this conflict there was also silence, for these books are about a myth – a myth of happiness.

MARRIAGE AND DIVORCE

Sociology was influential in suggesting to the public that the family was in good shape. It was conservative – although the sociologists concerned saw themselves as engaged in a radical enterprise of rooting sociology in the life of ordinary people and in rehabilitating the working class (Platt 1971) – in suggesting that nothing much needed to be done about the family, in emphasizing stability and tradition.

Marriage and the family were discussed together so that tensions between conjugal and parental roles were ironed out. The debate about divorce, on the other hand, did lay bare some of the conflicting social needs the family was expected to fill.

To talk about divorce was to talk about the family as an institution under threat. 'Broken homes' were feared because of the threat to the upbringing of children and to the fabric of society generally. To engage in discussion about the legal boundaries of family life, and the kinds of behaviour that were, or were not, permissible within marriage was both to recognize that such legal boundaries did exist, and also to question where the line was drawn between public and private behaviour. Elizabeth Bott found that most of her research couples were 'almost totally ignorant of their legal rights and obligations as a family'. Marriage, for those entering it, was – and still is – understood as a personal matter, as the result of an unique romantic attraction between two individuals. It was an individual's free choice. Problems over divorce caused special anguish in the fifties and sixties because the legal arrangements in some sense offended against conceptions of free choice and individualism which ran riot in the climate of affluence.

As more individuals sought the remedy of divorce, what seemed like the vagaries of the law became more offensive. As Lord Denning said in 1959, the law had changed or was changing away from the concept of husband and wife as one person and towards the principle of partnership. The partners however were not 'partners at will'. The partnership could not be dissolved at their wish. Yet up until the point of separation, the law would not interfere in the hundred and one small quarrels and disputes over the rights and obligations of a couple, and this showed how unclear the concept of partnerships was, since the rights and obligations of marriage were so ill-defined and since the law avoided interference: 'In respect of these promises, each house is a domain into which the King's writ does not seek to run and to which his officers do not seek to be admitted.'

What this meant was that the rights and obligations of the marriage partnership were increasingly and only being hammered out in the divorce courts, in precise terms, and this led to what appeared to be anomalies and injustices. This also explains why it is inevitable that we should discuss marriage in terms of divorce (Delphy 1976). The debate on divorce sheds light on views about marriage.

The high divorce rate of the later forties was partly the result of hasty wartime marriages and of lengthy separations that could not be repaired. By the early fifties the divorce rate had dropped. The anxiety surrounding divorce had not. The disruptions of the war had opened up cracks in family life and the argument around divorce was about how to repair these wounds. The debate, like other discussions of the family, was conducted within the parameters of liberalism and conservatism. The Report of the Morton Commission on Marriage and Divorce, in particular, illustrated the way in which the conflict between a liberal – a progressive reformist – point of view and a conservative – a paternalist and authoritarian – one, produced a new level of consensus.

In the early fifties both the Church and the lay public appeared split on the issue of divorce. In 1951 Eirene White, a Labour MP, introduced a Bill to make possible divorce by consent, but was persuaded to withdraw this in return for the promise of a Royal Commission. This, the Morton Commission, did not report until 1956. Its composition was overwhelmingly legal, no divorced persons sat on it, and the average age of its members was over fifty-five years. Mabel Ridealgh, trades unionist and Labour MP, alone represented a working-class point of view, and she was hardly a supporter of permissiveness. When it finally reported, it split down the middle on the question of whether the irretrievable breakdown of marriage should be the basis for divorce, so that while it was superficially united against the *idea* of divorce by consent, it was able to offer no guidance as to what *should* be done.

The Report, the evidence given to it, and the contemporary commentary in the press all suggest that questions of class were an underlying factor in the debate. The question of class meshed with the question of the equality of women because, as already suggested, the prevailing view of consensus enshrined the idea of democracy. Marriage, no less than 'society', was to be democratic. O.R. McGregor (later a member of the Finer Committee on One Parent Families) wrote (McGregor 1957) what amounted to a statement of the liberal position, and central to this was the conception of the modern family unit as democratic. McGregor believed that the Morton Commission wished to preserve the Victorian family code, and that in emphasizing the 'dangers' and 'insidious weaknesses' of the democratic family, had failed to understand 'its potentialities for free men and women whose loyalties are those of choice'. For him, the emancipation of women and the ideal of equal partnership 'ought . . . to be judged a new source of strength, rather than weakness for the instituion of marriage'. Other reformers also wished for the democratization of divorce, in the sense that all classes should have equal access to it.

The Morton Report stated firmly that the emancipation of women had been the major cause of new stresses in the home, and that an 'over emphasis' on a satisfactory sex relationship in marriage had resulted in a 'tendency to take the duties and responsibilities of marriage less seriously than formerly'. The evidence to the Commission reflected more distinctly the two different views. The conservative view was that the family was threatened with decay, and that any extension of the conditions in which divorce could be obtained must encourage this decay. As Mrs Erica Coombs, a voluntary social worker and member of the Mothers' Union expressed it:

> 'I find both husbands and wives lacking in a sense of duty and responsibilities to each other and to their children. It is hard to point out to them that, if love is growing cold, duty must take its place, for it is always a new thought to them; clearly anything else will lead to social anarchy.' (HM Government 1956 Minutes of Evidence: 278)

But those who were in favour of extending the divorce laws thought that *their* proposals would prevent family decay, about which they were an anxious as the paternalists. For example, the Women's Co-operative Guild, arguing for a revision of the divorce laws, began their statement:

> 'The good of the community is a first priority. The sanctity of marriage must be upheld but the law as it operates at the present time frequently brings marriage into disrepute. . . . [Our proposals] will uphold the sanctity of marriage and will

help to make people more conscious of their responsibilities as partners to a lifelong contract. . . . Homes are broken by [many] causes and the law should be allowed to give relief where these causes are serious and lead to the break up of marriage. Reasonable law, based upon human needs, is more likely to increase morality than to undermine it.' (HM Government 1956 Minutes of Evidence:278)

This position was shared by other supporters of reform. Both the Marriage Law Reform Society and the Daily Herald, for example (a newspaper that gave priority to the divorce issue during these years) championed the cause of those unfortunate couples who were living together but were prevented from marrying because one of them was still tied to a 'dead' marriage. Although some of the opponents to reform felt that the survival of marriage itself was at stake, the liberals never questioned the institution of marriage, and indeed saw divorce as promoting it. (We may speculate whether some liberals held views they believed it inexpedient to raise, but for whatever reason there was no radical opposition to marriage itself as an institution.)

The most extreme exponent of the 'optimistic' point of view was Ronald Fletcher, who argued that a higher divorce rate indicated that marriage and family life were flourishing and should be seen in the context of the greater availability of divorce through legal aid, and the increasing popularity of marriage. More divorce represented high expectations and a less fatalistic attitude. Couples were no longer prepared to tolerate an unhappy marriage, but demanded from marriage a high degree of affection and compansionship.

The conservatives admitted that women's position was not equal only when it was a question of punitive measures against them. They wished women to be made liable for costs and maintenance, and for women co-respondents to be named in divorce cases instead of being shielded by anonymity as was then the 'chivalrous' practice. It was also in this context that the recognition of lesbianism as a matrimonial offence was suggested, while the Bar Council looked with approval at the tough divorce laws in the USSR.

After the couples who were married 'in all but name', the second

group to suffer from the divorce laws as they stood were those
whose lives had been blighted by marriage to a violent or insane
spouse. Many of the contentious divorce cases of the period
centred round controversial definitions of what did or did not
constitute cruelty. Could insanity, for example, which led to
cruelty, be intentional? If it were not, could it be grounds for
divorce? Unacceptable sexual practices or demands became an
issue in cases of cruelty. In individual divorce cases there seems
habitually to have been an assumption by the legal profession that
a man's sexual requirements were likely to be greater than his
wife's, and that while he should exercise some restraint, it was for
his wife to respond to and adapt to his needs. Both a wife's
persistent refusal of sex and her persistent demands for it were, in
different cases, judged as constituting cruelty. This was a thorny
issue, for since 1923 an act of simple adultery by the husband had
been grounds for divorce. Before that, a husband could divorce an
adulterous wife, but a woman could not divorce her husband for
mere adultery. Therefore, since 1923, the law had not supported
the view that a man's sexual needs differed from those of his wife,
yet this was still a widely held belief. This contradiction was not
approached directly, yet we shall see later how sexual counselling
in the fifties and sixties tried to provide a remedy.

THE HOUSEWIFE'S INCOME – AGAIN

Women's organizations who gave evidence to the Morton Commission were on the whole more interested in women's economic
disabilities than in sexual satisfaction, and some did question the
extent of women's emancipation. In the opinion of the Six Point
Group: 'foremost among the causes of personal conflicts, broken
homes and the subsequent injury to children is the inferior
economic status of the wife and mother.' The Women's Co-
operative Guild suggested that women were not in practice equal
under the law and that it was more difficult for a woman than for a
man to prove a matrimonial offence.

The women's organizations argued that the remedy lay in the
equitable joint division of the family wage or of any property,
including the matrimonial home. The question of the housekeep-

ing allowance was raised. For instance, one woman lawyer seemingly with little sympathy for women nevertheless had this to say about social security:

'For the receipt of National Assistance you only have to prove need. While a person can prove need – "I have left my husband and have nothing to live on" – money must be paid. The . . . Assistance Board should be given authority to say, "There is no reason at all why this should be, and we must refuse you assistance unless you are prepared to take employment" . . . . At present these wives . . . just come and say "I am not going to live with my husband. I do not like him any more. . . ."
Q: And quite often husbands are willing for the wife to return?
A: Yes, and it does not follow that there is any serious reason why they should not live together. The thing is that a great many women like getting their money from the Post Office. You cannot rely on a working-class man to pay up the money and it is nicer to get it regularly from the Post Office. . . . The husband at present has got to maintain his children – it is the wife's maintenance that is the problem. I wonder if the right idea is not that we should make a charge on the husband for the wife's services.' (H.M. Government 1956: 493)

Many of the women who gave evidence expressed their confused feelings that, supporting as they did a traditional and approved view of family life, they were yet discriminated against by the state and also perhaps despised and neglected by those other articulate women whose energies had all been directed towards education, work, and equal pay. This sense of injustice was echoed by feminists such as Dr Edith Summerskill, who opposed divorce reform then and later on the grounds that the reform of the law came in the shape of a 'seducers' charter'. Helena Normanton, a QC, was another feminist whose feminism led her into a very conservative position on divorce. She initially prepared the evidence to be submitted by the Married Women's Association to the Morton Commission. The Association however refused to endorse her statement because she argued that a wife's right to knowledge of her husband's income must go with a corresponding responsibility on her part to maintain the home. Helena

Normanton's evidence went in as hers alone, and this heated dispute within the Married Women's Association showed how difficult, contentious, and confused an issue was the whole question of women's duties in the home and their corresponding 'right' to maintenance.

DIVORCE IN THE SIXTIES

The Morton Report was a stalemate. Between 1956 and 1963, when Leo Abse introduced another reform Bill into Parliament, the Marriage Law Reform Society continued to campaign for a change in the law. Public debate continued. Women who contemplated divorce were bound to become conscious of their economic dependence within marriage generally. Lena Jeger, discussing the 'Economics of Divorce' in the *Guardian* (21.6.63) pointed out that:

'There are economic difficulties which provide especially for older women a strong argument against bringing an action for divorce against a husband who has long deserted them. A divorced woman cannot be her ex-husband's widow. When a decree becomes absolute she reverts to the status of a single woman – pensions go to the second wife – and vice versa. A man can live for many years with a woman not his wife and she gets nothing.'

Thus both wife and 'other woman' were at the mercy of a social security system that invariably treated all women as the dependants of a man. In 1965 Mary Delane, again in the *Guardian*, put the point even more strongly:

'A right to maintenance is not automatic, whether she has children or not, and even if she has no income of her own during the period of the marriage. . . . If the husband marries again and has another family the first wife's allowance may well be reduced, and unless she starts paying her own contributions immediately following the date of the divorce she may not be able to qualify for a retirement pension by means of her subsequent earnings. . . . At one stroke she may lose the roof over her head, a sufficient share of a husband's income (an income that may have been adequate for one family but is certainly not for two), a father for her children, adult companionship for herself, and possibly the most meagre provision for her old age. And only those who have themselves endured this situation or have tried to mitigate some of the effects of it, understand how wholly suffocating and destructive of physical and mental well being it can be.'

Although there was no major change in the law until 1969, the fifties and sixties saw a series of minor changes. Judges and courts assumed greater powers in ensuring the wellbeing of children of divorced couples, for example. By the mid-sixties it was clear that it would be impossible to stop people voting with their feet. The divorce rate was just not going to drop back to prewar levels. The provision of legal aid after the war *had* democratized divorce, which was now no longer a course of action open only to the rich. Although many working-class couples opted for a separation order rather than for a divorce, the public discussion of a major moral issue meant that everyone was aware of separation and divorce as possible solutions for an unhappy marriage. By 1965 *The Times* (15.2.65) estimated that there were 40,000 divorces each year as against 28,000 in 1954. (In 1976 the figure was 136,000.)

Also, 90 per cent of these divorces were undefended. It had become clear that not only were there injustices within the law, particularly over 'cruelty', but also that different courts were interpreting the law differently. In cases – the majority – where both partners wanted a divorce the law was being brought into disrepute by the manufacture of 'evidence' against the 'guilty party'.

THE ROLE OF THE CHURCH

The power of the Church but also the limits of that power was nowhere more in evidence than over the question of divorce. When Princess Margaret renounced Group Captain Peter Townsend in 1956 because he was himself divorced, this had a symbolic significance for the whole nation and asserted the patriarchal authority of the Church. The ecclesiastical establishment had, however, itself been split on the issue of divorce and there was a progressive body of churchmen that supported liberalized divorce laws. Because of this split neither side had been represented on the Morton Commission. Ultimately, though, it was the Church that cut the knot. In 1964 the Archbishop of Canterbury set up a Committee to report on the state of divorce laws and to make recommendations. The Report referred to a National Opinion Poll printed in the *Daily Sketch* (18.9.65) which showed a 90 per cent support for divorce on the petition of either party after a seven year separation. Accordingly the Report bowed to the inevitable and proposed that the doctrine of the irretrievable breakdown of marriage should be substituted for the doctrine of the matrimonial offence.

The intentions of this Report, which eventually led to new legislation in 1969, with its emphasis on reconciliation procedures and on the need for the courts to establish in any given case whether or not a marriage had irretrievably broken down, were complex. In part it must have been a face-saving exercise for the Church in a situation in which divorce had ceased to bring social stigma and in which it was impossible to enforce lifelong monogamy. The Church also intended that the law should be rationalized. Yet while recognizing its loss of ideological grip, the Church did not intend that divorce should be made easier to obtain, although that is what happened. It distinguished the principle of the irretrievable breakdown of marriage quite clearly from the principle of divorce by consent. The Church remained opposed to divorce by consent on the grounds that divorce was not simply a private contract to be repudiated at will by either party but was a lifelong commitment so that some body representing 'the community' – in practice the courts – must have a say in the ending of all marriages. At the time there were radicals who criticized the Report precisely because they feared that it would undermine civil rights and replace legal criteria with the undefined and even more subjective judgments of counsellors with a psychiatric or psychologistic orientation.

CONCLUSION

Arguments about the condition of family life in postwar Britain always involved a fear of state intervention. Despite the seemingly widespread acceptance of the welfare state in the fifties and sixties, conservatives continued to fear that it undermined family life. As a grammar school head master put it, addressing representatives of the British Medical Association in July 1961: ' "In the kind of security state we are creating, the state does for the child many of the things that in my youth were the hallmark of good parenthood." ' (Fletcher 1966)

When it came to marriage, there was ambivalence towards the intervention of the state into the private area of marriage relationships, with no parties to the debate confronting this issue very directly. A higher incidence of divorce did nonetheless lead in practice to greater state intervention, both with the development of marriage counselling and social work services, and with the courts becoming more interventionist in the 'best interests' of children when it came to issues of custody and care. There was a great deal of legislation relating to children during this period too, which was also part of an enterprise to define more clearly how children should be reared (see Wilson 1977).

The relationship of public to private in the sphere of moral and sexual behaviour and the care of children was therefore clearly raised in these years. The relationship of public to private was to be transformed into the relationship between personal and political by the women's movement.

Secondly, discussions about the family raised the question of the status of women within marriage. The Church Report on divorce, *Putting Asunder*, discussed the security of wives and mothers and correctly argued that the economic insecurity of divorced women was a result not of divorce but of the economic inequality of the *wife*. It argued therefore that the laws relating to property, pensions, insurance, and other matters to do with the economic status of wives and children needed reform along with the divorce laws.

Putting Asunder and the legislation to which it led represented a victory for liberal opinion both within and outside the Church, but a defeat for the 'old feminists' as well as for conservatism. Lady Summerskill opposed the reforms to the end, but this was really the last stand of all the women who had tried in different ways to 'raise the status of the wife and homemaker' ever since the war, to protect her, and to extend her legal rights.

Changes in the customs surrounding marriage and attitudes to divorce must also be seen as one of the preconditions of the women's liberation movement. It is sometimes argued that women's liberation encourages divorce, but it would seem rather that high rates of divorce in the sixties created part of the pre-conditions for the re-emergence of a feminist movement. More and more women were experiencing life as deserted wife or lone parent. Although this situation affected only a minority directly, it had a powerful effect on the general consciousness simply by throwing into glaring relief the economic inequality and dependence upon which all marriage was based. Many women in the late forties had wanted essentially a reaffirmation of traditional marriage on lines that recognized more concretely the sexual division of labour and the value of women's 'equal but different' role. By 1969 a new generation of women was beginning to search for more radical solutions.

CHAPTER FIVE

The boundaries of sexuality

Our Ford – or Our Freud, as, for some inscrutable reason, he chose to call himself whenever he spoke of psychological matters – Our Freud had been the first to reveal the appalling dangers of family life. The world was full of fathers – was therefore full of misery; full of mothers – therefore of every kind of perversion from sadism to chastity; full of brothers, sisters, uncles, aunts – full of madness and suicide.

'And yet, among the savages of Samoa, in certain islands off the coast of New Guinea. . . .'

The tropical sunshine lay like warm honey on the naked bodies of children tumbling promiscuously among the hibiscus blossoms. Home was in any one of twenty palm-thatched houses. In the Trobriands conception was the work of ancestral ghosts; nobody had ever heard of a father. . . . Mothers and fathers, brothers and sisters. But there were also husbands, wives, lovers. There were also monogamy and romance. . . . Everywhere exclusiveness, everywhere a focusing of interest, a narrow channelling of impulse and energy.

'But everyone belongs to everyone else. . . .' (Aldous Huxley: *Brave New World*.)

'They say it takes two to make a baby, but it's not true. It takes one.' (Madeline Kerr: *The People of Ship Street*)

To talk of 'marriage and the family' as a single entity was to minimize the importance of marriage as a sexual relationship. Yet the importance of sexuality within marriage was covertly acknowledged in discussions of divorce, while women interviewed by sociological investigators hinted at sexual problems. Anchored within the family, sexuality was full of contradictions. Ambiguously, sex is most strictly forbidden within the family – between the generations – yet the family is also still the only legitimate site for sexual activity – within marriage. Women's liberation has certainly been linked with reassessments of sexuality and the meaning for women of their sexual experiences. According to one popular stereotype a 'liberated woman' is a sexually available woman. Another has suggested that 'women's liberation represents a demand for the return to female chastity' (Decter 1973). Yet other anti-feminists have accused women's liberation of making aggressive, castrating sexual demands on men, in response to which the unfortunate male has taken flight into impotence or homosexuality. The modern feminists have been accused of wanting too much sex and of rejecting their sexuality. Women are still caricatured as either frigid or whores. To refuse the penis is evil, but so is it evil to engage in the frenzied search for the multiple orgasm.

Such arguments and accusations are not new. The aim of many of the suffragists and suffragettes had been to be freed from sexual enslavement, and what they desired was for men to raise themselves to a state of 'purity' equal to that of women. Feminists struggled to bring to an end the exploitation suffered by prostitutes. They hoped also for a more healthy relationship between the sexes. Many of them campaigned for birth control. What they were disconcerted to find, in the twenties and thirties, was a new generation of young women who interpreted freedom differently. Young women in the West as well as in the Soviet Union put into practice the 'glass of water' theory of sexual behaviour and treated sex as a simple pleasure akin to smoking a cigarette – which was another symbol of their new freedom. Nor did these young women feel, as the older feminists had, that make-up and smart clothes were a sign of servitude. On the contrary, lipstick, silk stockings, short skirts, and bobbed hair symbolized liberation. The older women looked on, ambivalent, afraid that promiscuity and sophistication would lead not to independence but to a reinforcement of male values.

After the Second World War the debate continued but was recast. Popular manuals on sex and marriage openly rejected the period of women's 'false' emancipation, the Jazz Age of the twenties. Then a boyish appearance and a wish to ape men by swearing, drinking, and demanding too much independence had led women away from true democratic equality within marriage. The act of reconciliation attempted after the war, which has been discussed in relation to women's role in the home, also encompassed a sexual reconciliation between men and women.

This occurred, initially, in the aftermath of a war that had certainly given many individual men and women a very new experience of sexuality. For some women, beached high and dry in remote country areas or evacuated to a place of dull safety 'for the duration', it had meant total and unrelieved sexual abstinence (McCrindle and Rowbotham 1977). For others the threat of death dissolved restraints. In the bohemian atmosphere of wartime London many women as well as men, single or married, felt free to take their pleasure as it came. The exciting presence of American GIs, or Free Poles, Free Czechs or Free French in provincial towns too caused agreeable havoc amongst the local female population (Charles 1966, Longmate 1971).

After the war, even if most women returned to an acceptance of monogamy, they felt that as well as a right to employment theirs was the right to sexual fulfilment. The ideas of Havelock Ellis and of Freud, still considered avant-garde before the war, were beginning to reach a wider audience. Women also wanted some glamour after the drab days of the war. As Anne Scott James (1952) expressed it:

> 'As the last guns rumbled and the last all clear sounded all the squalor and discomfort and roughness that had seemed fitting for so long began to feel old fashioned. . . . I wanted to throw the dried egg out of the window, burn my shabby curtains and wear a Paris hat again. The Amazons, the women in trousers, the good comrades had had their glorious day. But it was over. Gracious living beckoned once again.'

Or, as one ATS character in a forces play near the end of the war put it: 'After khaki you want sky blue and frills' (Public Records Office 1941-1946). And Elliott Slater and Moya Woodside (1951) found that men and perhaps especially women wanted more good times after the war: 'I want some fun out of life – I'm not interested in raising the birthrate'. Alison Settle in the *Observer* said that young women were 'hungry for romantic dressing', and alluded to a 'depression of spirits such as was unknown during even the blackest days of the war'. And she further reported that 'many returned servicemen say they find British women tired, unglamorous, shabbily dressed'.

The recapturing of lost glamour and femininity crystallized around the New Look. Labour movement stalwarts such as Annie Loughlin (who had been chairman of the TUC), Mabel Ridealgh (later to sit on the Morton Commission) and Bessie Braddock, another Labour MP, raged against it in the name of women's emancipation, but they seemed to be as frightened of the 'over-sexiness' of the New Look as critical of it as extravagant and unpatriotic, although they also objected to it as symbolic of a return to a 'caged bird' attitude, and the curtailment of women's freedom. In fact, the New Look marked the beginning of an era in which sex appeal and work had to be combined, a period when the old division between celibate career woman and the little wife broke down. The division between Nice Women and Tarts was also about to go.

In the fifties the successful, although short-term, economic solutions of the Conservatives solved the problem of women's postwar blues. Within a few years there were no clothing coupons, but a plentiful supply of cheap, smart clothing and new cosmetics in the shops. Many women saw this as a real advance; for instance Anne Godwin of the TUC wrote in *Labour Woman* in 1963: 'One of the changes which has impressed me most of all . . . has been the disappearance of class distinction in women's dress. . . . Now thank goodness . . . all women have the opportunity of dressing well.' It was to take another turn of the wheel before women began once again to feel that glamour, too, was in its own way oppressive.

Although women activists moved away in the fifties and sixties

from the dismissal of fashion as frivolous, there remained notice-
able class differences in the ways in which women experienced
their sexuality and their femininity. Elizabeth Bott found that a
working-class wife seemed to feel that 'physical sexuality was an
intrusion on a peaceful domestic relationship rather than an expression of such a relationship. It was as if sexuality were felt to be
basically violent and disruptive'. But the couples with a more
middle-class life pattern seemed to feel 'a moral obligation to enjoy
sexual relations . . . successful sexual relations were felt to prove
that all was well with the joint relationship, whereas
unsatisfactory relations were indicative of a failure in the total
relationship' – which suggests a strong internalization of
ideologies and norms.

There are endless suggestions in the documentary literature of
the period that many working-class women knew sexuality only as
violent and coercive. One woman interviewed for the Mass
Observation study on population said:

> 'Some of these women, and some of them quite old, that were
> having their babies the same time I had Billy, they said their
> husbands wouldn't leave them alone, they didn't want to go
> out of the nursing home, some of them sobbed and cried, they
> didn't want to go home for fear of starting one right away.'
> (Mass Observation 1945:55)

The sociological studies of 'Ashton', the Yorkshire mining community, of 'Ship Street' in Liverpool, by Madeline Kerr (1958), and
two studies of Paddington (Paneth 1944, Spinley 1954), all testify
to the miserable lives led by many working-class women for whom
a brief, adolescent interest in romance and in their own
appearance died after marriage which brought the experience of
frequent pregnancy and often a lack of all tenderness and affection
from their men. Kerr, whose account was particularly
unsympathetic, and who was entirely critical of the women, especially the domineering 'mums', even managed to explain away
many examples of sexual violence in marriage, including one man
who tried to set fire to his wife. Naturally, in Madeline Kerr's eyes:
'in a community where the woman is dominant the male clings to
the vestiges of his power by refusing to allow his wife to be

sterilized or to use birth control methods'.

Although fear or rejection of sexuality may not be so much a thing of the past today as many of us might like to believe, sexual enlightenment was certainly a major project of the postwar years. Before the war, the invisibility of most sexual behaviour had meant that a high level of ignorance persisted. On the movies, the length of a kiss was timed and double beds were seldom shown. (This led to the furnishing vogue for twin beds, an interesting example of life imitating art.) But by 1960 it was possible for a French film director to photograph (poetically) the moment of a woman's orgasm, in *Les Amants*, although the shot of her face at the critical moment was censored in Britain. By 1971, in *Sunday, Bloody Sunday*, it was even possible for two homosexual men to be shown kissing in a film destined for the commercial circuit. So the advance of media representations of sexuality, usually presented in the style of realism, has gone hand in hand with the burrowing determination of psychiatrists, therapists, and sociologists who undertook a full scale exploration into the privacy and secrecy of sexual life in order to make the 'dark places light'. Current discussions of sexuality within the contemporary women's movement have to be understood as part of this unfinished investigation of unresolved problems.

THEORIES OF SEXUAL BEHAVIOUR

In industrialized society the idea of sexuality as natural (McIntosh 1977) – and the idea of children as innocent and asexual – have been powerful ones. It is not surprising if men and women have felt that in seeking sexual fulfilment they are reaching for the true core of themselves and to a kind of human essence that has been left free of the contamination of industrial life so evident everywhere else. Yet it is this 'natural' aspect of sex, too, that has been perceived as disruptive, dangerous, and destructive.

The work of Alfred Kinsey tended to fit in with the view of sex as a natural and as an animal activity, partly because he was a zoologist and partly because he presented his findings in a way that suggested that 'everybody's doing it' – like the birds and bees of the Eartha Kitt song. The two pioneering Kinsey Reports, appearing in 1948 and 1953, went against the grain of the prevailing social atmosphere and might seem to have been more in tune with the simpler and more optimistic faith in science characteristic of the prewar period when they had been begun.

Kinsey sought, perhaps naively, simply to catalogue what human beings *did* sexually, to divest it of moral meanings and to challenge accepted ideas about what was natural or unnatural. This naive empiricism had its own covert ideological assumptions and value judgments (Robinson 1976). But it was liberating in demonstrating just how diverse sexual behavoiur was (within the boundaries of the United States at least). His Reports called into question all kinds of beliefs surrounding the relationship between class and sexual behaviour and the differences between the sexes. He discredited the idea of a vaginal orgasm upon which Freud had laid so much emphasis and found that for women masturbation and homosexual relationships were more reliable as a source of sexual satisfaction than heterosexual intercourse. He also found that whereas men are at their most potent early in life, the sexual potentiality of women is at its peak in their thirties. Only in suggesting that women's sexual responses were more 'physiological' and less imaginative, that they responded more to touch and less to fantasy, did Kinsey support accepted views. In other respects his findings were of a nature to shatter the self-esteem of the American male and undermine the authority of the husband. Threatening and shocking in the moral climate of the late 1940s and 1950s, both Reports received massive publicity and both were strongly attacked.

It was said that Kinsey sought to treat human beings as mere animals – an objection made by Soviet as well as Western critics. Critics objected because Kinsey had used the simple measurement of 'sexual outlet' and orgasm as an indication of sexual satisfaction, whereas psychoanalysts made strong distinctions of a qualitative kind. But while there was some justification for criticisms of Kinsey's method, it was really his radical conclusions that were under attack, and especially what Lionel Trilling (1957), the conservative and anti-Communist critic, described as a 'democratic' view of sexual behaviour which showed 'intentional intellectual weakness' in denying values and consequences.

In 1966 the first report of the work of William Masters and Virginia Johnson appeared. In the heady climate of the sixties *Human Sexual Response* was welcomed by radicals and particularly by American feminists. Although Kinsey's work had undoubtedly been of great importance in breaking new ground and preparing a less hostile climate, in 1966 there was as there had not been in 1953 a constituency ready to make use of new weapons against the sexual oppression of women. Women were ready to unite against Freud and the 'tyranny of the phallus', yet American feminists seemed not to notice that while Masters and Johnson took a democratic view of relations between the sexes, while they emphasized the woman's right to sexual satisfaction, and her responsibility to control her response or even take control of the sexual act, their therapeutic endeavour was the maintenance of the marital couple (Robinson 1976). *Human Sexual Response* was, after all, not so far from the many books that attempted to domesticate the Kinsey findings and fit them to Western monogamous marriage.

SEX WITHIN MARRIAGE

Marriage is where sexual activity is supposed to take place. Only within marriage have sexual acts been regarded as positively legal (McIntosh 1977). It is impossible to overemphasize the importance of marriage as a central and organizing idea in both the 1950s and the 1960s. It appealed as much to progressives as to conservatives in the climate of postwar Britain (and North America), and equally to feminists and to those hostile to the equality of women. It was part of a hedonistic life style as much as of a puritanical one.

Conservative views on marriage were still powerful in the 1940s. Innes Pearse and Lucy Crocker, authors of *The Peckham Experiment* (1943), an account of a pioneer health centre in South London, were within the progressive stream of thought of the period which then still held strong overtones of puritanism and eugenicism. Nature, they wrote (Pearse and Crocker 1943:224–5): 'like a knitter, weaves her living fabric on two needles – the sexes . . . picking up loops of circumstances from the continuous flow of events, and through their mutual action the materialization of a specific design or pattern grows.' They extended this weird metaphor into an attack on sex equality:

> 'The only "equality" between Nature's hands is that, like our own hands they each have fingers. . . . Try to put a male glove on a female hand or vice versa and it will only "fit" if it is turned inside out – eviscerated. The only thing that *will* "fit" is a stocking-like garment, and that immobilizes all the "fingers", so that they cannot act discretionately! That is the biological price we pay for any attempted "equality" of the sexes – both hands desensitized and reduced to undifferentiated stumps.'

Not content with this eloquent symbol of castration, they went on to emphasize that 'in health or wholeness, the bias of sex in man and woman is brought naturally to balance in the unity of *family*.'

Postwar marriage more generally, though, aspired to a democratic ideal, although writers might introduce the idea of 'equality in difference' between the sexes. Georgene Seward (1953), for example, wrote that 'victory for the democratic way of living means a democratic reformulation of sex roles'. This, though, was the statement of an ideal and seemed far removed from the situation at the end of the war.

There was a scare – to be repeated at intervals during the fifties and sixties – about rising rates of veneral disease, and for the first time a public campaign to educate the populace into the idea that prevention and cure were possible – posters with VD in huge letters were plastered on hoardings. (Was it confused with V-Day?) There was also the old wartime problem of illegitimacy, evidently connected in the mind of at least one of Mass Observation's interviewees with women getting uppity:

> 'Look what's going on. I don't want to be rude to a lady – but there's a woman in the house where I'm staying bringing men home every night. And he knows – he *knows* what's going on – in the army he is. Who's going to come back to that? There'll be some messes there will – little kids and all. And what about them that's earning £4 or £5 a week – women – are they going to settle to nothing a week when their old man comes back?' (Mass Observation 1944:47)

When servicemen did return they brought many problems of readjustment, for as one marriage guidance counsellor pointed out (Wallis 1968): 'not only did many a young father return full of excited anticipation only to find himself resented as an intruder by children he hardly knew, and even by a wife who had got used to living without him', but the sexual aspects of marriage caused difficulty at a time when such matters were less freely discussed. In the early days after the war the Marriage Guidance Council received thousands of letters in response to which they issued a booklet which gave basic sexual information.

There were fears of population decline, but fears too of large 'problem' families, of broken homes, juvenile delinquents, and social anarchy. The 1949 Royal Commission on Population recommended that contraceptive advice should be available to married women. There was beginning to be an understanding that repeated pregnancies resulting from a failure to use birth control was often the symptom not of a joyous sexual life but of sexual coercion and distaste, and that it could be associated with the instability rather than the stability of marriage. Family planning clinics uncovered a horrifying secret life of sexual misery in the families of the nation. Dr Helena Wright, the pioneer campaigner for birth control and for sexual satisfaction for women, suggested that at least 50 per cent of women derived no pleasure from their sexual lives, and she too felt that women's lack of satisfaction, coupled with contraceptive failure, undermined marriage and family life.

One factor in the democratization of marriage was the very material change in the law that had since 1923 made simple adultery a marital offence for a man. Once this was the case it clearly became important for wives to be able to satisfy their husbands' sexual demands, and it would have been inhumane to suggest that they should do so without enjoying it. There was a point, then, at which women's *right* to sexual fulfilment might come close to being a *duty*.

It was after the war that the work of the Marriage Guidance Council started to expand. (It became the National Marriage Guidance Council in 1947.) It received encouragement from the Denning Report of 1947, which, mainly concerned with reconciliation procedures, suggested an important role for counselling services in preventing divorce by helping couples towards a happier experience of marriage.

The marriage counselling services were well aware that women were making new demands, and nothing illustrates more clearly the general changes in attitudes towards sexual behaviour than a comparison of the three books produced by the Council in 1948, 1958, and 1968. J.H. Wallis (1968) suggested that immediately after the war the idea of a wife 'as an equal and active participator in intercourse was still a novelty, for the subsequent crusade among sex writers in favour of orgasms for women had scarcely begun' but within twenty years the Council had moved from a conservative position to one in which the psychotherapeutic goal of self fulfilment appeared not even to need justification. In 1948, the Council's 'General Principles' affirmed its support for 'permanent monogamous marriage', condemned sexual intercourse outside it, and hardly even welcomed birth control. The Archbishop of Canterbury himself worded the Council's Principle 9, which stated:

> 'That scientific contraception, while serving a purpose in assisting married couples to regulate the spacing of their children, becomes a danger when misused to enable selfish and irresponsible people to escape the duties and disciplines of marriage and parenthood.' (Mace 1948:153)

By 1958 this had been changed to a statement that welcomed contraception within marriage as contributing 'to the health and happiness of the whole family', although it still gave unqualified support to monogamy, and opposed divorce. By this time the Council was heavily involved in sex education in schools, which to some members seemed 'healthier' than an involvement in the pathology of marriages that had gone sexually wrong. But by 1968 there was no statement of principles at all – it had been replaced by a bibliography of the literature on psychotherapy and sex.

THE HAPPINESS LITERATURE

The fifties in Britain saw the 'psychiatrization' of personal relation ships and the expansion of psycho-sexual counselling services along psychoanalytic lines, at the Tavistock Institute, in child guidance clinics, and in the more progressive psychiatric departments of hospitals (Wilson 1977). In retrospect these endeavours, and the literature they produced, have been judged by feminists and radicals of the seventies as conservative and stiflingly normative. Yet although a dogmatic insistence on heterosexuality prevailed, and although masculinity and femininity were narrowly defined, this work was rather heroic, ultimately, in its attempt to reconcile the individual and his or her disruptive sexual urges and unconscious immaturities to the institution of monogamous marriage. If the price of sexual fulfilment and heterosexuality were a general conformity in other areas of life, this price did not seem too high.

The psychotherapists were dealing with individuals who had specific difficulties, often defined as pathological, in their sexual relationships. The advice given to those not so afflicted, however, tended to adopt many of the sub-Freudian assumptions of the psychotherapeutic literature. These did not support a view of women as equal, if only because they were concerned above all with *differences* and with the problem, perceived as intractable, of the individual's 'identification' of him or herself as appropriately masculine or feminine.

The popular literature on marriage performed a delicate balancing act in combining these theories with the democratic ideal of marriage. An important part of the work of the National Marriage Guidance Council and the Family Planning Association was the sexual education of wives. The main responsibility for this education lay with the husband, so not for nothing was the Council's postwar booklet entitled *How To Treat A Young Wife*. The prevailing view of female sexuality was summed up by the Bar Council in its evidence to the Morton Commission (H.M. Government 1956, Minutes of Evidence:28):

'Intercourse and its results have a far deeper physical and emotional impact on the woman and we further stress that many a bride who would *apta viro** if understandingly and

* This may be translated as 'ready for a man'.

gently approached by her spouse, is panicked into frigidity by ignorant sexual approaches in the early days of marriage.'

Even Helena Wright took the view that it was the role of husbands to guide their wives towards sexual happiness. Although she understood the importance of the clitoris in the sexual satisfaction of women and believed that male definitions of sexuality had led to a 'penis vagina fixation' she also held to the traditional beliefs that women took longer than men to become sexually aroused, that they did not fantasize and so on, as well as encouraging women to do everything they could to develop vaginal sensations. (The clitoris should be saying to the vagina ' "wake up and feel" ' (1947).)

Other writers clearly did not share Helena Wright's enthusiams, yet felt it necessary to respond and adapt their advice to the views she represented as well as to the Kinsey findings. Mary Macaulay, 'a well known doctor and magistrate', who wrote the Penguin handbook *The Art of Marriage* (1957) was critical of books that 'lay such emphasis on the importance of a woman's sharing her husband's physical satisfaction' since this contributed to women's dissatisfaction with their marriages. For this author, too, since she assumed that men have a stronger sexual urge than women, it was both for men to restrain it, and to take charge in this area: 'just as the success of the erotic side of the marriage is chiefly the husband's responsibility, so the atmosphere of the home is chiefly the wife's.' But while the husband should exercise some sexual restraint, since women enjoyed being 'pursued and conquered' a man might use something approaching force in his love making, nor should a woman refuse her husband merely because she felt no desire: 'It is a shocking thing to hear a woman say that . . . she will not be raped even by her husband. Such an attitude would be impossible in any woman to whom loving and giving were synonymous' (Macaulay 1957:79). At the same time, 'whether or not the wife reaches what is known as the climax or orgasm, sexual intercourse between husband and wife can and should be utterly satisfying.' Another of Dr Macaulay's tips for husbands was that 'shy' wives are often most responsive when half asleep, and she suggested that while it should not be too difficult for the husband to give his wife a clitoral orgasm, the chief purpose of this was to prepare the way for a 'full and natural "vaginal orgasm" '. The clitoral orgasm was presumably not 'natural'.

The Power of Sexual Surrender (1960) by Marie Robinson, another book on 'the art of loving', also emphasized what was virtually a geisha role for wives, who should neither demand sex if their husband felt disinclined, nor refuse it if they themselves felt no desire. Response to a husband's desires was also the message of *The Sexual Responsibility of Women* (1957) by Maxine Davis. This started more explicitly from the 'democratic' viewpoint that 'woman has come of age'. This book is interesting as an attempt to accomodate Kinsey's findings to marriage. His discovery that women reached their peak of sexual interest much later in life than men was described as 'what seemed like mismanagement on Nature's part', yet his findings on women's responses led Davis to argue that women should still respond to their husbands' desires, while recognizing that they themselves have a sexual responsibility – they should not imagine that the man will 'do everything'.

All these manuals, and others, betrayed a horror of celibacy. Dr Macaulay felt it necessary to reassure her readers that celibacy did not necessarily damage your health. In 1953, in *Speaking as a Woman* Phyllis Whiteman could even justify homosexual attachments, because although inferior they might 'hold beauty for those concerned. . . . The thing to avoid at all costs is celibacy'. Another advice book, *Living Alone* (1956) by Beryl Conway Cross, suggested that for a woman to be living alone was not only the path to loneliness, bitterness, and frumpiness, but was likely to be the lot of women who were selfish and egocentric.

Such books repeatedly referred to marriage as an 'art', and the relationship between a man and a woman as extraordinarily delicate and difficult. Even Drusilla Beyfus, writing in 1968 of *The English Marriage*, a book of interviews with rather 'trendy' couples, described the state of marriage as 'totally and absolutely unlike the consciousness of being single' and spoke of its 'impenetrably private nature'. If today we have lost this sense of companionship between men and women as momentously difficult and mysterious, this surely represents an advance. Even in the early sixties, and certainly in the fifties there was greater segregation of the sexes amongst the young, and to a certain extent among adults. The legacy of the so-called 'permissive society' was not just promiscuity; the incursion of women into work and higher education did actually make it easier for men and women to be friends.

CONTRACEPTION AND FERTILITY

Family planning workers were forced into a more realistic view of what sexual relationships were like for many women by what they saw and heard day in, day out in their clinics. Lella Florence in her *Progress Report On Birth Control* (1956) could not be unaware of the inequality between men and women that caused many a woman to 'live in slavery with no control over her own body'. The Birmingham Family Planning Association workers of whom Lella Florence wrote found resistance among women to the cap as a contraceptive because they were expected to pay for it out of their housekeeping money, when it was the husband who desired intercourse – the wives would have been more than happy to do without it. A familiar story to the clinic workers was that of the wife who 'because of desperate fear of pregnancy withholds and rejects all endearments for long periods'. Husbands were seen to be often punitive, demanding and boorish, and sex looked on by large numbers of wives as a duty.

Yet contraception was almost a necessary accompaniment to the idea of female sexual satisfaction within marriage. The birthrate had begun to fall in the 1870s, but general social approval for contraception remained problematic until the importance of sexuality within marriage was accepted as an ideal. In the twenties feminists such as Helena Wright and Mary Stocks had braved abuse and physical assault to give working class women access to birth control help and advice – by the late 1940s, contraception was recognized as part of the welfare state. After the Second World War birth control, transformed into 'family planning', sought to locate sexuality firmly within marriage (Gordon 1978), minimized women's unequal position and emphasized the careful, spaced upbringing of children. There was a major expansion in the operations of the Family Planning Association. In 1938 it had been operating sixty-one clinics, and by 1948 this number had increased only to sixty-five. However, starting in 1949 new clinics opened at about the rate of one every five weeks, and by 1963 there were four hundred clinics in operation.

Lella Florence regarded 1955 as 'something of a turning point' in making birth control respectable. In that year Iain Macleod, then Minister of Health, visited the Kensington FPA (then the North Kensington Marriage Welfare Centre); the FPA chairman Margaret Pyke appeared on television; and the next day the work of the FPA was explained on Woman's Hour (the BBC radio programme for women). There was also a leading article in *The Times*, which welcomed contraception because 'a free community must have room for both schools of thought' (that is for those both for and against birth control). *The Times* leader, however, also believed that the family planning movement was rightly a voluntary one, since this best expressed the notion of individual choice and freedom and the coexistence of a plurality of views.

This increasing respectability may be explained partly by a growing fear of the world population explosion. In any case, in Britain by the mid-fifties the birthrate had begun to rise (although not to American levels) and this made birth control appear more reasonable. It was also more widely understood that most couples did attempt to control their fertility anyway, so again the provision of more efficient methods seemed only reasonable. The Marriage Survey of the Population Investigation Committee (1959-61) carried out by David Glass, Griselda Rowntree, and Rachel Pierce, showed that among couples married in the 1950s almost three quarters were 'birth control users', nearly half of these after marriage, the rest after the birth of their first child. Nearly half the users, however, relied on withdrawal, or, less often, on the 'safe' period. Among mechanical methods by far the most popular was the sheath. For most couples, therefore, birth control was the man's responsibility. (In this Britain differed from the USA.) But the family planning clinics catered largely for women and most commonly prescribed the dutch cap, which was used by about 13 per cent of couples.

The Birmingham survey showed how difficult it was for many women to use a cap. Lack of privacy owing to housing problems, and lack of a bathroom or even running water made it too embarrassing for many women to persist in using a cap, but research into alternatives were hampered because it was still not a wholly respectable subject for an ambitious scientist.

In 1958, however, the Lambeth Conference of the Church of England gave its positive blessing to the use of contraceptives for the first time, in announcing that family planning was 'a right and important factor in Christian family life and should be the result of positive choice before God'. No matter how few were in any real sense Christian, this statement gave birth control a respectability it had never previously had. Shortly afterwards, when the Pill first came onto the market, this generated widespread discussion, so that as C.M. Langford later noted 'It is quite likely that the considerable favourable publicity given to birth control during the last few years has had the effect of reducing the reluctance of women to acknowledge their use of contraception'.

Birth control use became virtually universal in the sixties and the major change in contraceptive use was the Pill, although it was still outstripped in popularity by the sheath. The Population Investigation Committee study (Langford 1976) found that 33 per cent of women married in 1966 or later were using or had used the Pill, but, like cap users, they were more likely to be middle class.

Ann Cartwright (1970) found that the Pill was favoured for its 'naturalness'. Comments such as ' "It's so natural" ' or ' "It's just like not using anything and you can really relax and enjoy it" ' were made and it was contrasted with the cap – ' "I'm not one for gadgets. It's not natural and that's what it should be" '. This demonstrates the continuing importance of the association of sex with the natural.

Ann Cartwright made the important point that:

'The Pill has surely had a most liberating effect by overcoming inhibitions. An oral contraceptive could be discussed more easily and with less embarrassment than methods related to the vagina, penis, or sexual intercourse. But once conventional barriers were breached all methods could be talked about more freely.'

It was in this way that the Pill changed consciousness, rather than, as was widely assumed at the time, because it for the first time separated sexuality from fertility. Juliet Mitchell and Helena Wright echoed this popular assumption which ignored two factors. First, men and women had for some time been controlling their fertility to a considerable degree, and secondly, it was over-rationalistic in assuming that total control was always desired by men and women.

But for a few years the popular myth was of the Pill as the solution to sexual problems – or alternatively as the harbinger of promiscuity. From 1967 on, however, the risks to health were being proven and written up, and Ann Cartwright commented that they seemed to have been taken more seriously than the well established link between lung cancer and smoking. Perhaps in the case of oral contraceptives, the health risks act as a justification for lingering doubts and guilt as well as a rebellion, possibly, against the image of women's constant sexual availability with which the Pill was associated.

The FPA Working Party Report of 1963 shared the general view that the Lambeth Conference and the later publicity surrounding the Pill had made birth control respectable, but this was virtually the limit to discussions of motivation. Birth control was treated as a wholly rational process, the problems surrounding it as problems of information and technology. The whole discussion of family planning took place within a framework that ignored not only the constraints of poverty and the inequalities between men and women but also the complex meanings of sexual behaviour. It was difficult, too, to have a meaningful debate on such an emotionally charged subject when it was seen so exclusively within the para-meters of reproduction – the spacing of children and regulation of marriage.

Because hyper-rationalism was so dominant in the discussions of birth control it was often difficult for researchers to understand the continuing failure of a small number of couples to use con-traception. The Birmingham FPA workers found that the 'social pressure exerted on women in the matter of child bearing is quite astonishing'. Their clients were uniformly apologetic about their wish to space their children and felt compelled to justify it. (The survey was carried out in 1948, when the scare about the declining population was still in the public mind.) A wide variety of writers has testified to the fact that large families were equally frowned upon. The 'norm' of a small family was firmly established after the Second World War. Families could in the fifties and sixties become 'problem families' almost by virtue of their size alone, and there was a lingering eugenicism in the bafflement of social workers and policy planners faced with these feckless families 'breeding like rabbits'. In 1968 a Labour Government minister caused a national uproar by mounting a direct verbal attack on such families (and since then Sir Keith Joseph has returned to the attack). What was never understood was the meaning of contraception to quite large numbers of women. It meant you were always available and sex became a duty. A study of 100 large families undertaken by Pauline Shapiro (1962) showed that the women, many of whom were depressed, anxious, or resigned, seemed to feel disapproved of and one commented: 'People think that if you've got a lot of children you're inclined that way (i.e. towards sex) but I'm not.'

Many of these women felt that if they used contraceptives they would have to 'go with' their husbands again. Eleven were openly refusing intercourse and many others were able to use the risk of pregnancy as an excuse for avoiding regular or frequent sex. Many of the husbands were hostile to birth control. Some objected to female sterilization because they thought their wives would be 'no use' to them afterwards; some equated fertility with potency, some saw it as a way of controlling their wives, others as a way of punishing them. To be 'on strike' was often the only possible method of birth control for the wives, and welcome when they were frigid after years of unsatisfying sex relations and repeated pregnancy.

And if feminism was absent from the report, at least one *New Society* reader drew a feminist moral, which appeared in the letters column (15.11.62):

'Opposition to family planning and reform of the abortion laws, based on the knowledge that the end of the double standard of sexual morality would ensue, is inevitable in a society whose dream is "every man a James Bond". Thus the reaction of the husband who said his wife was "now all ready to go on the streets" because she now had the same sexual freedoms he himself already possessed, is an indication of the psychological

reality – fear or lack of self-confidence – underlying the resistance to measures which would make marital relationships a
partnership rather than an assertion of power.'

There was considerable resistance to the idea of family planning
outside marriage. Leah Manning, a feminist Labour MP, turned
her attention to family planning after she had left Parliament, and,
in Harlow, was one of the first actively and openly to campaign for
access to contraception for the unmarried. In 1964 the Harlow
Executive of the FPA placed a resolution before the FPA Annual
Conference. Although, Leah Manning commented: 'no unpre-
judiced person could have any doubt that the floor was in favour of
the resolution . . . the platform, terrified that their public image
would be smirched, managed by a procedural sleight of hand to
have the resolution defeated' (Manning 1970). Leah Manning
nonetheless succeeded in raising enough money to start an independent clinic for the unmarried in Harlow. In 1966 the FPA
changed its policy. Helen Brook, president of the Brook Advisory
Centres and closely associated for many years with the FPA gives
this reason:

> 'The decision to help the unwed came with the West Indians.
> Before that the FPA would not give advice to the widowed or
> divorced, let alone the under 16s . . . Unmarried women seek-
> ing contraceptive advice were widely suspected of being
> prostitutes and therefore not to be encouraged. To everyone's
> general consternation, it turned out that many respectable
> women who followed the West Indian men, who had been
> recruited to work London's trains and buses, had not actually
> married them. It was normal cultural practice in the men's
> homelands.' (*The Guardian* 15.12.78)

While no inference of consciously racist policies should be drawn,
it is the case that racial tensions were growing with attendant fears
that ethnic minorities would reproduce themselves faster than the
indigenous population. It was also by the mid sixties felt to be a
question of weighing the evils of promiscuity against the greater
evil of illegitimate or unwanted children.

Leah Manning tended to justify birth control for the unmarried
in terms of the enhancement of marriage. It prevented shotgun

marriages and teenage divorces and indeed the common justification for sex before marriage was that it would improve marriage itself.

SEXUAL DEVIATION AND THE LAW

Sexuality was to flower within marriage. It was to be discouraged outside it. Human sexuality, evasive, fluid, ungraspable, was to be netted, confined like a shoal of fishes, within boundaries set by the interventions of the law and those of psychology.

In the political climate of the fifties to suggest that homosexuality might be a matter of moral indifference was heretical. Both in the United States and in Britain homosexuality came to be associated with moral unreliability, and, like Communism, with treason. Guy Burgess represented an archetype of the unreliable pervert, in whom one proof of his sinister nature was his sexuality, another his Communism. As Lord Devlin put it in his polemic *The Enforcement of Morals* (1959): 'the suppression of vice is as much the law's business as the suppression of subversive activities' and he believed that immorality just as much as treason might jeopardize a nation's existence – a popular Cold War view. Alternatively the homosexual was seen as weak and unmanly. Such a man, as the Vassall spy case of 1963 showed, could be blackmailed and was also therefore a security risk. (Yet in 1963 the British film *Victim*, starring Dirk Bogarde, made a plea for the reform of the law relating to homosexuality, and this represented part of the break up of the monolithic consensus view of morals and a widening of the parameters of the debate.)

Ironically it was the trial and imprisonment of three socially prominent homosexuals in 1953/1954, intended according to one of them, Peter Wildeblood, as the start of a 'new drive against male vice', that led to increased pressure for a change in the law. Individuals such as Robert Boothby, a Tory MP, campaigned for this, as did the Church of England by publishing a report on homosexuality which concluded that although sinful, homosexuality was no worse than adultery or fornication and that there were no grounds for treating it as a crime. In Wildeblood's words

(Wildeblood 1955): 'the Government was finally goaded into setting up a Committee to investigate the antique and savage laws under which we had been charged.'

This was the Wolfenden Committee, which issued its Report in 1957. Its task in examining both male homosexuality and prostitution, was in its own terms to explore the boundary between 'private moral conduct' and 'public order and decency'. It was not for the law to enforce morals unless these interfered with public order or with other individuals. Wolfenden recommended that homosexual acts 'in private' should no longer be criminal, but this did not mean they were to be sanctioned. Similarly the act of prostitution was not a criminal offence, yet was not sanctioned by the law. In general sexuality outside marriage belonged to the twilight area of 'unlawful sexual intercourse', and effectively the Wolfenden recommendations in relation to homosexuality meant that homosexual behaviour would also be included within this grey area.

Similarly the recommendations to get prostitutes 'off the streets' were simply intended to prevent offences against 'public order and decency', not to end prostitution. These recommendations, punitive to prostitutes, were rushed into law, whereas it was not until 1967 that the law relating to homosexuals was changed. The Committee was urged by feminists to look at the nuisance of 'kerb crawling' but made no recommendations because of the difficulties of proof 'and the possibility of a very damaging charge being levelled at an innocent motorist'. It did not seem to matter if 'a very damaging charge' were levelled at women. (For a short time there were occasional reports, for instance in the *New Statesman*, of 'respectable' women being picked up mistakenly by the police.) It was clear that if prostitutes were to be prevented from walking the streets a call girl system would be the result, but the Wolfenden Committee brushed aside the possibility that this might be more exploitative of the women themselves, involving as it was bound to a relationship not even only with a pimp, but often with an underworld organization.

Neither prostitutes nor women's organizations gave evidence to the Wolfenden Committee, but the 'old feminists' were represented indirectly, for Elizabeth Abbott and 1 iss E.N. Steel gave evidence for the Association for Social and Moral Hygiene. Mrs Abbott had been associated with the Women's Freedom League and was one of the two authors of its feminist critique of the Beveridge Report. Miss Steel was a moral welfare worker and had written of this work as having a descent from the work of Josephine Butler. The editorial of *Moral Welfare* (Autumn 1957) welcomed the Wolfenden proposals on homosexuality and gave a clearly feminist view of the proposals relating to prostitution, which was probably based on the evidence given by Mrs Abbott and Miss Steel:

> 'The Report pays insufficient attention to the men (and particularly the clients) who are involved in prostitution. Indeed, the brief paragraph on "kerb crawling" almost suggests a reluctance to face this matter. Consequently the proposals regarding street order are aimed almost exclusively at the women – though surely the presence of men on the look out for them is just as self evident a public nuisance. . . .
>
> Our aim is to see that justice is done in the matter of sexual behaviour as between man and woman, and that the public interest is consulted – and in this connection it is worth noting that in spite of the representations made to it, the Committee has treated homosexual offences primarily as a male question.'

It was not surprising that lesbianism was left out of this debate, which was about the relationship between morality and its legal enforcement. When divorce was discussed, the question of lesbianism as separate grounds for divorce was raised, but the Morton Report argued against this on the basis that there was no lesbian sexual practice that approximated to heterosexual intercourse in the way that sodomy did; while Wolfenden claimed that buggery was especially abhorred 'because it involved coitus and this simulates more nearly than any other homosexual act the normal act of sexual intercourse.' Legally speaking, then, heterosexuality *was* the penis vagina conjunction described by Helena Wright as an obsession and outcome of male dominance.

FREUD AND THE PERMISSIVE SOCIETY

A more or less Freudian account of psycho-sexual development formed the basis for the whole discussion of sexuality of which the Wolfenden Report was one part. The Report itself relied on a Freudian conception of homosexuality as a state of arrested development dependent upon unconscious elements in the psychological make up of the individual. It combined with this an acceptance of Kinsey's six point scale of homosexual/heterosexual preference. Homosexuality was not a disease (a more medical or psychiatric view). Prostitution also was seen as an essentially psychological condition, and economic explanations for it – after all this was the affluent society – were rejected. It was not for the law to change the psychological make up of the individual, nor could it. Change was nonetheless desirable, and the counselling agencies, both statutory and voluntary, were to effect this psychological change.

Here, the subject of lesbianism, invisible or virtually so within the law, *could* become a focus of moral concern. Liberal progressive opinion championed the cause of male homosexuals in the late fifties and early sixties – it was often the subject of comment in the *New Statesman*, where the oppression of women never rated a word – and there was a tendency to assume that because lesbianism was not criminal it neither attracted disapproval nor merited support. There was an inexplicit feeling that it was only an aspect of female sexual frustration and would fade away as women learned to enjoy heterosexuality and now that there was a sufficient supply of men. *A Quaker View of Sex* (Heron (ed.) 1963), the most advanced expression of 'permissive' views in its time, even displayed considerable hostility towards lesbians who were 'a menace to their friends' and 'spread unhappiness wherever they go'. It put up a staunchly liberal defence of the male homosexual but sternly accused lesbian relationships of being thwarted and neurotic and expressive only of frustrated maternal feelings. Even this 'shockingly' liberal document defined women in terms only of their biological reproductive powers. But this was consistent with the psychoanalytic framework within which the pamphlet was cast.

Progressive liberal opinion began to suggest quite forcibly during the late fifties and early sixties, that sex before marriage might not be a bad thing. It might actually make for better relationships within marriage. There was a national outcry when this view was put forward by Dr Eustace Chesser and Dr Winifred de Kok in the British Medical Association book, *Getting Married* (BMA 1959). Published in 1959, it sold 200,000 copies in the few weeks before it was withdrawn as a result of the hostility aroused by the views of the two doctors, though they had made only a mild plea for a reconsideration of the ideal of pre-marital chastity; and Chesser's work in general was conservative in its attitude to women's sexual role (Campbell 1980).

There was another national brouhaha in 1963 when Professor Carstairs, head of the Department of Psychological Medicine at Glasgow, made a similar suggestion in his Reith lectures. He gave a psychoanalytic account of the development of the adolescent, his need for an identity and his need to achieve a mature sexual life within marriage. He differed from traditionalists mainly in believing that 'sexual experience before marriage may actually help towards achieving these goals'.

It was widely believed that the young of both sexes had embarked on a rampage of promiscuity. The research done by Michael Schofield (*The Sexual Life Of Young People* 1965) suggested otherwise, but objective research could never stem the tide of fantasy. Popular reports of 'gym slip mothers' or of 'golliwog girls' (the tale went that at one school the girls chose a golliwog badge as a symbol of lost virginity) fanned the fears of parents.

Society *had* changed – because these subjects could now be discussed on the radio, on television and in the newspapers. In the fifties there had been uproar when Kathleen Nott had suggested in a radio broadcast that it might be possible for agnostics to bring up children satisfactorily. Now it seemed to the conservatives that anything and everything could be not only said but done.

Yet the boundaries of the 'permissive society' were quite narrow. This is clear from an examination of the beliefs of a public figure associated with 'permissive' views and hated by the traditionalists. Dr Martin Cole, for example, was a sex therapist who wrote on sexual matters and also produced an explicit film for sex education purposes. (Today the film seems excessively male-orientated in its approach.) Dr Cole's view on teenage sex was: 'I think that teenagers should be promiscuous. I think being promiscuous can, in many cases, be a vitally important part of growing up' (*The Guardian* 1.5.71). So he too was advocating pre-marital sex as a help towards maturity. And then his much publicized marriage to a young woman who had previously been a lesbian was presented (whether intentionally or not) as a triumph for his 'liberated' views. His bisexual bride represented the sixties' ideal of a sexuality that undermined traditional and rigid sexual roles yet reached ultimately, still, towards heterosexuality, *within which* even a bisexual tendency could be incorporated along with everything else.

The 'permissive society' was in a sense the creation of conservatives and of a mass media that was both conservative and prurient. It was also a shorthand phrase for various tendencies, not necessarily closely connected. One of these was the attempt of a number of pressure groups to minimize the legal penalties attached to disapproved of behaviour and suffered by minority groups, such as unmarried mothers and homosexual adults. These attempts carried through the fifties and were largely successful in achieving their aims in the sixties. They represented a belief that the law should not add to the pains of the deviant. At the same time it did not imply that promiscuous girls or homosexuals were *happy*. On the contrary they were lonely misfits (see *Twentieth Century* special issue on Loneliness, Summer 1964). Or they might be sick – for the only available 'progressive' view was this, and Barbara Wootton (1959) was almost alone in speaking out against what she called 'the concept of illness expanding continually at the expense of the concept of moral failure'. It was liberal opinion that was especially eager to use psychiatry and psychotherapy to fill the ambiguous area of private morality vacated or not touched by the law.

Secondly, there was an overt questioning of religion, of which John Robinson's *Honest To God* (1963) was the most famous example. This seemed at the time part of a general questioning of authority. It was not, obviously, directly connected with sex. Yet the undermining of religious authority when coupled with the arrival of penicillin and the Pill, which were to do away with the dreaded consequences of promiscuity, appeared to undermine the whole basis of *fear*, so necessary, the conservatives believed, to hold young men and women to the paths of virtue.

Thirdly, many older men and women found the abandonment of familiar 'masculine' and 'feminine' behaviour extremely threatening. Anthony Storr (Storr 1964), Jungian analyst and popularizer of conservative views on psychology, suggested that the emancipation of women had caused a loss of confidence in men and women and that 'the two sexes seem to make a better relationship with each other when their social roles are sharply differentiated in a way which reinforces their sense of sexual identity as man and woman'. But writing in 1968 Angus Wilson (Wilson 1968) welcomed the 'sexual revolution' of the sixties, which he understood as young people losing their hangups and getting away from rigid role stereotyping, even to the extent of losing the rigid division between heterosexual and homosexual behaviour.

This crossing of forbidden sexual boundaries was part of a wider imperative to break down the distinction between, say, sanity and madness, pain and pleasure, the 'real' and the psychedelic. 'Unisex' nonetheless remained largely a matter of appearance. It was primarily the extension of adolescent styles of dress to the adult population and although it included jeans or trousers for women, was mainly an increase in narcissistic glamour for men, so perhaps its main purpose was to bring even effeminacy within the wide embrace of the heterosexual.

Finally, the sexual discourse of the sixties was obsessively about youth. It was hardly about women at all. In a sense it was an argument about the right of the disenfranchised young, trapped in adolescence, to the sexual life for which they were physiologically equipped and ready. Young men and women continued to get married at an earlier age and at a faster rate than ever before. *This*, rather than CND (or later the student revolts) was the teenage rebellion. The young voted with their feet for the right of lawful sex.

The limits of liberal permissiveness may be illustrated by an anecdote in the *New Statesman* in 1966. Corinna Adam, a journalist, described how her daughter, aged nine, came home one day and reported that her school friend had told her 'People fuck for fun'. Was this really true? Corinna Adam confessed that, progressive parent as she felt herself to be, she could not bring herself to admit to her daughter that it was indeed the case, but felt compelled to stress how sacred and how serious sex must be.

CONCLUSION

In the postwar period marriage and the family were essential parts of a vision of the social democratic society. Equality for women was redefined as equality of sexual enjoyment between the sexes encompassed within a marriage that stressed equality in difference and the complementarity of roles.

The effect of Kinsey's work was to create a much greater awareness of the nature and extent of sexual activity. He emphasized individual sexual acts and 'outlets' rather than a coherent unitary 'sexual identity' (which gives his work something in common with the recent theorizings of Michel Foucault, although their work is theoretically worlds apart).

The response to Kinsey was to use a Freudian theory precisely to organize the manifestations of sexual desire that in Kinsey were, relatively speaking, disorganized. Freudian theory as it was utilized in the postwar period both affirmed and denied Kinsey, and thereby scotched the threat he represented. Freudian theory acknowledged and indeed emphasized the importance of sexuality not only in marriage but in the construction of the personality, but it located sexuality within the family, while Kinsey showed it as free-roaming. Not only did Freudians assert that the marriage relationship was the highest form of sexual experience, but in stressing the importance to the development of the normal sexuality of the child of a stable, two-parent family, the dangers of extra-marital and non-reproductive sexuality were emphasized in one way; in another way Freudians also undermined Kinsey's 'democratic' approach, and sought to re-establish a hierarchical view of sexuality, which, as elaborated in the work of Erik Erikson (1965), for example, re-emphasized the importance of growth towards a mature heterosexuality. This body of thought reaffirmed that all sexual experiences were *not* equivalent; to experience the best and most mature you had to be anchored firmly in your 'femininity' or 'masculinity'.

Freud did not appeal only to those who feared Kinsey. In the twenties the new science of psychoanalysis had seemed to offer a form of liberation of women. Today many women see it as a cornerstone of women's oppression. During the years between Freudian theory as it developed offered a reconciliation – perhaps not consciously recognized as such – between two conflicting sets of feminine, and sometimes feminist, aspirations.

Women aspired to sexual fulfilment. Women also aspired to high moral standards. As we shall see, women used their role as nurturers and as stabilizers to argue for peace. According to this view, the calling of women as mother gave her a superiority over men, and Freudian theory could be called upon to support this view.

In the fifties, marriage was more consciously sexualized, women more consciously feminine. Even then, some women were suspicious. Mary McCarthy (1960) argued that the price women were being made to pay for the precious orgasm was economic independence, and feminists as distinguished as Simone de Beauvoir have seen in the promotion of the female orgasm a conspiracy to chain women in even greater dependency on men.

In the sixties the American and later some of the British feminists rebelled against Freudian definitions of womanhood. Yet, at least since the twenties and thirties, the radical movement has consistently rejected Freud and simultaneously experienced a contradictory pull towards him, has time and again rejected him for his pessimistic, apolitical, and even reactionary conclusions, and yet after fruitless searching for some better theory has returned for a fresh exploration of his hypotheses on the construction of the 'gendered subject'. In the student movement of the sixties this pull was represented by Herbert Marcuse, whose *Eros and Civilization*, first published in 1955, attained its moment of fame in the late sixties as a key work of the American 'new left'. 'Make Love Not War' was a distillation of his thesis that the 'permanent arms economy' necessitated the narrowing down and the repression and control of sexual behaviour. If this was so, then part of the revolutionary task was to break out of this 'surplus repression' and liberate creative energy in a free, polymorphic, perverse sexuality no longer chained to the demands of capitalism or the death instinct.

The sexual reformists of the 'permissive society' almost all brought Freud to the centre of the stage, sometimes claimed their views were revolutionary, and then devoted themselves to the enhancement of heterosexual marriage. The sex education they wanted in schools was about how to have a legitimate baby, and they wanted planned contraception and women's sexual fulfilment because these would enhance marriage. Even youthful experimentation was dealt with by expanding the concept of marriage to incorporate it. Sex education was 'preparation for marriage', sexual intercourse by the unmarried was 'anticipation of marriage', even the idea of homosexual marriage gained ground.

This was neither an attempt to repress sexuality (on the contrary, there was a compulsion to *be* sexual and it was celibacy, as we saw, that was to be wiped out); nor was it a straightforward adoption of an ideal of non-reproductive, non-monogamous, 'liberated' sexuality as Ros Coward has suggested (Coward 1978). Rather, by an impossible sleight of hand, sexuality was both to expand and flower in liberated fashion *and* to be organized within marriage.

To study this huge literature of sexuality, which drew on legal, psychological, and social theories, suggests to the reader the question: what *is* sexuality? It seems almost like an absent centre around which the debate ebbs and flows. And the debates did, significantly, have as their object in many cases the construction of definitions of sexuality. The arguments connected with Wolfenden and with divorce were in part arguments about the boundary between public and private, about grey areas of state intervention. The concept of a sexual act was enlarged beyond the 'penis vagina conjunction' once held sufficient (and indeed obvious) as the definition of sexual activity. Here, the more reliable separation of sexuality and fertility *was* important. Once that happened sexuality became no longer a matter to do essentially with reproduction, at any rate before the law, but came also to involve questions of the boundaries of permissible pleasure.

British feminists rebelled against the exploding mass media images of woman as fetishized sexual object. On the screen a generation of stylish women with minds of their own – Lauren Bacall, Joan Crawford, Barbara Stanwyck – had long ago made way for a crop of *femmes enfants*. Brigitte Bardot was a 'sex kitten'. Marilyn Monroe's waiflike quality was repeatedly celebrated. In fashion also the elegance – adult even if backward looking – of the New Look made way for the *'petite fille sexy'* of Guy Laroche and the thumb-sucking Lolita of the glossy magazines, Twiggy, the fifteen-year-old model. Recently André Courrèges, the inventor of the mini-skirt and the trouser suit of the sixties has argued that his clothes represented freedom for women (*The Guardian* 15.8.79). But rebellion *against* this whole imagery of woman as both imma-ture and sexually available was an important part of the begin-nings of women's liberation, as was the moral revulsion against the excesses of the advertising industry that had driven Betty Friedan to write *The Feminine Mystique*. The women's movement has concentrated on a rejection of the 'sexual objectification' of women while affirming women's right to sexual enjoyment. Feminists speak to women of the moral issues of jealousy and possessiveness and of the economic functions of marriage. They speak of sexuality within marriage as a system of enslavement justifying violence and rape. American feminists especially, for example Kate Millett (1971) and Phyllis Chesler (1974), have portrayed women as enslaved, coerced, repressed, and punished by an ideology of feminine sexuality that has been forcibly imposed. Yet elsewhere feminists have spoken of women's sexual-ity as ecstasy and life force. This confusion mirrors rather than transcends a more general confusion, one that is by no means confined to feminists.

To say that the personal is political was to say that sexual re-lations were the site of coercion and power relations. But it came as a shock to some feminists to realize that many women – and they themselves – still felt seduced by the commercial images of women, clung to false eyelashes and high heels, felt and wanted to feel submissive to men, yearned for sexual surrender and chivalry. It was an attempt to understand this – women's own commitment to a traditional ideal of 'femininity' – that has led some British feminists back to Freud.

CHAPTER SIX

Sanity and madness

Within the chateau where Sade's hero confines himself, within the convents, the forests, the dungeons where he endlessly pursues the agony of his victims, it seems at first glance that nature can act with utter freedom. There man rediscovers a truth he had forgotten, though it was manifest: what desire can be contrary to nature, since it was given to man by nature itself? And since it was taught by nature in the great lesson of life and death which never stops repeating itself in the world? The madness of desire, insane murders, the most unreasonable passions — all are wisdom and reason, since they are a part of the order of nature. . . . There is nothing that the madness of men invents which is not either nature made manifest or nature restored. (Michel Foucault: *Madness and Civilization*)

The post-political world of the fifties was to free western 'man' from ideologies so that he could explore 'his' individuality. But this quest involved not only a recognition of the existential loneliness of the individual, but also the uncovering of pathology, irrationalism, violence. The cosy certainties of the welfare state left us spiritually unappeased. It was not the John Betjemans of the right alone who rebelled against the grey wastes of the 'socialist' utopia. Norman Mailer's 'white negro' and Kerouac's hero in *On The Road* rebelled against conformity, as did, perhaps, the Teds and the juvenile delinquents. The corrosion of socialism as an ideal was brought about in the US by a paranoid hatred of the Communist enemy 'out there'. In Britain the erosion was more subtle, and as deadly, and was achieved by the Fabian boredoms of the welfare state, as well as by the atmosphere of the Cold War.

Madness could be both one form of rebellion against the inertia of the affluent society and simultaneously a depoliticization of the political. The predicament of the mental patient was similar to that of the Kafka hero. He or she is lost in the world of non-sense. In a brilliant novel, *The Ha-Ha* (1960), Jennifer Dawson's heroine lived this experience from the inside. Seen through her eyes the cruelty around her in the hospital was itself insane. Since she was completely isolated, though, escape could only take the form of hopeless flight. At the same time, the reader experienced a double vision, or double understanding, sympathizing wholly with the heroine yet wholly aware that she was in fact 'mad'. The rebellion of the madman was hopeless and doomed – that was the message, the consequence of identifying rebellion with insanity.

MENTAL HEALTH, PUBLIC POLICY, AND PSYCHOLOGICAL THEORIES

The Royal Commission on Mental Illness and Mental Deficiency reported in 1957 (the same year as Wolfenden) and the 1959 Mental Health Act carried out the spirit of its recommendations, in seeking to change the law so that while patients could still be detained compulsorily, the old permanent stigma of 'being certified' was done away with. It was made simpler and easier for a patient to enter a mental hospital voluntarily or 'informally', and these changes were backed up by a call for more community services to assist the patient and his family at home.

Concepts of 'community' and 'preventive' treatment were not peculiar to the mental health field, since they were popular also in the field of child care after the war, but in the case of mental illness were made possible by advances in drug treatments. Once it had been possible to control the bizarre or violent behaviour of patients only by constraint or punishment. Since the war a range of drugs has made it possible for their behaviour to be chemically controlled. Consequently, many patients who would formerly have rotted for years in institutions are able, for a time at least, to return to the world outside.

Traditional psychiatry with its emphasis on drug and other physical forms of treatment was reflected in the opening words of the Report on Mental Illness: 'Disorders of the mind are illnesses which need medical treatment'. Orthodox psychiatrists explained mad behaviour as an effect of illness. The cause and cure of these illnesses were not fully understood, it was true, but the way to understanding lay through the investigation of the brain and its chemistry. Taken to their logical conclusion, such views rendered behaviour meaningless, and certainly devoid of moral significance. An extreme proponent of such views was William Sargant, a psychiatrist who wrote a popularizing book on 'brainwashing', *Battle For The Mind* (1957). Sargant advocated brain surgery (leucotomy and lobotomy) for mental disorders. Operations in which the frontal lobes of the brain were severed were said to alleviate overmastering impulses, whether aggressive or phobic, and to tame uncontrollable anxieties and compulsions which lost their obsessive quality so that the patient could return to normal life, although there was always the danger that she or he might become something of a vegetable. Enthusiasts for leucotomy even recommended it for social problems, such as the depression of a woman with a violent husband.

Although it dealt with the moral issue of 'brain washing' *Battle For The Mind* similarly gave the impression that the individual was at the mercy of physical and mental techniques of manipulation, which made liberal ideas of the 'personality', 'free will', and 'human dignity' somewhat meaningless. This too was the world of Kafka, the grim world of the 'totalitarian' societies. Psychiatric violence was the archetypal violence of the post-atomic world. Just as the nature of war had taken a qualitative leap into the horrors of radiation and mutation, so had torture taken a qualitative leap in horror too. Not only could a man's body be tortured, mutilated and destroyed; his very personality could be wiped out. The Soviet trials of the thirties, and later the Slansky trials in Czechoslovakia,

Arthur Koestler's novels, and George Orwell's *1984*, all testified to this new horror.

The 'message' of orthodox psychiatry was then in one way a message of pessimism, in spite of the fact that it came disguised as a promise of cure. It individualized the patient past the point of moral responsibility.

The behaviourist school of psychology also tended to do away with the autonomy of the individual who was conceived of as an essentially passive entity conditioned, shaped, and moulded by the environment. Again, motivation and choice were discounted as unscientific and therefore meaningless concepts.

Politically, the history of behaviourism has been an interesting one. Its attraction for leftwingers in the thirties had been that it claimed to be able to explain psychological behaviour in terms of conditioning and learning. The individual therefore was a product of the environment, and could also be influenced and changed. This led to utopian hopes that unhappiness could be virtually abolished, especially in a socialist society where the environment, it was hoped, would exert a benign influence. Divorce, homosexuality, and juvenile delinquency, those ugly by-products of capitalism, would be no more. The seeming optimism of the behaviourist creed was in glaring contrast to the home truths of psychoanalysis, itself understood as part of the decadence of capitalism.

But after the war, when psychological manipulation came to be associated with brainwashing, it was feared that the malleability of the human personality would be one feature not of an utopia but of a nightmare society. While Pavlovian behaviourism continued to dominate the British Communist Party, and hampered attempts to develop some more adequate theory of the functioning of 'personality' from the left, it was also popularized by H.J. Eysenck who used it to discredit both politics and psychoanalysis from the right. The tone of Eysenck's best selling, popularizing books (Eysenck 1954, 1957) was commonsensical. He took a commonsense view of males as dominant and females as submissive, but also supported Kinsey's efforts to find out 'what really happened' in sexual behaviour, and was critical of the Royal Commission on Divorce for relying on value judgments and failing to do experimental research in the area of marital relations.

At this period, though, he was more interested in political behaviour and beliefs than in differences between the sexes, and the thrust of his writings was to depoliticize and to reduce political behaviour to an effect of the personality. Eysenck did not rule out the idea of innate characteristics of introversion/extraversion. He developed the theory of the existence of authoritarian/democratic or toughminded/tenderminded personality types whose political beliefs could be predicted, and managed to have personality tests carried out on eighty-six individuals; forty-three members of the British Communist Party and forty-three members of a Fascist group or groups. The difficulties for his research assistant (a young woman) of carrying out the tests without any of the individuals concerned realizing their purpose was poignantly described by Eysenck, but while the validity of these findings might be questioned, Eysenck was successful in popularizing the idea that extremists, whether of left or right, are 'all the same'.

Eysenck also attacked psychoanalysis on the basis that it was 'unscientific' and that its rate of cure was no higher than that to be expected by spontaneous remission. But psychoanalysis had shifted its ground. Freud himself had been clear that his treatment was for those who were 'ill':

> 'When I have promised my patients help or improvement by means of a cathartic treatment I have often been faced with the objection: "Why you tell me yourself that my illness is probably connected with my circumstances and the events of my life. You cannot alter these in any way. How do you propose to help me, then?" And I have been able to make this reply: "No doubt fate would find it easier than I do to relieve you of your illness. But you will be able to convince yourself that much will be gained if we succeed in transforming your hysterical misery into common unhappiness. With a mental life that has been restored to health you will be better armed against that unhappiness." ' (Freud and Breuer 1974:393)

But many of those who sought help from the latter-day followers of Freud were unhappy rather than ill. The search for happiness at the hands of these therapists, who appeared to be replacing the priest, was also a symptom of a spiritual search in a materialistic and greedy world, or so it was believed.

Paradoxically, while those who were manifestly mentally disordered were more and more directed towards orthodox psychiatrists and behaviourist psychologists, and while it was those suffering from 'common unhappiness' who sought the help of the psychotherapists, the influence of psychoanalysts in the field of child psychiatry led to a subtle 'medicalization' of a wide field of behaviour. I have already mentioned Barbara Wootton as one of the few to criticize this tendency from the point of view of social science. The effect of psychoanalysis in both the discussion and treatment of a range of social problems after the war was again to demote these to an effect of the malfunctioning of the individual. This may not have been the intention. The behaviour of juvenile delinquents, school failures, unmarried mothers, bedwetters and prostitutes *were*, however, explained in terms of a failure to reach an appropriate level of maturity. The depressed housewives, homosexuals, thwarted artists, and hyper-anxious businessmen who sought help for their unhappiness *were* accepted as patients. Many psychoanalysts and psychotherapists *did* simply seek to help individuals to adjust. They shunned the moral problems raised by issues of deviance and conformity, and the political problems raised by poverty, economic injustice, and educational impoverishment.

It was not a political system or the dominance of men that caused these problems, they said. It was the mother whose dark shadow lay across these sad lives. In part, this was due to the influence of the Kleinian school of psychoanalysis in Britain. Melanie Klein herself lived in this country for many years and her work influenced a number of psychoanalysts who have themselves been influential: Donald Winnicott, John Bowlby, and others. The theoretical interest of Melanie Klein's work and that of her followers was its exploration back into the infancy of the child.

Psychotic illness (e.g. schizophrenia) was held to be rooted in this very early period, so the mother's initial relationship with her child was of vital importance. In practice the father was edged out of the picture (this is very obvious in Bowlby's work, both early and late).

THE POLITICS OF EXPERIENCE

Yet psychoanalysis was the liberal, the humane, the progressive wing of the psychiatric profession. For the silent violence of ECT* and drugs it substituted the 'talking cure'. The patient was listened to, not chemically gagged. His life was seen as a moral enterprise, as meaningful. Freud had elevated even – and indeed especially – what he called 'the refuse of the phenomenal world' (dreams, slips of the tongue, errors, the forgotten) to a central place in the construction of meaning. It was on this base that the 'radical psychiatrists' of the sixties were to build.

While Eysenck was equating Communism and Fascism at the Maudsley Hospital, a Glaswegian psychiatrist was studying the meaning and significance of schizophrenia. R.D. Laing later came south to work at the Tavistock Institute. His first book, *The Divided Self*, was published in 1960. In it, Laing took off from the Kleinian proposition that the seeds of psychosis lay in infancy, and he wanted, initially, to 'make madness, and the process of going mad, comprehensible'. At the same time, influenced by Existentialist thought, he sought to gain a better understanding of the psychotic patient by seeing him as a 'real person' and this brought him to criticize the way psychiatrists habitually treated their patients:

> 'The current psychiatric jargon . . . speaks of psychosis as a social or biological *failure* of adjustment, or *mal*-adaptation of a particularly radical kind, of *loss* of contact with reality, of *lack* of insight . . . This jargon is a veritable "vocabularly of denigration". The denigration is not moralistic, at least in a nineteenth century sense; in fact, in many ways this language is the outcome of efforts to avoid thinking in terms of freedom, choice, responsibility.' (Laing 1965:27)

It therefore came close to the behaviourist position in denying rational choice and moral meanings.

For the relationship between analyst and patient – the transference relationship – Laing substituted the 'real' 'I–Thou' rela-

* Electro convulsive therapy – electric shocks are passed through the brain of the patient.

tionship of the existentialists in which the patient was simply accepted and recognized as a real other person. Juliet Mitchell suggested in *Psychoanalysis and Feminism* (1974) that this substitution effectively oversimplified the Freudian theory. It was 'essentialist' that is, it suggested the existence of a prior 'real' person overlaid by the distortions caused by a repressive civilization. The therapeutic process then became the simplified process of uncovering the 'truth' about the patient and revealing his real human self. As Laing himself describes it:

'Freud insisted that our civilization is a repressive one. There is a conflict between the demands of conformity and the demands of our instinctive energies, explicitly sexual. Freud could see no easy resolution of this antagonism, and he came to believe that in our time the possibility of simple natural love between human beings had already been abolished.' (Laing 1965:11)

This view has more in common with the work and aspirations of the 'cultural radicals' – for example with Raymond Williams and Richard Hoggart, whose work is to be discussed later, than with Freud, who certainly did not believe in something called 'simple natural love' but in the creation of a capacity to love as part of a complex process, the development of the baby into an adult.

Even though the schizophrenic was truly 'mad' Laing from the start recognized that when the schizophrenic patient was not involved in an 'I–Thou' relationship, he was often instead treated in a depersonalizing fashion, as a thing, or as fragmented. The psychiatrist started off from an assumption of his own sanity; but his sanity was only in the words of David Cooper, 'the compulsive non-madness of the sane' – a successful conformity to outward convention, a false self in many ways as false or more false even than the false self of the schizophrenic.

This insight opened the way for the development of the idea of the patient into the 'hero as victim', the teenage rebel whose family is trying to hold him (or, more frequently in Laing's work, her) in its grip and prevent the necessary escape into self discovery and freedom. Juliet Mitchell suggests that Laing spoke strongly to the adolescent and to the 'teenage thing' in this way. His descriptions of the psychotic experience are insightful and poetic. Yet in the end he sought, and found, a 'sane' person underneath the false, 'mad' self. Writing of 'Julie', the 'ghost in the weed garden' in *The Divided Self*, he suggested:

> 'There was something of great worth deeply lost or buried inside her, as yet undiscovered by herself or by anyone. If one could go deep into the depth of the dark earth one would discover "the bright gold", or if one could get fathoms down one would discover "the pearl at the bottom of the sea".' (Laing 1965:205)

From this it was not a long step to an inversion whereby the schizophrenic became the sane one in a mad world. In this transposition the mad person was also close to the artist. Kafka and Francis Bacon were mentioned early in *The Divided Self* as artists of the experience of depersonalization, alienation, and existential terror. The experience of the creative artist and that of the schizophrenic then could be conflated, both seen as having a superior 'take' on reality.

From this Laing went on to develop a 'political' interpretation of the schizophrenic experience. This, in the early sixties, was part of a search, almost, for new ways of *being* political. Peter Sedgwick (1972) saw the early sixties as a quiescent period politically, a time of 'impasse for mass movements and of immobility for radical thinkers', and therefore thought it an odd time for Laing to have moved leftwards. Yet what seems, or seemed like an impasse, was part of new movements. Some of those who had been active in CND turned towards other forms of community activity. Left intellectuals such as those involved with the *New Left Review*, who took up Laing's work early on, were trying to develop more sophisticated theories of the interaction of the individual and the environment, the structuring of the individual subject, and the relationship between the individual and ideology than those previously available to the left. There was a more general search for spiritual alternatives.

This was the turning outwards again of the whole preoccupation with private life so characteristic of the fifties. It was the partly unintended outcome of the sociology of the family of which Talcott Parsons was the predominating representative. Parsons and his followers described both the family and society in organic terms, stressing its functions and properties of self regulation in descriptions that relied in part upon Freudian theory. This imperceptibly led to explorations of the *dys*functioning of the delicate mechanisms of family life, and there was more and more emphasis on the pathology of family communication. Laing himself became interested in the schizophrenic not as an isolated sick person, but as one member in a system of faulty familial communications. The mad nuclear family and the mad nuclear-bomb-ridden world were alike part of the same conspiracy against the lonely individual.

The effect of family on individual was described especially vividly in the book Laing wrote in collaboration with Aaron Esterson, *Sanity, Madness and the Family* (1964), and in relation to how *women* patients experienced their family relationships. The description of the eleven women diagnosed as schizophrenic in this book provided a vivid description of problems facing many young women. As Juliet Mitchell pointed out, in this respect Laing's work was bound to have a huge appeal to the women's liberation movement when it came, because: 'many women who join the women's liberation movement are young and are trying to leave one or other of their family homes'. But women in our society are supposed to become adult by leaving their family of origin simply to form, and remain protected in, another: the family they create with a husband and where they rear children. What Laing and Esterson were describing was the way in which 'abnormal' families prevent seemingly quite sane young women from leaving. These women were not allowed to become sufficiently and appropriately sexual to leave the nest and embark on normal, adult sexual relationships. In these families, the mothers by denial, the fathers by incompletely suppressed incestuous impulses prevented the 'natural' flowering of their daughters into 'real women', and this gave Laing's work further resonance in the climate of the mid-sixties with its emphasis on the importance of young women *being* sexual. This was how sexual liberation for women was then perceived.

Laing and Esterson emphasized the mother-daughter relationship and many of their interviews were joint interviews with mother and daughter. Yet the 'bad' illness-inducing mothers were

themselves victims. 'Mrs Blair' described the lot of women in
almost schizophrenic language herself:

'Oh, the decorum and all the rest of the unreality and artificial-
ity, there's no doubt about it, women were so limited in thought
because of over-doing this, but nowadays it's different and they
don't find that outlet so – discussing people quite so much. I
don't think so. And of course a lot of women have the privilege
of going out to work, instead of staring at the walls and waiting
for the next bit of criticism about how they live – that's what a
woman's life used to be – just waiting for the next piece of
criticism – that's how I see it. And as I say I never really got into
the subject of what I'm like, because, as I say, I've had such a
dose of it.' (Laing and Esterson 1964:40–41)

CONCLUSION

Finally, Laing was driven towards the mysticism of the
psychedelic experience, where in a wholly alienated world, the
schizophrenic alone made sense: 'We are all murderers and
prostitutes. . . . Humanity is estranged from its authentic
possibilities. This basic vision prevents us from taking any
unequivocal view of the sanity of common sense, or of the madness of the so-called madman' (Laing 1967:11). The aspirations of
Laing's work found their fullest expression in the Dialectics of
Liberation Congress in 1967, an event which strove, however
ineptly, towards a form of cultural revolution.

Laing expressed as well as anyone the contradictory aspirations
of politics in the sixties. He *assumed* the irrelevance of 'East' and
'West'. Political difference in this sense was depoliticized by Laing
to become a kind of mistake, a form of alienation in which the
nations of the earth were prevented from recognizing their essential brotherhood.

Such an analysis would apply too, although this is never made
explicit, to relations between the sexes, which in the authentic
I–Thou relationship would transcend sexual divisions and gender
difference. The whole concept of alienation was romantic on its
stress on the individual. The 'individual' and the 'real person'

were sexless spirits, the authentic relationship a communion of souls.

Laing's insights created fissures and cracks in the surface of the social crust. Part of the volcanic eruption that was to come was the women's movement, and Laing did speak for women, in however limited a way.

Those limitations were taken into the women's movement and its practice, where 'the personal is political' might be understood as meaning that *anything* personal was immediately political and that any personal solution was therefore a political solution too. It is the women's movement in particular – after all, the majority of mental patients are women – that has taken forward and carried on the continuing struggle against oppressive and inhuman methods of treatment and mental institutions, particularly where this struggle takes the form of attempts to find and create alternatives. In this area, as in so many others, women struggle with the unresolved problem of what it is they want and are trying to create, struggling at one and the same time to participate in the world as it is and to suggest, in a 'prefigurative' way the entirely different kind of world that might exist if 'feminine' values dominated.

CHAPTER SEVEN

Culture and humanism

Whether or not there is more discontent in the world than was formerly the case, there is no doubt whatsoever that the means of fanning it and exploiting it are infinitely greater than they used to be, because of the increase in literacy and the introduction of wireless and television sets in large numbers. . . .

There is no doubt that from a mechanical point of view the ability of men to influence each other by the printed and broadcast word will increase as more and more people learn to read and as small cheap wireless sets become available in ever greater quantities. There is of course no technical reason why this should work to the advantage of the organizers of subversion since their propaganda could be nullified by more effective propaganda put out by the other side. But this would involve more thought, effort, and money being devoted to the purpose than has usually been the case in the past.
(Brigadier Frank Kitson: *Low Intensity Operations*)

As chunks of the British Empire broke off and floated away down the tide of history, progressive sections of the British intelligentsia attempted a reaffirmation of a British culture and identity tainted neither by élitism nor by Americanism. The regeneration of a radical tradition in the mid-fifties was an understandable reaction to the gentility and pessimism of the postwar cultural scene, the snobbery and parochialism so disliked by visiting Americans, and described, for example, by Edward Shils in *Encounter* (April 1955):

'Continental holidays, the connoisseurship of wine and food, the knowledge of wild flowers and birds, acquaintance with the writings of Jane Austen, a knowing indulgence for the worthies of the English past, an appreciation of "more leisurely epochs", doing one's job dutifully and reliably, the cultivation of personal relations – these are the elements in the ethos of the newly emerging British intellectual class.'

In relation to culture, the position of women as a separate issue was raised even less often than in discussions of the family, because discussions of culture were embedded in a form of humanism that denied the difference it simultaneously expressed. Yet these hidden representations insidiously created and sustained powerful and restricting images of women.

Celia Johnson in *Brief Encounter* portrayed the ideal English-woman of the 1940s. She was John Newsom's gracious hostess, conforming with her well-cut tweeds and chintz drawing room to the tastes of her class, prepared to suffer romantic, girlish pangs of love in Fuller's tearooms, but too refined for the squalor of sex in a borrowed bedroom. Her brittle, perfect porcelain face and voice called forth British male protectiveness but froze lust. Virginia McKenna, in films made after the war, enacted the more imperial, 'plucky' side of this image of the English lady, confronting jungle, desert, Jap and torture with unshakeable British *sang froid*. In British films of this period the sexy girls were all lower-class. Diana Dors was no lady.

By the end of the fifties British actresses such as Rachel Roberts in *Saturday Night and Sunday Morning* and *This Sporting Life* had superseded the more class-bound images of women characteristic of the early fifties, and were portraying women who although more or less working-class were not 'common'. These heroines came out of a new realist literature that tried to explore and validate working-class life.

This was in contrast to the late forties and early fifties when there was greater emphasis on the desirability of extending middle-class taste and standards to the newly – and perhaps rather dangerously – literate and educated masses. This was John Newsom's project (as we saw), and was evident too in the influential writings of Talcott Parsons, the American sociologist, who described rather than theorized women's 'expressive' role (though his descriptions were uncritically accepted as theorizations):

'. . . a conspicuous tendency for the feminine role to emphasize broadly humanistic rather than technically specialized achievement values. One of the key patterns is that of "good taste" in personal appearance, house furnishings, cultural things like literature and music. To a large and perhaps increasing extent the more humanistic cultural traditions and amenities of life are carried on by women. . . . These things are of a high intrinsic importance in the scale of values of our culture.' (Parsons 1964:194)

Women were to have a stabilizing and civilizing influence, and this was particularly important in a period haunted by the fear of destruction, and of the ending of *all* civilization.

THE RETREAT FROM RADICALISM

The postwar atmosphere of pessimism was a whole cultural climate, which did not simply discredit the progressive ideas and the socialism, however flawed, of the thirties, but perversely drew sustenance from it. Many writers, intellectuals, and political activists had turned away from the Soviet Union before the outbreak of the Second World War. This was not a simple turning from left to right. In writers such as George Orwell there had always been a tension between left-wing views and a distrust of the masses and of activism, a dislike if not of socialism, at least of intellectuals who were socialists. By 1939, intellectuals endorsed what Cyril Connolly expressed when he wrote of war ' "as a justification for the artist to retire and concentrate on his work – to withdraw into his ivory shelter" ' which somehow freed him from ' "the burden of anti-Fascist activities, the subtler burden of pro-Communist opinions" ' (Hewison 1977:11).

Coming from Orwell, who had after all fought 'totalitarianism' in the shape of fascism in Spain, such views were even more powerful. His essay *Inside the Whale* (1941) was a defence of quiet-ism and in the late forties he was the voice of disillusion and created a nightmare projection of the 'totalitarian' state in *1984*, a projection based on the Soviet rather than the Nazi experience (Williams 1971). Orwell equated the creativity of the artist with individualism and liberalism. The writer, he felt, could never be a socialist or a 'party man'. In his work, though, were seams of thought that were to be mined by a new generation of socialists in the later fifties. In both *The Road To Wigan Pier* and *The Lion And The Unicorn* he described class in terms of styles, accents, tastes – as the sociologists of the fifties were to do when they argued that we were all middle-class. But there were also those like Raymond Williams, who took Orwell as some sort of starting point, 'who agreed with him about Stalinism and about imperialism and about the English establishment, and who made a new socialist politics out of his sense of failure' (Williams 1971:83).

THE REVIVAL OF RELIGION AND THE DISCREDITING OF SCIENCE

If Orwell expressed an urge towards passivity and disillusion in the negative sense of withdrawal, there was also a positive intellectual movement to create or to develop the idea of 'western civilization' or the 'western European tradition'. Series of talks on BBC radio popularized these ideas. So did campaigning individuals such as Victor Gollancz (publisher of the Left Book Club before the war), whose Save Europe Now campaign was an embodiment of the civilized, religious principle of the forgiveness of enemies. He saw this as essential to the survival of the western ethic in the face of totalitarian thuggery. Liberal humanists such as E.M. Forster and Arthur Koestler supported these views, as did, most strongly of all, Christians such as C.S. Lewis, a broadcaster and popular writer.

C.S. Lewis (Carpenter 1978) had never been sympathetic to socialism and was associated at Oxford with a group of right-wing friends that included J.R.R. Tolkien, author of *The Lord of the Rings* and a Roman Catholic, and Roy Campbell who had fought for

Franco in Spain. C.S. Lewis had been converted to Christianity (he was an Anglican) long before the war. But his views reached their full influence and flowering in the postwar atmosphere. John Wain, the novelist, who was an undergraduate at Oxford soon after the war, described in his autobiography the atmosphere there then and the great appeal of Christianity:

> 'The war had made normal life an affair of constant crisis and suffering, the anti-clerical and rationalistic left-wing generation were dispersed, and – as it seemed to many – discredited, and a suitably presented Christianity met with no real opposition among either the uneducated or the intelligentsia. . . . Lewis had won a huge following with his BBC talks, his addresses to schools and to servicemen, by his insistence that Christianity was reasonable. . . .
>
> Not only Oxford, but all England, had recently come round to the position that T.S. Eliot was after all a great poet. . . . The *Four Quartets* was on everyone's table . . . Anglicanism, for years regarded as a quaint, intellectually dowdy set of attitudes . . . associated with the silver teapot on the vicarage lawn, suddenly became the adventurous spearhead of English intellectual and artistic life. . . . The interpretation of English poetry along Anglican lines was carried in those years to extraordinary lengths.' (Wain 1960:140-2)

The revival of religion came at a time when science (Wood 1959; Werskey 1978) was deeply tainted and discredited by the very invention of the atom bomb. The Soviet system was itself associated with science or its misuse and with a 'scientific' or 'materialist' philosophy of life, characterized as an attitude that denied or denigrated the spiritual. At the same time it should be stressed that this is an oversimplified account and that the move to the right and away from science was not universal. J.B.S. Haldane, for example, one of the best known spokesmen for the left, *joined* the Communist Party in 1942, and spoke and broadcast (he appeared regularly on the Brains Trust) for a number of years, expounding his beliefs in popular vein to a huge audience.

Nevertheless the trend was in the other direction, and left-wing scientists were themselves partly responsible for the caricature of science as soulless. In many cases their views were tinged with eugenicism and positivistic empiricism, and there was a widespread tendency amongst them to regard scientific advance as the prototype of revolutionary advance and as revolutionary in and of itself (Werskey 1978). F. Le Gros Clarke for instance wrote: 'science has no politics; it stretches out to pervade and at last control with its mild influence every sphere of human life, politics among the rest. Then science is, if you like, supremely political after all.' But after the war this sounded too much like the nightmare of *1984*, with 'thought control' and Big Brother. Aldous Huxley's *Brave New World* became the dominant vision – or rather nightmare – of a world controlled by science.

T. S. ELIOT

An alternative and less hostile view was to see science as valid in the 'external' sphere and religion as valid in the 'internal' or spiritual sphere. This was the doctrine of the 'two truths'. Yet even when science was in this way given its own sphere of influence there remained a feeling that the scientific revolutions of the seventeenth century had begun a process described by T.S. Eliot as the 'dissociation of sensibility' (Nott 1953). The poets of that period were the last, Eliot believed, to have been able to 'gather up and digest into its art all the experience of the human mind'. From then on, he argued, English poetry had suffered from a specialization of experience and a deterioration of values.

T.S. Eliot desired a return to Anglican Christian values, and indeed for him there was literally no such thing as a civilization that was not Christian. He had held these views long before the war, but his influence was most potent in the late forties and early fifties, when his poetry was widely read, his plays performed in the West End, records made of him speaking his own verse, and when he broadcast and gave interviews. It was during this period that he made his most definitive statement, *Notes Towards The Definition of Culture* (1948).

He intended this as a contribution towards a philosophy opposed to the 'getting on' mentality of the welfare state, that incarnation of the Fabianism to which he was deeply opposed. He objected to the educational principle of equality of opportunity and to 'meritocracy', because while emphasizing differences in ability and function, he himself was anxious to include the 'masses' the meritocracy excluded. He also believed that the 'dogma of equal opportunity' undermined the family, indeed could only arise when the institution of the family was already no longer respected, when its responsibilities had already passed to the state. In this he was voicing a familiar anxiety of the period and a familiar antithesis between family and state. But for him the family was not merely the nuclear family, site of personal affection, but the generational continuity that ensured the transmission of culture.

Eliot said little about the place of women, yet the belief that the transmission of culture centred around the family through the generations implied that the role of women would be a traditional one. Yet Eliot's concern was simply not with women at all, but with the strengthening of Anglican church and community. That his silence on women and his political views generally were little discussed is indicative of the atmosphere at the time, when the implications of his views in the wider sense were simply imbibed along with the general atmosphere of religious pessimism.

There *was* a contradiction in his work, for, like the pop artists of the sixties he used the flotsam of daily life to create his poetic vision of the world and made – or had made in his earlier poetry – a collage of the vulgar and the banal in order to represent the fractured, mass world he hated – the Wasteland. Written in 1922, *The Wasteland* spoke to the fifties. Impossibly kitsch, with its subliminal echoes of forgotten classics, collage of conversational débris, industrial and metropolitan imagery and bits and pieces culled from other religions, it reeked of the atmosphere of the post-Bomb world and in one way was curiously at odds with the views expressed in his essay on culture since it evoked with far more vitality just that disintegration of culture to which he alluded in his essay with such dismay.

Women did figure noticeably in *The Wasteland*. There was the neurosis of the idle rich woman: 'My nerves are bad tonight. Yes bad. Stay with me. Speak to me. Why do you never speak.' Her bored search for sensation and her repressed impulses were immediately contrasted with the working-class woman gripped by the brutal necessities of male sexual demands, abortion, and illness: 'Well, if Albert won't leave you alone, there it is, I said: What you get married for if you don't want children.' Between these extremes was the mistress of the house-agent's clerk:

> She turns and looks a moment in the glass,
> Hardly aware of her departed lover;
> Her brain allows one half formed thought to pass;
> Well now that's done; and I'm glad it's over.

These women, sexual victims, were also repellent, stupid, and amoral, and led de-centred and fragmented lives. Yet Eliot's vision of 'love' in his later poems was abstract; the hollow grandiloquence of *Four Quartets* – 'All shall be well, and all manner of thing shall be well', comes weakly as an antidote to the vivid images of pessimism, waste, and decay.

THE CHRISTIAN VISION OF WOMAN

A positive Christian vision of womanhood did exist, all the same. However little the majority lived by religion, positive Christian ideals of relationships between the sexes permeated the social fabric. The whole debate on divorce was one in which both sides, however far apart they might seem, not only acquiesced in but positively promoted an essentially Christian ideal of marriage as the lynchpin of life for both society and the individual. And Christian marriage was based on the Platonic view that marriage is the union of two halves, two beings that are incomplete without each other, the masculine and the feminine.

Denis de Rougemont, in *Passion and Society* (1938), had developed the idea of a necessary conflict between romantic passion and bourgeois marriage, yet had ended his book with a call for their reconciliation in the interests of the married love he had demonstrated for several hundred pages as impossible. Father M.C. D'Arcy, a Jesuit, used this book as a jumping off point for his own, *The Mind and the Heart of Love* (1945) and wrote of Christian

marriage as the central reality of Christianity itself. In the relationship of marriage alone (on earth at least) could the two oppositions
of life be united. The 'mutal creation' of a married couple transcended the essential nature of each individual, of essential
masculinity and essential femininity, or Animus and Anima
(Jungian terms for the male and female principle, used by D'Arcy).

D'Arcy argued that Christian marriage had raised the status of
woman, since, whereas other religions and civilizations had simply confined her within her feminine nature, Christian marriage
offered the partners the opportunity to rise above the purely
masculine or feminine and unite as *fully human* in Agape, the
highest form of love. At the same time, he forcefully repeated –
many times – all the essential differences between Animus and
Anima. Reason was the male attribute, as also the 'instinct to
dominate and take' – which included intellectual mastery. Anima,
the feminine principle, expressed almost everything else in both
its good and its bad aspects; the surrender that is altruism, 'service
and affection for family and society', on the one hand; irrationalism, obscurantism, mysticism on the other, ultimately reaching
towards romanticism, melancholy, and the death wish. This was a
traditional and very familiar view of the male/female duality and of
'woman's nature'. It was found too in Robert Graves's *The White
Goddess* (1946), in which Woman, the poet's Muse, was a powerful
and often terrifying life force: 'The New Moon is the white goddess
of birth and growth; the Full Moon, the red goddess of love and
battle; the Old Moon, the black goddess of death and divination.'
Graves felt that: 'woman has of late become virtual head of the
household in most parts of the Western world, and holds the purse
strings, and can take up almost any career or position she pleases'
but that this merely equal status in the patriarchal world was far
inferior to her former divine power.

D'Arcy however argued that only in Christian marriage did the
feminine principle become 'human':

'At its most human the anima acts as the handmaid of the mind,
serving it and coaxing it, running ahead to make contacts with
the world which the reason has to meet, 'warming the house of
the soul so that the visitor may enter not as a stranger but as a
friend. But beyond all other services it creates a world of

persons. The mind (male) . . . reproduces on a higher level the characteristics of the acquisitive, masterful, self-centred love. It tends therefore to exploit the world and all whom it meets: it leaves out the homely and personal and lives in the abstractions.' (D'Arcy 1962:288)

Anima warming Animus's slippers when he comes home from work sounds like John Newsom's or Talcott Parsons' ideal of the wifely role. But it was strictly illogical or indeed meaningless to talk of woman's position as inferior or subordinate, since within Christian marriage two individuals become literally 'one flesh', although at the same time since Christian marriage symbolized the union of Christ and the Church, the man was head of the family at the social level, and in the sexual act played the part of – as C.S. Lewis put it – 'Sky Father' or 'Form' to the woman's 'Earth Mother' or 'Matter'. For Lewis as for D'Arcy the Greek belief that Form was masculine and matter feminine was incorporated into his Christianity after his conversion, but behind his intellectual arguments lurked what reads like old-fashioned prejudice: 'If there must be a head (of the family), why the man? Well, is there any very serious wish that it should be the woman?. . . . Do you really want a matriarchal world? Do you really like women in authority?' (Lewis 1952:98-9). In his discussions about sex, too, Lewis sounded like an old-fashioned scout master with his talk of fighting lust, being 'cured', suggesting that 'surrender to all our desires leads to impotence' and of these desires as an enemy that we must learn to know, in order to conquer it, as 'Wellington knew Napoleon or as Sherlock Holmes knew Moriarty'.

Lewis and the Christians said that in Christian marriage men and women met as 'two immortal souls, two free-born adults, two citizens'. At this level their relationship was perceived as democratic and egalitarian. Simultaneously within marriage they became one flesh and enacted the 'Pagan sacrament' of sex with its ultimate reduction to essential masculinity and essential femininity; mastery and surrender. At a third level they represented the marriage of Christ and Church. The (sacred and sacramental) ways in which the relationship between men and women was 'asymmetrical' had nothing to do with the freedom and equality of the two adults they also were. But for women this could mean a fragmentation of their experience and it did not give the disjointed parts of women's lives – juridical equality, economic dependence, sexual surrender, the female role – an overall coherence. It simply denied the contradiction it expressed.

Yet C.S. Lewis and T.S. Eliot spoke against the fragmentation of modern life and mass society. They shared these anxieties with many of those whose political views were far to the left. Raymond Williams just as much as Eliot was convinced that our society must degenerate without a 'common culture' although he defined it in a very different way. And one writer more than any other spoke to the fifties and voiced that desire to return to a more organic society.

LAWRENCE AND THE FIFTIES

Lord Longford, looking back from the end of the sixties (Beyfus 1968), thought that Lawrence had dominated the views of his own generation, in the thirties, in regard to sexual relations between men and women and the whole question of marriage. Today, his spirit seems also to have brooded over the fifties. His vision of male-female relationships was compelling because alternative representations of sexuality were tainted with vulgarity. Marilyn Monroe, draped across the Niagara falls in a strapless scarlet gown possibly symbolized a new sexual freedom for the girls of 'Ashton' the Yorkshire mining town, as she beamed down on them from the hoardings; but there was about her an atmosphere of the exploitation and commercialization of sex. With Lawrence's young women, on the other hand, the educated young could identify or fall in love. Gudrun and Ursula were made to be heroines of the fifties:

'Gudrun, new from her life in Chelsea and Sussex, shrank cruelly from this amorphous ugliness of a small colliery town in the Midlands. . . . If this were human life, if these were human beings living in a complete world, then what was her own world, outside? She was aware of her grass-green stockings, her large grass-green velour hat, her full soft coat, of a strong blue colour. And she felt as if she were treading in the air, quite unstable, her heart was contracted, as if at any minute she might be precipitated to the ground.' (Lawrence 1959:8-9)

Gudrun with her dark red, her grass-green, her bright yellow stockings, and her dresses from 1913 – made of Morris design materials, like the ones that Liberty reissued in the mid-fifties – was sexually experienced and sexually free, as was Ursula her sister. Lawrence in his novels not only offered men a justification for their sexual drive, he offered girls and women a richer female nature, and a sexuality that was neither vulgar nor aseptically repressed. Gudrun and Ursula were not in the Celia Johnson mould. They also after all were human beings with complex aspirations and an interest in their work. Gudrun was even an artist. As one aspiring young woman artist expressed it (Dunn 1965): 'He's very extraordinary Lawrence, one should read him all the time.' And like many of the young women who read Lawrence's novels, his heroines had become upwardly mobile through education, escaping in the process the narrowly puritanical confines of a working-class or lower-middle-class home. And they sought, and found, passion.

In 1970, Kate Millett, in one of the first books of the new feminist movement, *Sexual Politics*, wrote a blistering condemnation of Lawrence, of his phallo-centrism, his sadistic demand for submission from women, and his ultimate hatred of them. Readers in the Britain of the fifties did not and could not respond in this way because Lawrence was all that was offered and at the imaginative level the best that was offered to those who rejected the pin-up and the strangulated débutante. The work of Lawrence was attractive because he was English, working class, and a profoundly sexual and sensual writer in a period dominated by self caricatures of Britishness, and threatened by the cultural advance of America. F.R. Leavis, who taught English at Cambridge for many years and had been editor of the influential quarterly review *Scrutiny*, did much to popularize Lawrence. Generations of his pupils left Cambridge to teach his 'radical' criticism in new universities, colleges and schools. Lawrence was part of this 'radicalism'.

Equally, Raymond Williams admired Lawrence because he explored the relationship between industrialism and personal relationships, so that decadent sexuality became an image of industrial society itself:

'The real meaning of sex, Lawrence argues, is that it "involves the whole of a human being". The alternative to the "base forcing" into the competition for money and property is not sexual adventure, nor the available sexual emphasis, but again a return to the "quick of self".' (Williams 1961:212-13)

Lawrence, then, offered a way out of the commercialized wasteland of industrial civilization. His escape route was 'personal relationships' and in the case of women these were defined as sexual relationships with men. The latent political implications and the overt concern with the personal made him intensely sympathetic to the new left.

The nature of his attraction was dramatically demonstrated in the *Lady Chatterley* show trial of 1960. The trial was at one level a test case for the 1959 Obscene Publications Act, an act which its liberal supporters had hoped would reinforce the division between straight porn, and works of art, henceforth to be protected against prosecution. So the decision by the DPP to bring a case against *Lady Chatterley* angered and alarmed the liberal establishment. The first English edition of the unexpurgated version of *Lady Chatterley's Lover* was to be published by Penguin Books. The trial, which resulted in an acquittal, seemed at the time a triumph for liberal good sense and for progressive views in what Penguin themselves described as a battle between generations and between classes. It also illustrated how a Puritan, humanist view of marriage dominated radical intellectuals and Christians alike, and brought them very close together, so that there could be, even in progressive discourse, no space for women to speak with a separate voice. A view of sexual relationships as relationships 'between whole persons' as David Holbrook (who took Leavis's views off in a more clearly rightwards and anti-feminist direction) expressed it, could be counterposed to all that was brash and shoddy about postwar Britain. It implied an attack on industrialism itself, and therefore drew on a tradition of romantic or Christian socialism, yet was also compatible with the more Marxist elements of the new left, and with the views of R.D. Laing. It straddled political boundaries and rendered women non-problematical. E.P. Thompson, the historian and Communist Party dissident (he left the Party in 1956), who briefly mentioned the 'woman' problem (Thompson 1977) spoke of it entirely within humanist terms, although he did not support the idea of 'equality in difference'. Humanism just as much as David Holbrook's or Laing's psychoanalytic viewpoint, or even C.S. Lewis's Graeco-Christianity, was wholly consistent with a Lawrentian view that placed the union between man and woman above all else, the 'quick of self' at the heart of a heartless civilization, and made it a form of testimony and rebellion against it.

The trial of *Lady Chatterley* itself had farcical overtones, with a parade of Christian and literary notables brought to bear witness as to the book's uplifting nature, against the chief prosecutor's attempt to label it as smut ('Is it a book that you would even wish your wife or your servants to read?'). Over against the legal view of marriage, as expressed by the judge (Rolph 1961:219): 'What *is* a marriage if it is not in a legal sense? What *are* we talking about? This is a Christian country and quite apart from Christianity there is a lawful marriage even if it is only contracted before a registrar' – was set the puritan humanist view of the relationship between Mellors and Lady Chatterley as a 'true marriage', a 'very carefully worked out picture of relationships between the sexes which are based on tenderness and compassion', and a book to raise the status of women, since it did not depict them as mere sexual objects. In this way *Lady Chatterley's Lover* was seen as an antidote to corrupt and superficial sexual values, a view endorsed, for instance, by Richard Hoggart, who spoke of the 'enormous reverence which must be paid by one human being to another with whom he is in love' and of the importance of retrieving the true tradition of British puritanism. This was certainly the view of marriage expressed by Lawrence himself in one of his last works, *A Propos of Lady Chatterley* (1929), a defence of the then banned book. The Lawrentian marriage ideal seemed to offer a way back to the 'connectedness' that might otherwise be lost.

Nor did women themselves reject the potent Lawrentian vision. What better experience was there, after all, than a great love?:

'I see in Cambridge, particularly among the women dons, a series of such grotesques! . . . They are all very brilliant or learned . . . but I feel that all their experience is *secondary* and this to me is tantamount to a kind of living death. I want to . . . move into the world of growth and suffering where the real books are people's minds and souls. . . .

Don't worry that I am a "career woman", either . . . I am definitely *meant* to be married and have children and a home.' (Plath 1975:198;208)

So while working at her writing, Sylvia Plath was also acting the part of a Cambridge belle, yet was hopeful of or longing for a deeper relationship. And when it came:

'I have never known anything like it. For the first time in my life I can use all my knowing and laughing and force and writing to the hilt all the time, everything. . . .

I accept these days and these livings, for I am growing and shall be a woman beyond women for my strength.' (Plath 1975:234)

Sylvia Plath might seem an unfair as well as an obvious woman to choose as an example, since we are mindful of the black ending of that love, of her suicide, of her final knowledge of the masochism of those Lawrentian loves – 'Every woman adores a Fascist'. Yet her feeling was representative, and we do not know how many women may have died smaller, unnoticed, spiritual deaths in acting out that ideal.

THE CULTURAL CRITIQUE

However imprecise, the word 'culture' is itself rather evocative of the late fifties. David Marquand described the new left intelligentsia of Oxford as placing culture at the heart of the new socialism:

'Oxford socialists . . . are scarcely concerned at all with politics as usually understood. What are they concerned with instead? The short, superficial answer is, culture. *"Look Back in Anger"*, one prominent university left winger shouted at me recently, his voice almost shaking with passion, "is a more important political document than anything the Labour Party has said since 1951". . . . Culture and politics are bound together; politics is about people, not the economic men of the laissez faire text books.' (*The Guardian* 18.8.58)

Dennis Potter (1960) condemned the stuffy and élitist Oxford educational system. He had experienced it as a boy from the Forest of Dean mining community and as one of the first meritocratic children of the welfare state. He attacked the contradiction of that welfare state, built, it had been believed, on socialist foundations, yet supporting an élite and conservative culture.

Yet, hostile to élitism, the 'culturalists' approached the whole idea of mass culture with suspicion. Along with an attempt to return to the wellsprings of working-class culture was a fear of vulgar Americanism. F.R. Leavis (1933) had been writing on this theme already in the early thirties and took his images of mass society from American sociological and documentary literature. 'Mass society' brought the degradation of work, the destruction of crafts, the impoverishment of social life and communities and the breakdown of family life with predictable effects on youth and education.

Richard Hoggart's *The Uses of Literacy* (1958) was perhaps the most complete expression of all the themes latent in the enquiry into the nature of British – or English, it was not always the same – culture in the late fifties. His work had similarities to the work of the Institute of Community Studies and links with the left-wing tradition that was represented by the *New Reasoner*, started by E.P. Thomspon and John Saville as part of what became a revolt against Stalinism in the British Communist Party, by the *Universities and Left Review*, and by the Campaign for Nuclear Disarmament (Platt 1971).

His was a romantic, subjective evocation of working-class culture that gained rapid authority. His name was almost an incantation in earlier issues of the *Universities and Left Review* and the subsequent *New Left Review* and in Dennis Potter's book. Hoggart's special area of exploration was the role of popular mass literature, the radio, and popular music, but he personified working-class culture in the person of the 'working-class Mum' – also the dominant figure in the partly fictional world of Bethnal Green, and in Madeline Kerr's hostile descriptions. Almost sentimental about this powerful yet put-upon figure, Hoggart contrasted her with the symbol of the new American culture, also symbolized by a woman, the Mickey Spillane type of broad or dame – 'for page after page big-thighed and big-bosomed girls from Mars step out of their space-machines, and gangster's molls scream away in high-powered sedans'.

But the link between the two cultures, old and new, was a man, the 'scholarship boy'; the Dennis Potters; the grammar school boys made good who were for Hoggart the representatives of the 'uprooted and anxious', and for whom Colin Wilson spoke in his bestseller, *The Outsider* (1956). These uprooted and anxious intellectuals were all outsiders. So in the end, Hoggart's attitude towards a 'meritocratic' educational system was one of ambivalence, since it meant a loss of the traditional in return for the uncertain benefits of 'a precarious tenancy in several near-intellectual worlds'.

Education and youth culture were pivotal themes within the general culture debate, of as much concern to T.S. Eliot as to those on the left. For Talcott Parsons and conservative American sociology, the youth culture had been male and middle-class. As developed, the idea was that it overrode both class and sex, although the anthropologists of modern Britain were effectively describing working-class boys. Even in studies of delinquency the convergence of class was emphasized. The Albemarle (1960) and Ingleby (1960) Reports on the Youth Service and on Delinquency drew the same picture of the 'teenage consumer', of bored, alienated, and affluent youth, no longer fully contained within the family and living in a threatening world in which the overwhelming realities were the Cold War and the H–Bomb. The official remedies tried to give them a 'sense of purpose' with Duke of Edinburgh Award Schemes – or home care classes for the girls; the 'alternative' was to identify with youth, which meant accepting their aspirations on their terms. Either way the girls got screwed.

Ray Gosling, who for a time ran a youth club in Leicester, took the second position; he argued for a club run by those who used it and one that did not censor out sex:

> 'The result? Virgins may be raped. A club may have the reputation of a public brothel. Stolen goods may be received. Thieves and murderers may have a hideout. Decent folk may be intimidated. Teenage prostitution may have a place from which to operate.' (Gosling 1961:18)

Ray Gosling was right, though, to realize that for the young sexuality was definitely associated with revolt and rebellion; typical in accepting the contemporary definition of the rebellious girl as a *sexual* rebel. For this was also the definition found within the sociology of delinquency where girls appeared as criminals only in so far as they *were* sexual. For girls their sexuality *was* a crime.

HOMOSEXUALITY

Jeff Nuttall (1970) was later to describe the Mods as representing sexual ambiguity in so far as both sexes used make up, dyed their hair, and wore outrageous clothes. 'Kinky' was the fashionable word used to describe clothes of the early sixties, the black leather, PVC, and boots. There were: 'a thousand overtones of sexual deviation, particularly sadism, and everywhere, mixed in with amphetamines, was the birth pill'. He saw Elvis Presley as the 'queer boy's pin-up' and was well aware of the homosexual flavour of the youth culture. This was noticed by commentators much closer to a traditional view of youth. T.R. Fyvel, who wrote regularly for *Tribune*, the left Labour weekly, wrote in *The Insecure Offenders* (1961) of teenagers as victims of an ersatz and commercialized culture, of the insecurity of the Bomb, and of the thoughtlessness of 'latch-key mothers' who should have stayed at home. Fyvel noted that:

> 'It appeared to be the essence of the Teddy Boy cult that its members were more interested in each other and in their group life than in girls. . . .
>
> It could be argued that the combination of obsessive violence and obsessive interest in personal adornment betrayed not only a social but a sexual unsureness among the gang members in general. It was certainly the case that in the inner Teddy Boy circles homosexualism was regarded as one of the ubiquitous facts of life.' (Fyvel 1961:64-5)

The theme of homosexuality, running close to the surface yet never really in the open links D.H. Lawrence, C.S. Lewis, and the pop culture. There is no suggestion (Carpenter 1978) that Lewis was homosexual, but both he and Lawrence placed a very high value on male friendship and bonding, and Lawrence's ideal of love between men certainly bordered on the erotic, notably in *Women In Love*. Lawrence and Lewis also *shared* with many homosexuals a denigration of women as intellectual companions (although some male homosexuals have enjoyed women as intellectual friends and have rejected them only sexually). This attitude was also of a piece with the acceptance of what was perceived as manly in the working-class culture in which men as a matter of course despised, exploited, and beat their women. Colin MacInnes, in his documentary trilogy of novels that explored London at the turn of the decade, displayed women from both black and white communities as accepting brutality as evidence of love, or just as part of the unremarked and normal exchange between men and women (MacInnes 1958; 1959; 1960).

Homosexuality was also expressed in the 'camp sensibility', which Susan Sontag (1967), the American critic, attempted to define. Conceding that camp was 'disengaged, depoliticized – or at least, apolitical' she delighted in its strange mixture of naivety and knowingness – the child prostitute aspect of it; in its strange detachment from feeling, its role playing, its 'sensibility of failed seriousness, or the theatricalization of experience. Camp refuses both the harmonies of traditional seriousness, and the risk of fully identifying with extreme states of feeling'.

The camp sensibility was not synonymous with homosexuality, yet clearly had a relationship to it, and, even more, to the androgyne. Perhaps the homosexuality was less important than a general atmosphere in which what was lawless, ambiguous, ugly in conventional terms, or extreme was valued for those very qualities.

POP ART AND POP CULTURE

While Raymond Williams and Richard Hoggart condemned mass-produced, commercialized entertainment as offered to a passive mass public, artists themselves delighted in the daily life images and symbols of commercialized, Americanized culture.

Hoggart and Williams looked towards the working class and its institutions for the creation of a popular culture that came from the people itself; pop artists explored what actually *was* popular – even if it was imposed and its values suspect.

An interest in the language of the popular – advertisement hoardings, cartoons, Hollywood – had featured in the work of some English photographers before the war. In the early fifties the Institute of Contemporary Arts was, according to George Melly (1972), the centre of the birth of the British pop art movement, although this was also rooted in the surrealist tradition. An 'intellectual attempt to come to terms with the Americanization of our society', pop art could not but explore the adman's ubiquitous imagery of womanhood. Richard Hamilton, whose exhibition of paintings at the Whitechapel Art Gallery in 1956, *This Is Tomorrow*, did not simply display his works, but created – like the Diaghilev Exhibition of 1954 – a total environment anticipating the 'Happenings' of the sixties, saw Woman in her new relationship to things:

> 'The worst thing that can happen to a girl, according to the ads is that she should fail to be exquisitely at ease in her appliance setting – the setting that now does much to establish our attitude to woman in the way that her clothes alone used to. Sex is everywhere, symbolized in the glamour of mass-produced luxury – the interplay of fleshy plastic and smooth, fleshier metal. This relationship of woman and appliance is a fundamental theme of our culture'. (Russell and Gablik 1969:73)

Richard Hoggart dismissed the pin-up in characteristically puritan language:

> 'The sex has been machined out of them. . . . Put them alongside a Degas dancer and the unreality comes out strikingly. Are such things likely to increase sexual immorality among young people? I find it hard to imagine much connexion between them and heterosexual activity. They may encourage masturbation; in their symbolic way they may promote that kind of sealed-off response.' (Hoggart 1958:164-5)

But pop art seemed liberating to many who had felt stifled by the high culture of the late forties and early fifties – the verse plays of Eliot and Christopher Fry, the vogue for Regency furniture and interior decoration, the romanticism of Paul Nash and Oliver Messel, whose theatrical sets created an impression that *all* glamour and richness of experience lay in the past, the plays again of Anouilh, which like films such as *Madame De. . .* and *La Ronde* promoted an atmosphere of *fin de siècle* French romanticism, titillation, and sentimental adultery.

The rebels thumbed their noses at the stuffy, high church atmosphere of that kind of high Kunst. They preferred to immerse themselves in the vulgarity, but also in the angst, fragmentation, violence, and madness which seemed to lie at the heart of metropolitan life. In this exploration women's experience was revealed, although seldom discussed or explained, much less struggled against.

CONCLUSION

Throughout a decade, sophisticated audiences sat through movies by the Italian director, Antonioni. These explored the fashionable alienation of a bourgeoisie for whom marriage and eroticism were dry and brittle, and the industrial landscape simply a backdrop, suffused with romantic melancholy, for these amoral moralities. There was a more feverish atmosphere in the films of Federico Fellini, who also explored a decaying bourgeois society, particularly in *La Dolce Vita*. Part of the feverishness was the very presence of women who were sexual objects or sexually 'free'. It seemed daring simply to state that women could be sexual. Sexuality in any shape or form was equated with rebellion. No longer was it tucked up safely within marriage; it was on the rampage. The very attempt to wrench the sexual act from all context of sacrament, deep relationship or love, abhorrent to the humanists, was part of the liberating element. Richard Hoggart and the Bethnal Green sociologists were in the end wedded to a world that was passing. The new sensibility more accurately bore witness to the brave new H–Bomb world.

We should still however salute in their enterprise its understanding of what was being done to the working class. 'Culture' was the incantation; but the working class was above all in the process of being gutted *politically*. Raymond Williams was right to care about the preservation of the cultural/political institutions of working-class life. At the same time the cultural blindness of these writers in failing to understand or confront the reactionary aspects of what now seems in some cases a sentimental stereotype of working-class life, or the cruel side of the Lawrentian approach to women, was itself part of the cultural decadence they were trying to arrest; whereas the new sensibility took hold of that decadence and, apolitical or pre-political to begin with, twisted it towards new forms of political understanding. There was in the cultural climate of the sixties an attempt to confront violence. This attempt might be completely amoral, or even sold on its glamour, as in David Bailey's *A Box of Pin Ups* (1965) where the caption to a portrait of the gangsters, the Kray brothers, described them as: 'an East End legend . . . to be with them is to enter the atmosphere (laconic, lavish, dangerous) of an early Bogart movie, where life is reduced to its simplest terms yet remains ambiguous.' But there might be a recognition that to admit the existence of the cruelty was a step forward from the anodyne world of the fifties. Sheila Rowbotham (1973b) thought that the overt contempt and brutality towards women found in the Rolling Stones' songs and those of Dylan were better and more honest than the sugary sentimentality of Cliff Richard and the drooling ballads of the fifties. And it was only when the violence came to the surface and art and politics began to be centred on personal and collective attempts to come to terms with it, that women began to say: 'Now, wait a moment'.

CHAPTER EIGHT

Novelists

I want you to imagine me writing a novel in a state of trance. I want you to figure to yourselves a girl sitting with a pen in her hand, which for minutes and indeed for hours, she never dips into the inkpot. The image that comes to my mind when I think of this girl is the image of a fisherman lying sunk in dreams on the verge of a deep lake with a rod held out over the water. She was letting her imagination sweep unchecked round every rock and cranny of the world that lies submerged in the depths of our unconscious being. Now came the experience, the experience that I believe to be far commoner with women writers than with men. The line raced through the girl's fingers. Her imagination had rushed away. It had sought the pools, the depths, the dark places where the largest fish slumber. And then there was a smash. There was an explosion. There was foam and confusion. The imagination had dashed itself against something hard. The girl was roused from her dream. She was indeed in a state of the most acute and difficult distress. To speak without figure she had thought of something, something about the body, about the passions which it was unfitting for her as a woman to say.
(Virginia Woolf: *Professions for Women*)

In the years after the war the imminent death of the novel was often announced. Writers who had been on the left before the war perceived the breakdown of the novel as connected with the more general breakdown of liberal humanism. Orwell had said this as early as 1941. In the aftermath of war Storm Jameson (1950) and Mary McCarthy (1960) made similar predictions, and a number of writers and critics saw the traditional novel as splitting down into two tendencies; 'social realism' and 'stylism' to use Storm Jameson's labels, 'social' and 'personal' for Raymond Williams, 'journalistic' and 'crystalline' for Iris Murdoch. Harold Nicolson started a long debate in the columns of the *Observer* with an article called *Is The Novel Dead?* (29.8.54).

The Two Cultures debate initiated by another novelist, C.P. Snow, in the fifties was a different path to a similar conclusion, since in discussing the split between the arts and scientific culture Snow was also describing a fragmentation of experience, an inability to 'know' the whole of modern experience. So the 'death' of the novel was related to the feeling that life in mass society – homogenous in one way – was also fragmented.

The decade after the war was marked in British fiction by a general sense of retreat and nostalgia for a prewar world that had been lost. Elizabeth Bowen's war story, *The Square*, expressed the feeling that came upon the refined upper-middle classes during the war as part of wartime; a sense of decay, of slipping social norms, even of a yawning void beneath the surface politeness. At first assumed to be temporary, this unease turned out to be permanent. After the war the disillusionment and sense of loss were reflected in a literature that turned to religion, to the past, to private moral visions. There were many novels that relied largely on the rendering of exotic places, and some that described the long-drawn-out British retreat from Empire. There were novels about generations of families, usually charting decline, such as *Brideshead Revisited* by Evelyn Waugh and *Through the Valley* by Robert Henriques.

In *Hemlock and After* (1952) Angus Wilson satirized the clash between the older liberals left over from the thirties, and their children, 'neo-Victorians' with authoritarian affectations, living in a world on the one hand dedicated to rising standards of living and snobbery in the shape of foreign food and foreign travel, on the other corrupted by the wide boys and the decadence of those who were either consciously trying to wreck the welfare state or else too evilly anarchic to compromise with it. No wonder many writers took flight into the past.

Angus Wilson satirized the cult of Jane Austen too; and her influence, like the influence of D.H. Lawrence, was part of the atmosphere of the forties and fifties. She held up a mirror to a middle class that felt itself subjectively to be in retreat, and who longed – for a time at least – to return to a world as ordered, as polite and as carefully ranked as hers, where conversation, manners, and wit could be used as measures of both charm and breeding, and where leisure gave ample opportunities for the cultivation of those civilized relationships and happy marriages that formed the backbone of society and reinforced its rightful hierarchy. The enormous popularity of Angela Thirkell (see Sissons and French 1963) fed the same needs at a more popular level.

Neither was the Cold War absent from literary criticism. Whatever the objective merits of their books, Boris Pasternak and Solzhenitsyn were heaped with praise as great writers at least partly because both appeared to bear witness to 'western values' from within a totalitarian state. At the popular level the spy story operated on crude cold war assumptions (though Ian Fleming's 'James Bond' books were an intellectual cult before they became bestsellers and films). John Le Carré (1960) described an alienated, 'outsider' hero, a man for the times who moved in a bleak and Kafkaesque world on both sides of the Iron Curtain. In these thrillers women played a predictably feeble role. The general effect of the genre was to discredit all politics. Important as part of postwar ideology, they confirmed a cynical view of politics as *only* about power, and of human nature as essentially low and self seeking.

In singling out a few novels and a few authors I have run the risk of considerable distortion. In any case, it might not be relevant to relate novels too closely to the period in which they were written. I have suggested already that Kafka, Jane Austen, and D.H. Lawrence were important influences. In the sixties, Herman Hesse and Tolkien's *The Lord of the Rings* enjoyed a vogue in the 'countercultural' underground. Also, the novel was such a popular literary form in spite of its anticipated demise, and so much has (already) been written about some of the novelists active in the fifties and sixties, that it has seemed best to do no more than sketch in a few of the ways in which these novels seemed to relate to other social and cultural trends. I have also run the risk of using them as documentary evidence of the state of feelings (women's in particular). Although most remained within the realist tradition of the psychological, confessional, sometimes openly autiobiographical novel, this approach does raise problems. I can only say that I am aware of them.

WOMEN NOVELISTS AFTER THE WAR

The women most likely to become novelists – from the upper-middle and middle classes – were just those likely after the war to be most preoccupied with loss of status and the dreariness of austerity. Working-class women were then, as they still are now, largely excluded from literature. Autobiographical accounts, such as *Not Like This* by Jane Welch (published in 1953 and now completely forgotten), a straightforward account of poverty in the twenties and thirties, only occasionally gave working-class women a direct voice. Even the documentary writing of the prewar period seemed to vanish as a tradition.

Rosamund Lehmann in *The Echoing Grove* (1953) was successful in connecting the general atmosphere of retreat to a special sense of women's peculiar situation. The novel hinges round a relationship between two sisters, and while obsessed with all the trappings of 'good' manners and 'good' taste and with upper-middle-class family relations, the author was aware that women's problems were not simply due to the advent of the welfare state:

'I can't help thinking it's particularly difficult to be a woman just at present. One feels so transitional and fluctuating. . . . So I suppose do men. I believe we *are* all in flux – that the difference between our grandmothers and us is far deeper than we realize – much more fundamental than the obvious social economic one. Our so-called emancipation may be a symptom, not a cause. Sometimes I think it's more than the development of a

new attitude towards sex: that a new gender may be evolving –
psychically new – a sort of hybrid. Or else it's just beginning to
be uncovered how much woman there is in man and vice
versa.' (Lehmann 1953)

It is not always clear at what point a minute and sensitive
recreation in detail of the texture of daily life slips into snobbery
and obsession with social nuances. The novels of Elizabeth Bowen
could easily cross this blurred line, and moral judgments become
confused with the socially 'correct'. Several of her heroines have
lost their social bearings, and, denied the supportive framework of
a recognized place in society, and sometimes the support of a man
as well, they become pure individual sensibility, and the author's
task the impossibly accurate pinning down of the minutest sensations and gradations of atmosphere and feeling – a 'woman's'
sensibility taken to excess.

Elizabeth Taylor's novels, less well known, discuss the position
of women more openly. Her women, like the heroines of Doris
Lessing's novels, depend on their friendships with other women.
But these, so dear and necessary at one level, are in some deep way
negated by the physical realities of love, marriage, children, and
domesticity. In both *A View of the Harbour* (1947) and *A Wreath of
Roses* (1949) the view is examined, but at once put aside, that there
might be a lesbian element in the close and possessive friendship
of two women. In the end marriage had to win in any case, since it
was economically necessary for women. Beth in *A View of the
Harbour* is a successful novelist, but only because her husband
keeps her; the price of this is his contempt for her 'scribbling' and
his thwarted hope that once she had children it would cease.
Husband and wife can only frustrate each other, and, for Beth,
men are simply 'artful': 'they implant in us, foster in us instincts
which it is to their advantage for us to have, and which, in the end,
we feel shame at not possessing.'

Her friend Tory, bitter because her husband has left her, is
equally clear about women's unequal status and economic
dependence: 'He pays me money, as he should and must. A man
cannot be allowed to reserve a woman's beauty for himself until it
is gone, and then throw her on to the market again with nothing
left to sell.' Saddest of all is Harriet in *A Game of Hide and Seek*

(1952). Harriet is untrained for any career except marriage. Yet marriage itself for a middle-class woman – certainly for one with a single child, a prosperous husband, and daily help – was no longer a career; so Harriet's life is one of idleness and daydreaming, leading to a doomed and pathetic romance. To herself, her life seems pointless in comparison with the lives of her mother and her aunt, suffragettes who had fought for the Cause; with bewilderment she sets her formless hopes and longings against their real, if antiquated, purposes. In her later novels, Elizabeth Taylor seems to move away from her interest in the position of women, but in these earlier books she seems very close to what feminists were saying at the same period.

Many women writers chose to locate their novels in the past, or wrote of obviously abnormal marriage relationships, or of madness as a female response to life. This may have been partly coincidence. Antonia White's trilogy of novels, written between 1950 and 1954, combined these three themes, but they were avowedly autobiographical, so that in a sense the material was chosen for her. Yet it is as if in the early fifties women novelists wrote about women in the past, lost in madness, deprived completely of autonomy, because in the modern world it was not possible to suggest that a woman's *normal* lot was dependence and captivity, sexual frustration, and the battle with patriarchal authority. It seemed as if many women were so bemused by the prevailing ideology of emancipation achieved that the actual, contemporary female predicament had to be described in terms of insanity, or of Victorian or Edwardian patriarchalism, or perverse abnormalities in men.

BOHEMIANS AND ANGRY YOUNG MEN

However in 1954 Iris Murdoch's first novel, *Under The Net*, appeared. This is narrated in the first person by a man, and harks back to the atmosphere of Fitzrovia in the forties. Here are no country houses or fretfulness at the lack of servants, but a world of minor film directors, binges in Soho pubs, affairs with blues singers, and the efforts of would-be writers to survive by living on their wits.

Several male writers have described London bohemian life: Robert Hewison as a part of literary history, Anthony Powell and Julian Maclaren Ross fictionally. Women figured in Fitzrovia as sexual objects rather than as artists in their own right, and the atmosphere of emancipation concerned sexual rather than intellectual or economic emancipation. At the same time, these male novelists had an appreciative and friendly approach towards women, unlike the 'angry young men'. At least some of Anthony Powell's women characters do participate in intellectual and political as well as in social and sexual affairs. If most are *femmes fatales*, mistresses, and artists' models, some are Party members, novelists, and actresses. They achieve a certain independence while retaining a cementing function in social life, a function that denotes the limits of their autonomy, since most do ultimately depend on the men to whom they relate. Women as mothers necessarily do not figure largely in Powell's novels, since they are for the most part off stage giving birth and bringing up families (the narrator's wife falls into this category).

Anthony Powell treated his women with urbane detachment. But then he wrote of a fairly privileged, if sometimes seedy, section of society, and his characters could afford, perhaps, the niceties of chivalry. The bohemians of the fifties were not always so kind. Caitlin Thomas wrote about what it was really like to be the 'wife-mistress' of a genius, she and Dylan Thomas acting out an extreme version of the great bohemian myth, capital-A artist chained to earth mother and beauty/slut (Thomas 1957). Bernard Kops, playwright, certainly had no respect for his girl friend's independence, especially since this involved allegiance to the bourgeoisie:

> 'I thought to myself, "how strange that I, from Stepney, from my background, should be sitting here with a girl who had gone to a public school, who had been born into certain luxury, who had never known material poverty." Yet so we absolutely, so simply loved each other. . . .
>
> Was I entitled to take what I wanted? The answer was always "yes." First I had to break her from her analyst. . . . It was a great victory for me . . . I became a man with her, wanted her to lean on me. . . . I felt so protective towards her. If anyone in

Soho so much as touched her on the shoulder I would growl like a wild beast. . . . In her basket I noticed her medical books. She said she had no intention now of being a doctor, so we took the books to Foyles and sold them . . . Erica had left the hospital, chucked in her lot completely with mine and we both felt completely free for the first time in our lives. We were our own masters' (sic).

It is easy to understand the attraction for a young and sheltered woman of a bohemianism that came in the guise of her own sexual and social liberation. But beyond this kind of male egomania was a realm in which contempt for women shaded into hatred. J.P. Donleavy's *The Ginger Man* (1958) describes a boozy bore who bullies his wife and treats women as cunts on the assumption that he is a Great Writer. In *Look Back In Anger* John Osborne felt justified in letting rip at women as if this were in itself an attack on convention and bourgeois values. The rebellion against the Establishment came in the guise of – amongst other things – an attack on traditional chivalry. But the tirades of Donleavy and Osborne went far beyond that, suggesting that just below the surface of this obsessively heterosexual world lay an absolute loathing of women. If women were chaste, then men hurt and bullied them. If they were martyred, they were further humiliated. If they were predatory, they became comic and contemptible, and the sight of a woman sexually aroused appeared to be threatening, obscene, and horrific to these womanizers.

The so-called 'Angry Young Men' amongst whom John Osborne and at one time Iris Murdoch were classed, were a well documented phenomenon, partly created by the media. (It was front-page news, for example, when Colin Wilson went off with a young woman whose father threatened to horsewhip the writer.) Some were closer to the bohemians and the beats. Others were seen as a product of the welfare state, their collective voice (which in any case was never really collective) interpreted as the brash voice of the new Keynesian 'socialism' – although their rebellion was primarily a demand for social recognition by a new and at first not quite socially acceptable voice (Allsop 1964). By the mid-sixties many of them were already voicing the opinions and supporting the causes of the far right; and many of their novels were about success and social advancement rather in the manner of H.G. Wells or Arnold Bennett.

Perhaps the most interesting was Kingsley Amis, who described the stuffy awfulness of provincial life with almost as much attention to detail as Elizabeth Bowen. For him, as for her, vulgarity had moral connotations, and if his heroes were actively and determinedly philistine it was because they were caught in a no-man's land between the vulgarity of commercial taste and the pretentiousness of the intellectual 'establishment'. These men had to acquire some money and success simply to escape suffocation. If they took it for granted that beautiful women represented status and that sexual permissiveness was one of the perks of the rich, then that simply reflected what was the case. Yet the Amis hero is not without compassion for women. On the other hand he seldom seems sexually at ease with them. In *Take A Girl Like You* (1960), one of the last – or one of the few – novels whose central theme was heavy petting, Patrick is supposed to be a young man of the world, aged nearly thirty, yet he spends the whole novel hung up on a virginal young woman from whom his only relief is a call girl. In *I Want It Now* (1968) the hero is plainly terrified of the rapacious mother and daughter who pursue him. He finds the daughter (significantly named Simon) flat chested and scrawny and although by the end of the book they have entered on a more permanent relationship, she never seems to be the hero's cup of tea.

WOMEN NOVELISTS OF THE SIXTIES

Two women, Doris Lessing and Iris Murdoch, shunted in with the 'Angries' in the fifties were then to be found in what was seen as a movement of women novelists in the sixties. It would be interesting to explore further the whole way in which the media orchestrated these 'movements' of writers and also the way in which it turned some writers into media stars. A forerunner was the French novelist Françoise Sagan, whose 'scandalous' first novel *Bonjour Tristesse*, written when she was only eighteen and published in 1958, became a best seller and not only made her famous but turned her into the symbol of western, fast-living, cynical amoral youth.

It was now possible to read about the young girl escaping the bonds of adolescence and virginity, instead of about the young hero finding himself in life. Most of these novels stayed within the realist tradition of the psychological novel. Their originality resided rather in their subject matter. The loss of virginity, the experience of motherhood, the portrayal of young women from the inside, these experiences were freshly described. These novels were part of the general obsession with youth. The novels did not suggest new roles for women, nor did they discuss or describe the world of work (but then few novels of any kind did that). The essentially 'feminine' predicaments of these women centred round romantic love, sexuality, childbirth. But with a difference; for these writers the novel became a medium within which they could attempt a confrontation with contradictory experience. Searching for their 'freedom' they turned back to the traditionally feminine world that their individualism might have led them to reject. This traditional sphere, though, was seen through new eyes. It was problematized.

In spite of the attempt to describe the family as a unity, there was a counter-tendency, not confined to the novel but found, say, in the sociology of the family, to break down the 'family' into its component functions, and within that to differentiate out women's multiple roles. In the sixties women began to write about this. In *Woman's Mirror* (15.5.65) Katherine Whitehorn suggested that women's roles were incompatible – how could you be mother, mistress, and wage earner all at the same time? (The same theme was recently taken up by Jill Tweedie in the columns of the *Guardian*.)

Women novelists went back into this hitherto taken-for-granted world of domesticity in order to sort it out into its component parts. But the institution of marriage was less important than the raw, personal edge of experience of childbirth, motherhood, orgasm, and love for a man. (It was never a woman, for as *Nova* naively put it: 'few would wish to end up their days like Lakey, Mary McCarthy's heroine in *The Group*, who opts out of the sex war completely to become a glamorous Lesbian.')

Nova (September 1965) explained women's writing in terms of the 'sex war'. Hostilities had broken out again because just at the point when women had achieved economic independence they had simultaneously discovered that they had sexual desires 'just like men'. In which case: 'how can you dispense with male domination when man is the bearer of this new found pleasure?' This was the theme of some of Edna O'Brien's novels. For her heroines, sexual desire repeatedly led to betrayal at the hands of men. For both Edna O'Brien and Doris Lessing, erotic love for men created a dreadful dependence and vulnerability which in turn could lead to hatred both of self and of the male.

By 1968, Angus Wilson (*The Listener* 10.10.68) feared that this sex war would be more violent than ever, akin to 'Black Power', 'total war of an Amazonian kind'. Some women, however, seemed more urgently to wish to re-establish or at least to explore the relationship between sex and childbirth. Margaret Drabble in *The Millstone* (1964) seemed to be doing something highly unusual simply by suggesting that to have an illegitimate baby might be not only possible, socially, but that it might be far more important than the simple sexual act that led to it. Penelope Mortimer in *The Pumpkin Eater* (1963) implicitly protested at the way in which sex had been divorced from childbearing. Her heroine cannot in fact do this, and so has an ever-larger family that infuriates and alienates her husband, who is in any case a compulsive womanizer. But why does everyone – the heroine's parents, her husband, her analysts – see her desire for many babies as a problem? Why does she have to be aborted and sterilized? It was as if merely to be a woman was to be a little mad; and mad even to call in question the longed-for separation between sexual acts and consequent fertility.

In the fifties Penelope Mortimer wrote an *Evening Standard* column about her experiences as a mother bringing up five children. In the sixties Margaret Drabble wrote articles in the *Guardian* about the trials and tribulations of motherhood, calling into question what had long been taken for granted – the burden it was to hump a heavy little child about; the horror of clearing up vomit and faeces. This may have been part of a reaction against the way in which birth and child-rearing had been glamorized in the fifties.

In the fifties, efforts were being made to make childbirth less painful. For the first time the idea was widely accepted that women had a *right* to the relief of pain in labour. The movement to promote natural childbirth, of which Sheila Kitzinger was a pioneer, went beyond this in emphasizing all the positive aspects of the experience, as well as women's own capacity to control and master the pain. Natural childbirth became such a vogue, especially amongst more intellectual women, that those who experienced pain and resorted to anaesthetics often felt guilty, as if they had failed. For these women, some of whom had abandoned careers, temporarily or permanently, natural childbirth techniques offered an intellectual way of retaining control over this most physical of experiences. But by 1966 Gillian Tindall, also a novelist, was writing in the *Guardian* to question the natural childbirth cult, and this was part of the swing away again from the exaggeration of women's roles within marriage.

Many of these women's novels were made into films, which presented them to a much wider audience. Some of the novelists themselves became well known media figures – Edna O'Brien, for example is *still* treated as a lovely Irish colleen (see the *Telegraph* Sunday magazine 8.7.79). Sometimes they were exploited as a popular image of liberated womanhood, although Brigid Brophy and Iris Murdoch had novelty value as intellectual women.

These last two wrote novels that were rather more artificed, which relied less on the fresh backgrounds – Irish girlhood, the young girl at Oxbridge, the first affair in Paris – and tended to write about sexually dominant women of ambiguous gender. Brigid Brophy wrote of deliberate role reversal in which women were sexual initiators, predators, and Don Juans. Iris Murdoch's philosophical preoccupation with right moral conduct led her away from the problems of women as 'special' and gender appeared relatively immaterial in many of the sexual encounters that littered her books. In more than one she described relationships between male homosexuals. But while lesbianism seemed to tinge many of her female characters this was rather as an aspect of their powerfulness as individuals than to do with sexual orientation.

Maureen Duffy's *The Microcosm* (1966) was one of the very few books during this period to confront lesbianism openly and to describe the social life of lesbians. Indeed the whole subject was shunned during the permissive sixties – it was the one 'problem' about which *Nova* never ran an article. It simply was not fashionable. But neither Iris Murdoch nor Maureen Duffy really explored the ambiguities of male identification in women. They only described it. Maureen Duffy's lesbian heroine, Matt, is simply referred to throughout as 'he' and is given to differentiating himself from the female:

> 'Matt laughs . . . . "I keep on hammering at the same point with all the reasons, the abstractions, the isms and ologies while Rae just steps right into it and deeper, lives it all and beyond, leaving me still shouting about, finding a system, a scheme that'll fit it all in. It's the old traditional difference, I suppose between masculine and feminine ways of approach, both necessary, complementary but irritating to each other." '
> (Duffy 1966:173)

But perhaps for many women, not only lesbians, intellect and reasoning *were* equated with masculinity and maleness. Maureen Duffy and Iris Murdoch bore witness to this tension and although it seems a pity they did not confront it more directly this may have been very difficult in a cultural climate in which the uniqueness of the Artist's experience was constantly emphasized, in which the atomized individual was more fashionable than the collective experience, the movement, the group. It was in a way a breakthrough for Maureen Duffy even to have described the social world of lesbianism and not to have confined it to the level of a unique and very private experience.

DORIS LESSING

Of all these writers none came so near the 'quick of self' as Doris Lessing, who alone connected the difficulties of being a woman with major political and intellectual problems. *The Golden Notebook* remains perhaps the most complete exploration possible of what it 'meant' and 'means' to be a woman today. Doris Lessing herself wrote about it in 1972:

'Some books are not read in the right way because they have skipped a stage of opinion, assume a crystallization of information in society which has not yet taken place. This book was written as if the attitudes that have been created by the women's liberation movements already existed. . . . If it were coming out now for the first time it might be read and not merely reacted to: things have changed very fast.' (Bradbury 1977:172)

Yet the book said many things that have been shunned and avoided by the British women's movement.

Doris Lessing came originally from Southern Africa and was one of the minority of white colonials who recognized racism as evil – a minority within a minority. In the West all those sympathetic to socialism have, in greater or lesser degree, this minority consciousness, a special view of life that comes from always seeing the reverse side of their own culture, a special bitter vulnerability from always swimming against the tide. Women often have this minority consciousness too.

Doris Lessing's two longest novels, *The Golden Notebook* (1962) and *The Four Gated City* (1968) attempt to go to the limit of this exposure and vulnerability. Doris Lessing is close to the existentialists, for, like Iris Murdoch's first hero, she is always trying to get 'under the net' of the structures and patterns and theories of social existence to the 'real' matter, the bedrock, and *The Golden Notebook* is all about the tensions between the 'raw, unfinished quality' of life and the (necessary) attempts to impose both theoretical (Freud, and Marxism) and artistic coherence on it.

Insanity is one way of getting to this raw bone of experience. For Doris Lessing, since bourgeois life is itself, in all its seeming compulsive, clockwork sanity, actually mad, by contrast madness, as with Laing, comes to be in some sense a more naked appreciation of the truth.

In her earlier books this sombre preoccupation with the heart of darkness is less evident; but her women characters always face lonely choices. They want to be 'free women', women not constrained by bourgeois convention, not conformist just out of fear. So – they get hurt, because unfortunately neither as wives nor as mistresses can women trust men:

' "What's the use of being free, if they aren't? I swear to God,
that everyone of them, even the best of them, have the old idea
of good women and bad women."

"And what about us? Free, we say, yet the truth is they get an
erection when they're with a woman they don't give a damn
about, but we don't have an orgasm unless we love him. What's
free about that?" ' (Lessing 1962:449)

This for Doris Lessing is the contradiction central to women's
experience of sexual love. Especially for her heroine in *The Golden
Notebook* (called Anna and Ella in different sections of the novel)
'integrity is the orgasm' and it is a vaginal orgasm:

'When Ella first made love with Paul . . . what set the seal on
the fact she loved him, and made it possible for her to use the
word, was that she immediately experienced orgasm. Vaginal
orgasm, that is. And she could not have experienced it if she
had not loved him. It is the orgasm that is created by the man's
need for a woman, and his confidence in that need. . . . A
vaginal orgasm is emotion and nothing else. . . . There is only
one real female orgasm, and that is when a man, from the whole
of his need and desire takes a woman and wants all of her
response.' (Lessing 1962:212-13)

There could be no more intense statement of sexual romanticism
nor a more traditional description of female sexual response. Yet
since it is so widely accepted that men and women *do* differ
fundamentally it is also a description of how women in our culture
'instinctively' feel about sex and about love with a man. At the
same time the situation itself is stereotyped – Ella's lover casts her
in the role of mistress with all that that implies of impermanence
and limitation, while she casts herself headlong into the relationship as a 'great love'. (*The Second Sex* is full of similar tales culled
from nineteenth- and twentieth-century literature and history.)

Doris Lessing's women, although they heartily despise lesbianism, are often left to support each other emotionally without men.
Indispensable, the friendship of another women is simultaneously
only possible in the light of their greater commitment to men. The
great thing in life is a Lawrentian love. And the pain is especially
intense for Doris Lessing's heroines *because* she/they see that

objectively men cannot relate to women in the way women want, so that instead of love there is betrayal, in a world that is no longer the longed for world of 'real women' and 'real men':

> 'I thought that somewhere here is a fearful trap for women, but I don't yet understand what it is. For there is no doubt of the new note women strike, the note of being betrayed. It's in the books they write, in how they speak, everywhere, all the time. It is a solemn, self-pitying organ note. It is in me, Anna betrayed, Anna unloved, Anna whose happiness is denied.' (Lessing 1962:582)

CONCLUSION

Anna Koedt's *The Myth of the Vaginal Orgasm* and a whole series of demolition jobs on Freud have blasted the Lawrentian ideal of phallocentric sexual love. This strategy has failed to acknowledge the extent to which the romantic myth still holds sway, not as a form of 'conditioning' which can be stripped off, peeled away, but inside us, part of us. The women's movement has sought a collective solution and looked to a new kind of solidarity amongst women. Doris Lessing has turned wholly away into the private experience of the individual, and in that respect her work remains, not a prefiguration of the women's movement, but very much a body of work from before the women's movement, reflecting the atomized, mad world of the sixties.

Yet the women's movement, in trying to censor out those aspects of Doris Lessing's writings that women did not want to hear, has run the risk of being pulled back into the dark ebb and flow of the longing for surrender of self in love and abandonment – in all senses.

CHAPTER NINE

The cause of reasonable feminism

We ought to remember that there has been one time pre-viously in the history of the world when women achieved a considerable measure of equality. It was in the Roman Empire, and it should serve as a warning of the dangers to which equality may give rise. . . . This freedom . . . proved to be disastrous to the Roman society. Morals decayed. The marital tie became the laxest the Western world has seen. Bertrand Russell . . . has expressed the position in a sentence: Women, who had been virtuous slaves, became free and dissolute; divorce became common; the rich ceased to have children. This decay of morality was indeed one of the factors in the fall of the Roman Empire. Let us look upon this and take heed. (Lord Denning: *The Equality of Women – Eleanor Rathbone Memorial Lecture 1960*)

After women had won the vote many of the activists felt that their task was completed, and that their future efforts should be directed towards the bringing together of men and women in greater understanding of the role both shared as citizens, regard-less of sex. So, in the twenties, the National Union of Women's Suffrage Societies renamed itself the National Union of Societies for Education in Citizenship. Although in the thirties Winifred

Holtby (1934) feared an anti-feminist back-lash in the midst of unemployment, fascism, and the threat of war, the war itself renewed the optimism of the feminists, who felt that women had once again proved their worth in the labour force, and their ability to combine work with the domestic role.

Victory came, but where were its rewards? The austere utopia that was at first welcomed soon became irksome to many. And at the same time as the domestic illusion of a new society began to be eroded, so another illusion on a much larger scale was or had been shattered: the Soviet utopia. Yet despite a general fear and hysterical vituperation against the Soviet Union, so recently our 'gallant ally', in one crucial respect the West continued to have nothing but praise for the Soviet state. A later generation of feminists has violently rejected Stalin's Russia for the family code introduced in the mid thirties as part of a population policy that was blind to women's needs. Many women in the thirties and forties, however, reacted otherwise. Many of the admirers of the Soviet Union in the thirties had especially welcomed Stalin's family code because it was held to have freed women from economic need so that they could more easily and happily fulfil their special role as mothers. Even in the period of the general revulsion against the USSR after 1946, there remained an inconsistent but equally strong admiration for her legal provisions with regard to the family and – perhaps – a sense of relief that, as it was felt, her experiment with the abolition of the family had failed. The Soviet family code seemed enlightened to planners, to politicians, and to some feminists. It was mentioned approvingly a number of times by groups and individuals who gave evidence to the Royal Commission on Population for example, for it was seen as a stabilizing force and as an encouragement to women to reproduce. Today, it is more widely viewed as an authoritarian betrayal of the sexual liberation of the twenties.

The tendency amongst modern feminists has been to characterize the reversals of the Stalin period as a well thought out attack on the sexual liberation of Soviet women and to idealize Alexandra Kollontai in particular for her attempt to work out a position on revolutionary love and for even having attempted to express her feelings. This is not surprising, since in the present phase of the struggle for women's liberation there has been a similar preoccupation with the nature of revolutionary love, attempts to abolish jealousy and possessiveness, explorations of women's true sexual feelings, and a questioning of the relationships between men and woman. But the sexual revolution was not crushed in the Soviet Union; rather the whole attempt was so difficult and involved so much that was unknown that it was gradually abandoned. It may well be abandoned again, in the West. And it was not even being attempted by most of the British feminists of the period in between.

FEMINISM AND FABIANISM

After the war feminism was, in fact, imprisoned within the constellation of social democratic beliefs that were for a time very powerful. Feminists fully shared the general optimism of the progressive sections of society and many had great expectations of the welfare state. For Vera Brittain, this was the mechanism that would finally dissolve feminism into the general progressive movement:

'It is only a beginning for in every country the old aggressive values still dominate at the top. . . . But the welfare state is dedicated to social service, and in it women have become ends in themselves and not merely means to the ends of men. . . . The welfare state has been both cause and consequence of the second great change by which women have moved within thirty years from rivalry with men to a new recognition of their unique value as women.' (Brittain 1953:224)

Vera Brittain traced three stages of feminism: the old original pioneers who had begun by demanding equality and rights; a second generation of feminists (her own) who had between the wars gone on to value the idea of self support and economic independence; and, finally, a third that emphasized the special values women could bring to a society menaced by destruction, who had 'perceived the importance, not of educating women to equal or excel men but of educating men to respect and adopt those women's values which emphasize the principles of love and toleration.' And she cited the examples of both the Soviet Union and of Denmark in making a plea that education should recognize the differences between men and women: 'Why not make some provision for the education of modern women as women?'

Once this line of argument began to be equated with 'modernity' the ideas of the feminists became 'old fashioned'. The new and often anti-feminist ideas were discussed as though they were a new form of feminism, a more advanced form. This transformation of ideas suggests that 'feminism' is not a wholly established, static, and assured world view with its own internal coherence, but has a certain fluidity and ambiguity.

After the war the themes that emerged to embrace narrower notions of feminism were the themes of peace; of democracy and its preservation; and of citizenship; and within this of a transformation of marriage into a partnership with a 'helping and co-operative father' and a wife who was a friend and companion. Charlotte Leutkens in *Women And A New Society* (1946) wrote of women's new role in this threatened postwar society, wrote of the general wish to restore the 'honour of homemaking' and to raise the status and conditions of housework to that of the factory job. These themes were evident elsewhere. What is interesting is to see them taken over so eagerly by women who were feminists. Why should this have been? It is easy to understand what Anne Scott James (1952) called the 'general malaise' which, combined with the practical problems of tax and lack of domestic help, gave middle class women little incentive to remain at work. But why the *ideological* reinforcements?

In the context of longing for a real peace, and terror of a new and far more horrible war, feminism as a separate political issue may have seemed sectarian. For those feminists who saw themselves as part of the progressive movement, now that a Labour government was in power, they were dedicated to its support, while in principle it was dedicated to many of the views and policies pursued by feminists. For some women activists this meant that if the Labour Government did not make equal pay or nurseries a priority, ostensibly at least because of the general economic crisis, then they too felt compelled to try to understand this, rather than harrying a government that was never free from harrassment from the right.

Then the theme of 'women's special qualities' was an attractive one in itself. It stressed the positive virtues of a feminine approach and this must have appealed to many women who had no wish to fit themselves to the mannish stereotype of the prewar feminist. To this was added the Freudian emphasis on the important womanly qualities of sexual responsiveness and mothering, and the importance of children's emotions as the primary consideration in child care. As the Birmingham Feminist History Group has recently (1979) pointed out, at least the Freudian approach made the mother's role seem important.

The idea of women as equal companions to men may also have appealed at an emotional level to women who had never wholly got over their belief that women were inferior. To be the equal companion of a man was almost to be a man, was better by far than to be a spinster, condemned to the narrow life of companionship only with her own kind. And paradoxically, at a deeper level again, the emphasis on women's special qualities could also express a rejection and hatred of men, of aggressive masculinity, of the destructiveness that seemed to have spread over the world in the late forties and early fifties.

Finally, it was difficult for educated, progressive feminists to complain about their status when it was in part the result of the advancement of their working-class sisters. Feminists of the twenties and thirties had debated the significance of the class composition of the feminist movement, as Ray Strachey in *The Cause* (1928) made clear. They had not realized that just as working-class women were beginning to enjoy the independence of the wage packet, they themselves would be thrown back into the position of a new 'proletariat'. Their attempt to make a virtue of domestic work was their adjustment to this situation.

Yet as expressed by Judith Hubback 'reasonable modern feminism', building on 'the diversity of the sexes', and not 'crudely egalitarian', was an impossible ideal:

'The educated wife of today . . . must be both feminine and masculine. . . . She must try to combine in herself some at least of the attitudes which were once believed to be found only in men, with a liberal allowance of the qualities that marriage and motherhood engender. In a predominantly masculine world she must restate feminine values and she must insist on the importance of human relationships.' (Hubback 1957:159)

THE BRITISH HOUSEWIVES' LEAGUE

Given these factors, it might almost seem at times, at least in the immediate postwar years, that feminism was an aspect of right-wing politics. It is salutary to recall that one of the most effective organized groupings of women in the late forties was the British Housewives League. Led by Dorothy Crisp, an extreme right-winger and anti-semite, this organization mobilized huge numbers of women in demonstrations and petitions against the Labour government and these were used as yet another stick by the largely right wing press with which to beat the 'socialists'. In 1946 a deputation of housewives met with Dr Edith Summerskill, then permanent secretary at the Ministry of Food, but she was able to offer them only sympathy, so in July a London meeting of 1,000 members of the League passed a motion of no confidence in the government's food policy. In the same year a petition against bread rationing collected 300,000 signatures and was presented to the King. In June 1947 there was an even larger rally at the Royal Albert Hall, at which the Communist Party tried to make clear the true political nature of the leaders at least, by dropping leaflets from the gallery in an attempt to wreck the meeting. Their slogan was 'Never mind the label on the packet; the stuff inside is a Tory racket'.

The Labour Party paper, the *Daily Herald* wrote off this and other clashes at some of the rallies and marches as simply a battle between left and right. A later commentator (Sissons and French 1963) has dismissed them as 'amazons'. Yet although the leadership and its squabbles may have been ridiculous, and the organization was certainly a Tory front, the support on which it drew was evidence of real feelings of anger and desperation amongst many women. Partly on their account the government had to hold a debate on housewives. The organization was able to set up a whole network of local groups and to hold large rallies in many cities. In

1951 their activities even included the ritual burning of ration cards. The organization must therefore have represented a real rebellion against their domestic plight by many women. The response of the left and even of progressive women's groups such as Women for Westminster was largely a moralistic call to help worse-off third-world and defeated countries. There was no *feminist* response to the anger of housewives. That this rebellion was orchestrated by the right does not prove that it spoke only for the right, nor that women are innately conservative, simply that postwar labour Fabian welfarism did not, despite the optimism of women like Vera Brittain, speak adequately to women's needs.

In general, the right, in the shape of the Tory party in the postwar period, had a record on women that was no worse and at times marginally better than that of the Labour party. In the period of consensus the issue was seldom raised officially on either side. The family was simply assumed as central by everyone, feminists included. One of the few Tory pronouncements on the subject was the Conservative Research Department paper, *Family Policy* (1952) which quoted Margaret Thatcher as saying: ' "It is possible to carry on working, taking a short leave of absence when families arrive and returning later" ' (Phillips 1978). In other words the Tories in the period of 'Butskellism' accepted women's dual role and in any case despite the tendency for the Tory party to emphasize 'traditional values' there has always been for it an ideological tension between these and its equally strong belief in 'freedom of choice' (which included choice for women) and 'free enterprise' (which often in practice meant small firms employing cheap female labour).

An examination of the postwar period can only serve to make the relationship between socialism and feminism *more* problematical, not less. In the context of the 1979 Tory government the immediate and unquestioned assumption by a number of feminists of the imminence of an anti-feminist backlash and the implementation of 'back to the home' policies for women suggests an oversimplified understanding of the relationship between feminism and the wider political spectrum. There has not been in Britain a simple relationship between right wing views and anti-feminism, nor between unemployment and practical attempts to eject women from the workforce, except directly after 1918. Indeed it was the period of the boom, in the fifties, that saw the elaboration of an ideology of motherhood. The interaction between ideologies and practical policies and politics is a complex matter and their relationship dependent on specific circumstances.

WOMEN AND THE TRADES UNIONS

Feminists today tend to be highly critical of the postwar labour movement and especially its leadership, male and female alike, for a failure to implement policies that would have favoured women. This is held to have been due in many cases to active hostility towards women's emancipation. Yet the situation seems more to have been one of uncertainty and of conflicting opinions, which not surprisingly led to ambivalence on issues such as equal pay and nursery provision. There was both conflict *and* uncertainty as to what women's role was or ought to be, and similar uncertainties as to what the role of policy should be. It was never clear, for example, within the labour movement, whether nurseries should be provided because the country needed female labour, or because nurseries were a right for all mothers. Nor was it clear whether wives and mothers should have a right to work, or whether they and their husbands had a right to a wage – for him – that adequately met the needs of the whole family.

It was recognized that women workers were playing a dual role and for some trades unionists nursery schooling was part of the drive to compensate for the strains this caused. This was stated at the Women's TUC of 1950, when one speaker acknowledged that women had not 'shed their domestic responsibilities' and argued that the work of the Women's Advisory Committee to the TUC was to 'ease their burden' by way of welfare, nurseries, canteens *and* part time work. No one at this time mentioned the idea of men sharing the domestic burden.

The whole question of nurseries was debated again at the 1953 TUC Congress when Miss Blake of the National Union of Hosiery Workers moved a motion against the closure of nurseries. This motion was remitted after two very hostile speeches, from Anne

Godwin of the General Council and Mrs A. Horan of the National Union of General and Municipal Workers, who expressed the more conservative view within the Labour Movement:

'The cost (of nurseries) is and should be prohibitive to the two wage-earning family. . . . We have not had many women on the rostrum and I am rather regretful that I have to oppose the previous speaker. . . . day nurseries were only a wartime expedient accepted very reluctantly by responsible women's organizations who all believed that the place for the child under two was at home with its mother. . . . It is unfair to ask the one wage family to subsidize the two wage family.'

It is interesting that the speaker should regret the absence of the women from active union politics without connecting this to their situation as child rearers or as a group still semi-excluded from work. But this failure to connect was far from unusual. All the same, active women trades unionists were certainly aware of and concerned about the 'trades union backwardness' of women, and took steps, some bizarre, to combat this. Activist women recognized that their working but non-unionized sisters faced objective difficulties that hindered union participation or even membership. Some women believed that unions were for men only (as some had been, until 1943), but the two greatest obstacles were 'the short term outlook of the young women and the fear of the older women'. Margaret McKay who was women's officer of the TUC in the early fifties thought that 'If many thousands of eligible lads in the Movement were to let it be known that they were looking for sweethearts in the trades union movement more young girls might become members'. Efforts were made in the mid-fifties to attract women to trades unions by staging fashion and cosmetics shows, but by the late fifties there seemed to be a growing awareness that women's domestic responsibilities were the main barrier. By that time it was clear that there was to be no development of a comprehensive welfare system embracing domestic work, such as had been envisaged immediately after the war, and it therefore became possible to talk about domestic work in a new way and to raise the issue of men helping in the home and helping with child care.

By this time, an increasing number of women in the workforce, and in the trades unions, was making some impact. Trades union membership amongst women rose throughout the fifties, and then more rapidly between 1959 and 1964, twice as fast as the increase in women employed. And this was in spite of the contraction of the textile industry, traditionally an area of unionized employment for women. After about 1963 there was considerably more interest throughout the labour movement in equal pay for the ordinary woman factory or shop worker.

EQUAL PAY

In the first decade after the war the winning of equal pay in the Civil Service and in the teaching profession was the major victory for women on the employment front. The postwar Labour government accepted the arguments for equal pay in principle but in practice refused to give them priority. There was a strong case, especially for women civil servants, that their work was identical to that of men. The campaign was accordingly fought on the ticket of 'equal pay for equal work' and not 'equal pay for work of equal value'. The women in the Civil Service had the support of male colleagues and fellow trades unionists, many of whom looked on the lower pay of women as a residual anomaly that should be eliminated.

One woman who participated in these struggles has described the atmosphere and attitudes at the time. She had always been aware of the existence of prejudice. As a member of the Women's Timber Corps during the war she and her mates used on occasion to go to pubs from which as likely as not they would be ejected, since the idea of women in pubs on their own or in a gang was far from acceptable in rural areas. But she regarded this as a joke rather than as something to get angry about. After the implementation of equal pay in the Civil Service she found that there could still be problems when the time came for her to be appointed above men. It was important not to appear too 'bossy'. With similar quiet discretion she would circumvent prejudice surrounding hire purchase and mortgages for women by finding firms that *would* make loans to single women. This desire not to make a fuss (partly, perhaps a legacy from wartime) and the view that tact and gentle determination would get women further than strident militancy was perhaps typical of the period.

The situation of women teachers was rather different, since they had to contend with the strong, organized opposition to equal pay from the National Association of Schoolmasters, whose strongest argument was that if equal pay were granted to women then the single woman would be at an advantage by comparison with her married male colleagues to whose dependants the situation would be unfair. When the issue had been raised towards the end of the war a storm of controversy had swept up, with the most bitter expressions of resentment against spinsters who were said to be able to afford holidays to Italy and expensive hobbies such as riding. This reads today as a strangely petulant and irrational outburst of anger and envy of the unmarried who all the same more often led narrow and impoverished lives. At the back of this was the vexed question of the economic position of a man's dependent family.

The failure of the Attlee government to implement equal pay was a bitter blow to the women activists within its ranks. Some, like Alice Bacon, back-pedalled on the issue as long as Labour was in power; although others such as Eirene White and Leah Manning, herself an ex-teacher, pressed for action throughout the period of Labour rule. Hugh Gaitskell appeared to reject even the principle of equal pay when in 1950 he was arguing, as Chancellor of the Exchequer, that the main effect of equal pay would be to improve the position of the employed woman at the expense of her dependent married sisters. When the Labour Party was returned to power in 1951 with a much reduced majority, Irene Ward, a Conservative Party feminist, felt that the time had come to take action, and with other women MPs from both sides of the House of Commons she organized a large equal pay demonstration in 1951. It has even been suggested (Partington 1976) that the failure of the second, and shortlived, Labour government to support the equal pay struggle may have contributed to its downfall in the autumn of that year, since, even if women activists in the Labour Party did not withdraw their vote – as some feminist organizations argued that they should – they may have withheld the active electoral support needed during the run up to the General Election.

Perhaps the incoming Conservative government took note of the high feeling, for they did implement equal pay. The campaign came to a climax with the presentation of two equal pay petitions on 9 March 1954. These had been organized by the Equal Pay Campaign Committee, formed by feminist organizations spearheaded by the strongly feminist National Union of Women Teachers, and by the Co-ordinating Committee on Equal Pay, which included the most important unions and staff associations. The feminist petition, though smaller, got more publicity because it was taken to Westminster in three horse-drawn carriages decorated with the suffragette colours and accompanied by Irene Ward, Barbara Castle, Edith Summerskill, and Patricia Ford, all MPs.

Both in the Civil Service and in teaching equal pay was implemented gradually, in a series of stages up to 1961; but although this caused some resentment the victory was essentially won in 1954. The easing of the economic situation must in part have made the victory more likely. The Conservative government may also have hoped for the support of women whose cause they had espoused, whereas the Labour government had always had to be mindful of its trades union constituency where even the principle of equal pay was not wholeheartedly accepted at all levels, and where the problems of a small number of 'middle-class' women might not appear as a priority. Another important factor in the granting of equal pay to teachers was the great shortage of teachers in the fifties and sixties. The rising birthrate in the 1950s meant more children in the classroom. Since women teachers, like other women, were marrying earlier and producing babies earlier, they too were more quickly leaving gaps in the teaching ranks that proved difficult to fill.

Later, other trades unions began to take the problems of women more seriously. The engineering unions were to the fore and a special working committee was set up to look into the structure of women's wages in the industry. One result of this was the 1963 engineering agreement under the terms of which women received a rise of 1/6 and men of 1/- in the £. In the same year the House of

Lords debated the revived Industrial Charter for women, and this became a major campaigning feature within the unions in the sixties. Throughout the sixties the impetus towards planning and the rationalization of industry, together with the pull towards the EEC meant that equal pay became more acceptable, since the Common Market supported the principle.

In the sixties the British economy began to be seriously plagued by the problems that had been postponed by short term measures in the fifties but now began to come home to roost. Both inflation and unemployment began to rise. The Labour government that held power from 1964 to 1970 made equal pay part of its campaigning platform in 1964 but did little to pursue this aim once in office, and the failure of the Labour Party in office vigorously to back equal pay is hard to understand, since by the sixties even at the level of political expediency to do so would have been in tune with stronger demands from within the trades union movement.

Inflation and unemployment affected women both in the home and at work. Other factors in the sixties also contributed to an increased sense amongst women of their unequal position in both these spheres. By 1967 the TUC's attitude towards nurseries had been modified by widespread knowledge of increasing poverty, family breakdown, and unsatisfactory childminding. There was a much greater sense of social crisis and no longer could nursery and national insurance provisions be easily seen simply as an addition to 'normal' family care. Amongst women trades unionists too a far more militant spirit was being displayed, with talk even of suffragette tactics; and the fighting speech of Miss E. Whelan of the GLC Staff Association at the Women's TUC in 1968 was only one example of women's growing awareness of continuing injustice in spite of – or more evidently because of – the implementation of equal pay:

'When you do achieve equal pay the battle will be only half won. There are still very few women in the higher echelons of local government and those who do achieve the higher paid posts usually have to be outstandingly better than the men against whom they are competing for promotion. . . .

Why should so many women in the second half of the twentieth century still have to choose between marriage and a career? A man does not. Why should young wives feel guilty about their lack of enthusiasm for household chores?' (TUC 1968)

ATTITUDES ON THE LEFT

The postwar record of the Labour Party in relation to women was not, then, a glorious one, although in the fifties there was a higher level of particpation by women in traditional politics and in the Labour Party. Individual women in the Labour Party carried on the fight for women's advancement in a variety of ways that related primarily to their position at work, their position within marriage, their position in relation to the social services, and their position as consumers. Most of these women saw women's right to work only within the context of full employment and women's right to protection within marriage only in the context of the sexual division of labour within the family as it was. Nor did they question that it was women who were interested in consumer issues. The 'woman's point of view' in Parliament was by and large a domestic point of view.

The left was no better. By the 1950s Communist parties all over Europe were emphasizing woman's role as wife and mother rather than combatting sexual discrimination and in this respect the British Communist Party was typical. Women were caught between the family and socialism; women's problems were the problems of *capitalism*. At the same time individual women Party members were active in a whole range of community struggles, in the peace movement and in the trades unions, where the Communist Party always supported struggles for equal pay. (Interesting accounts of union work by Communist Party women are 'That Bloody Section's Out Again' by Jean French in *Red Rag* no. 3, Spring 1963, and 'Minority of Millions' by Betty Harrison in *Red Rag* no. 6, Spring 1974.) Marie Betteridge has described how, with other activists in Islington, she struggled for the right to painless childbirth, against the cutbacks in free orange juice and cod liver oil, and for proper care before and after childbirth to prevent the unnecessary gynaecological problems from which so many working-class women still suffered. Her main involvement was with the tenants' movement and in the housing struggles of the fifties and sixties, first to get electric light installed in old tenement blocks, later around the host of evictions created by the 1957 Rent Act. 'We were like a fire brigade on eviction cases.' Eventually the Labour Council agreed to take responsibility for the private tenants evicted by slum landlords under the Act; later they took over and redeveloped or rehabilitated many private properties. Then came the struggle to extend democratic participation in the borough, with the right to form tenants' associations – not won without a struggle. Women were always to the fore in the tenants' struggles and deserve credit for the way in which the sights of working-class people were raised and for the extension of democratic rights in this period. Such women integrated their understanding of women's special difficulties into their general political work.

Some women Party members saw their emancipation rather as being able to combine work with marriage and child rearing, leaving political work by default to their husbands. Another woman described the 'closet' atmosphere in the fifties in which adultery and divorce occurred but could not be talked about since no-one really knew what the 'correct' socialist attitude towards such behaviour was. This was not Stalinist tyranny, but simply the difficulty many Marxists experienced in coming to terms with social changes that could not be explained in any simple way as the consequence of capitalism.

For some women, conscious of their right to emancipation, involvement in any sort of feminist organization seemed merely dreary. To be emancipated was to be among the men, in a man's world. The most 'advanced' position for a woman was to have got beyond feminism and to have achieved recognition and respect in the world of men. For individual woman this was possible; but there were others caught in a tradition that excluded women from politics.

The attitude of the British Communist Party is worth mentioning for two reasons. Although small it had an influence beyond its numbers. While some of its members were 'Party wives' no doubt, many were enthusiastic activists whose experience was taken into the community and the peace movement and influenced women who were later to move towards feminism. Then also in 1956 came the rebellion within the Party over Hungary and Stalinism. One result of this was the regeneration of a non-aligned left and of political debate and activity, a widening out of politics where eventually a space was created for the problems of women to re-emerge. For as E.P. Thompson (1977) has pointed out, this generation of rebels was not lost to the progressive movement in the way that so many of those in the pre-war left had been lost.

THE PEACE MOVEMENT

The revival of left radicalism in Britain took fire over the Campaign for Nuclear Disarmament. This was at its height from 1959 to 1963.

Even in the depths of the Cold War there had been some who had been prepared to speak as pacifists, Dr Donald Soper, head of the Methodist Church for example. Marie Betteridge tried to get signatures for the Stockholm Peace Petition in 1951, but the table she and a friend set up in Chapel Market, Islington, was overturned amid angry shouts of 'go back to Moscow' – although they had been born and bred in London. Another woman taking round the same petition in South London was chased down the Battersea Road. The National Assembly of Women, an organization in which Communist Party women were active, was always concerned with the position of women as an international issue and was very active in organizing around the issue of peace.

In the early fifties, as knowledge about the effect of nuclear bombs spread, so did unease (Driver 1964). Marghanita Laski wrote a play for the BBC which was performed in 1954 and was widely discussed. Anti-bomb groups formed outside London. Then in March 1955 two women in a North London branch of the Co-operative Women's Guild, both of whom were on the left and one of whom had been a suffragette, took up the issue of radiation and were instrumental in getting what became CND off the ground. Meanwhile two other women became secretaries of the National Committee for the Abolition of Nuclear Weapon Tests. So from the beginning women were centrally involved in the campaign against the bomb and one of the early demonstrations consisted of 2,000 women with black sashes and flags walking on a pouring wet Sunday from Hyde Park to Trafalgar Square. Once under way CND always attracted large numbers of women.

Often, anti-bomb activities by women were explicitly seen as not political. For example, the *Manchester Guardian* commented of a women's rally in 1957: 'The first of the women speakers said they represented ordinary housewives and mothers who were *not* Communists or fellow travellers but who wanted to stop the tests on Christmas Island in the interests of humanity.' Yet although CND transcended traditional politics by reason of its status as a moral campaign, nonetheless participation in it was often the expression of a general political position well to the left of centre. Frank Parkin (1964) estimated that many participants also supported the abolition of capital punishment, reform of the laws relating to homosexuality and abortion, anti-apartheid, and the abolition of censorship. Yet the position of women never became an overt focus, although CND derived so much of its support from women. Many of these women were the wives of 'middle-class radicals', who felt isolated and out of place in the coffee-morning lives they were compelled to live in their suburbs or provincial towns. Some of these were active at grass roots level as organizers; others simply gave their support because as mothers with young children they were greatly hampered in their ability to act on many issues about which they felt deeply. But on anti-nuclear demonstrations the presence of children had a very specific point.

CND also had a number of well known women supporters who lent their prestige to the cause. Some of these used the arguments popular amongst feminists in the thirties and forties – that women had a greater aversion to violence, cruelty, and war, and a greater care for the individual. Jacquetta Hawkes, the writer and archaeologist, summed up this view in a poem she wrote for the *New Statesman* in 1958. In this she argued that since war had now come to the civilian community in a new and most horrible form, women *must* be concerned and could no longer sit quietly, patiently seeing their men off to war and waiting for their return:

'Women have seldom been the great creators
Rather we have been the continuers, the protectors, the lovers of life'

– but precisely because of this it was for women to influence men:

> 'A few men seem possessed by a devil. . . .
> But many more . . . have remained as boys, just boys
> Heedlessly playing. But the spring of the toys they are winding
> is death.
> We must take power from these madmen, these prisoners, these
> perilous children.'

This belief in women's special role in the peace struggle was a very important one and together with a related appeal made to women as mothers, was constantly repeated throughout the sixties. One woman activist suggested that this was partly because to present the issue in this way always drew immediate and wide support – the idea of children dying from leukaemia from radiation, possibly from Strontium 90 imbibed through milk was such a horrible and nightmarish one. Many women, though, certainly believed wholeheartedly in women's special mission to bring peace. Of these perhaps the best known was, and is, Dora Russell. In 1968, in connection with the revival of interest in feminism attendant on the celebrations to mark the fiftieth anniversary of the vote, she wrote in *Call To Women* that there had always been a divison of opinion between those who claimed equality 'because women are rational, thinking individuals just as men are' and those who felt that women's claim to rights was based on:

> 'women's difference from men, more especially their function as mothers, which the Suffrage pioneers were, of necessity, obliged to play down. But they did believe nonetheless, that the entry of women into political life would bring a fresh and important contribution. . . . Nor could I see any point in fighting to get women into politics, if they were just the same as men.'

She went on to lament the persistence and increase of aggression in what was still so much a man's world, and the continued denigration of women as subjective, illogical creatures, when their preoccupation with personal relations and their natural role as defenders of biological life should rather be seen as being to their credit. She regretted that many modern women seemed to share an 'atrophy of instinct' which meant that they were bored by home and small children, and she felt this clash of values, the overvaluing of work outside the home came about because modern society undervalued work in the home.

This is part of a still unresolved argument, and ten years later, in 1978 when Dora Russell wrote in the same vein to the *Observer* many women wrote letters in her support, although there was one letter which pointed out that there was a danger in such ideas since the logical conclusion of the belief that women had a special biologically determined role as nurturers and protectors of life was that men had a biologically determined role as aggressors and this, if biologically programmed into them, might be very difficult to change.

Call To Women was the newsletter of the Liaison Committee for Women's Peace Groups, of which there were a large number in the sixties, and these continued the struggle for peace as it merged into the wider struggle against the Vietnam War. In reporting women's activities *Call To Women* put forward a consistently radical viewpoint on a variety of issues and was not narrowly pacifist. Women's groups pioneered original forms of demonstration such as were to become popular in the seventies – for instance during the Christmas period in 1966 there were demonstrations at big stores in London against war toys (supported by Anne Kerr, a Labour MP, amongst others), when women picketed the stores and distributed leaflets in the toy departments. *Call To Women* took a radical stance on juvenile delinquency, was critical of police violence in the 1968 Grosvenor Square demonstrations against the Vietnam War, and did also comment frequently on the political disabilities still endured by women. Women's Peace groups organized events to mark fifty years of women's suffrage in 1968 and it is clear that out of this ferment of political activity came part of the impetus for the revival of feminism.

WOMEN'S ORGANIZATIONS AND FEMINIST ORGANIZATIONS

A wide variety of women's organizations existed and I lack the space to summarize their work satisfactorily. Since the war, one important social change, however, that has affected most of them has been that fewer and fewer women have been able to undertake voluntary work. Many organizations – the FPA for example – had relied for many years on voluntary labour. In practice this voluntary work was for the most part a hobby for the wives of middle class men, who could afford not to work and who – before the war at least – had leisure to spare because their housework was done by a maid or daily helper. During the postwar period these women both lost their domestic help and started to take paid work in larger numbers and voluntary organizations have suffered from their absence.

Whereas the peace groups were often in practice associated with left-wing politics, there were a number of important groups that pursued traditional social democratic aims. Women For Westminster, the Status of Women group, and the Open Door Council (the latter mainly concerned with women's position at work) all campaigned for women to have improved access to the political process and desired that they should participate more fully in parliamentary politics and in the professions. They aimed at the advancement of women through the traditional methods of pressure group politics: lobbying and gradual advance towards the centres of power – although these methods were in practice those of the Communist Party as well.

The National Council of Women was an umbrella grouping to which many women's groups affiliated, and its objects included the resolve 'to work for the removal of all disabilities of women whether legal, economic or social'. It was customary for the NCW at least to express a view on matters of social policy relating to women and children. It campaigned on issues to do with the special disabilities of women as dependants; widows' pensions, the plight of disabled wives, the divorced. It organized a conference on single women in 1955 and on working mothers in 1958. It was also much concerned about the media. A number of women's groups gave evidence to the Pilkington Committee on Broadcasting, which reported in 1962, and they objected to too much violence and sex on television, and to the portrayal of commercial and materialistic ideals. The Townswomen's Guild could not affiliate to the NCW because it was resolutely non political, whereas the NCW did aim for the equality of women. Yet the Townswomen's Guild had been formed by feminists from the National Union of Societies for Equal Citizenship, among them Eva Hubback and Marjory Corbett Ashby. It had been the wish of the founders that the Guild should operate as a meeting ground for all women and therefore the sometimes divisive creed of feminism could not be actively expressed in the Guild. In seeking some form of grass roots organization for women it perhaps turned its back too resolutely on anything that smelled of politics, and Mary Stott (1977) has suggested that it operated in practice as an organization for the happily and stably married, and not one in which women's grievances or doubts could surface.

The two most consciously and wholeheartedly feminist groups in the old tradition were the Six Point Group and the Women's Freedom League. The Six Point Group, which continues its work today, had been founded by Lady Rhonnda (of *Time and Tide*) in 1921. It always had six points relating to the position of women and children for which it was fighting. It worked simply to establish equality between men and women, and its middle-class base was reflected in its preoccupation with married women's property rights and legal disabilities. In the sixties it was supported by a number of women in the media, and in 1968 produced a book, *In Her Own Right*, to which a number of well known women contributed. This expressed a view of women's position similar to the 'reasonable modern feminism' espoused by Judith Hubback and Viola Klein, for whom women's dual role was not the problem, but the solution.

The most militant feminist group from the old days was the Women's Freedom League, the breakaway suffragette group formed by Teresa Billington Grieg when she rebelled against the iron hand of the Pankhurst organization before the first world war. She lived to see its death in 1961 at the end of her own life, because there were no younger women to carry on its work as her generation of feminists died off, and when it disbanded she spoke passionately and even bitterly of the work still to be done.

Although its main focus in the fifties was the equal pay struggle, the Women's Freedom League reported in its *Bulletin* any militant action by women around any issue. It reported working-class women's strikes, actions against discrimination by militant teachers' groups, attempts by women to gain admittance to the Stock Exchange, and discrimination against girls in the Eleven Plus examination. Not content with equal pay for professional women it turned its attention to the position of women in industry. It also monitored what we now call sexism in the media – the use of the word 'girl' to describe adult women, for example. This group emphasized equality rather than women's special role, and the right of all women, whether married or not, to full time work. But these feminists differed from today's women's liberationists in defining their activities as 'non-political' – their explanation of women's disabilities did not involve either a general critique of society and a preoccupation with class differences, nor a concern with 'consciousness' and subjectivity.

Finally, there was an assortment of groups that came out of the discontent of a new generation of women, the 'housebound housewives' and 'miserable married women' about which the *Observer* and the *Guardian* began to write in the early sixties. The National Housewives' Register started in 1962 as the result of a letter written by a young housewife to the *Guardian*, complaining of her isolated state as a young mother stuck at home. She received thousands of letters in response and started a network, the aim of which was mutual support, and activities such as talks and coffee mornings. It was very loosely organized on the basis of small groups, and although neither political nor feminist, this form of organization anticipated the women's liberation movement rather than copying the more committee-like campaigning organizations in which women had hitherto organized themselves.

The Pre-school Playgroups Association was similarly founded in 1962 after Belle Tutaev had written to the *Guardian* in 1961 inviting readers to join the Nursery School Campaign, which not only petitioned for more state nursery school provisions, but also encouraged mothers to start their own schools to form playgroups. Then there was the work of the National Childbirth Trust, already mentioned, and the work of those mothers who campaigned to get better conditions for children in hospital and the right of mothers to spend more time with these children. In their development these groups, which still flourish, were initially at any rate primarily orientated towards helping mothers to do 'their' work more happily and were often more concerned with the rights and the suffering of children than women, although obviously mothers also suffered from being parted from their hospitalized children, and suffered from alienating obstetric practices. They did not challenge the sexual division of labour, but on the other hand they were self help groups that campaigned against the inadequacies and authoritarian practices of state welfare provision. Along with organizations such as the National Council for One Parent Families, they have maintained a distance from contemporary feminism yet they have been motivated by some of the same grievances and in turn no doubt influenced by the dissemination of more explicitly feminist views in the 1970s. For instance at the beginning of women's liberation to argue that nursery provision was for mothers as well as for toddlers – that is that mothers had a right to a rest from their children and that nurseries were not simply to be justified because they enhanced the child's development – was regarded as quite subversive. Today such a view, although not universally accepted, is certainly both more familiar and more acceptable.

CONCLUSION

The fiftieth anniversary of women's suffrage in 1968 does seem to have acted as some sort of catalyst. It was the year of the women's strike at Ford's Dagenham factory as well as of the great Vietnam demonstrations and of student upheavals all over the Western world. There could, though, have been no catalyst had women's grievances not been swelling under the surface.

Why had the long standing feminist groups seemed unable to harness the sense of grievance to their cause? A note of slight bitterness crept into the Women's Freedom League *Bulletin* at times when its editor contemplated the hordes of young women who seemed blithely indifferent both to the advantages an older generation had secured for them, and to the disabilities still besetting them. As Jill Craigie wrote in the *Evening Standard* in 1956: 'Today, the spirit of the old pioneers is so dead it seems a miracle that it ever existed.' Typical of the 'modern' women of the fifties and sixties was Shirley Williams, Vera Brittain's daughter who, interviewed in the *Guardian* in April 1960 said: 'I'm not a pacifist but I admire my mother's pacifism; I'm not a feminist either, but that's a matter of generations I think, don't you?'

It ceased to be a 'matter of generations' as women drawn into widening general political struggle came up against the prejudices of the macho revolutionary in the Civil Rights Movement and the SDS (Students for a Democratic Society) in the United States, and in the student movement, in the Vietnam Solidarity Campaign, and in left wing groups such as the International Socialists (now the Socialist Workers Party) in Britain. The Black Movement – importantly – gave women the beginnings of a theory of their oppression, for the works of Frantz Fanon and others who explored the experience of colonization and its effects on the *consciousness* of the oppressed race could be used to help understand women's experience too. There was also the 'relative deprivation' theory (Freeman 1975). This suggested that the revitalization of feminism came about because women's increased participation in education created rising expectations which were then not fulfilled or rewarded in the workforce.

There is also the possibility that simply women's increased participation in all kinds of political struggle heightened their awareness of their own situation. There were more of them in the Labour Party, but fewer women in Parliament. In the struggles for equal pay they suffered the prejudice and contempt of men. (The bile of the National Association of Schoolmasters makes for particularly unpleasant reading.) In the Peace Movement they suffered – paradoxically – assault, arrest, and imprisonment. In community struggles such as those in Islington and Notting Hill (O'Malley 1977) they defied the bailiffs, the councillors and sometimes the police, buttonholed cabinet ministers, and disrupted meetings. They were not passive. They *organized* – around major political issues and around their own and their children's rights to improved childbirth facilities and nursery schools. They formed nationwide friendship networks. They were everywhere – and yet they were nowhere.

CHAPTER TEN

Feminism: the return of the repressed

Why do we idealize sacrifice in mothers? Who gave us this inhuman idea that mothers should negate their own wishes and desires? The acceptance of servitude has been handed down from mother to daughter for so many centuries that it is now a monstrous chain which fetters them. Every woman at some point in her life, realizes how much she owes the woman who gave her birth, and at the moment of recognition feels intense remorse, aware that she has never really recompensed her mother for the damage done to herself in doing good for us. But as soon as she becomes a mother herself she stands her wish to repay this debts on its head: she denies herself in her turn, providing a new example of self-mortification and self-destruction. Yet what would happen if this dreadful cycle was broken, once and for all? What if mothers refused to deny their womanhood and gave their children instead an example of a life lived according to the needs of self respect? (Sibilla Aleramo: *A Woman*)

So feminism did not die in the years after the war. There continued to be women's organizations that made feminist demands, even if there was no movement to combat the general oppression of women, and there were certainly many women who struggled as feminists, although they often felt isolated. What made their struggles difficult and lonely was that this oppression was invisible and was silenced. Feminism led an underground or Sleeping Beauty existence in a society which claimed to have wiped out that oppression. The assertion first that women had 'equality in difference' and then that women had 'choice' repressed but did not resolve the conflicts surrounding the position of women, which necessarily resurfaced again, exploding – so it seemed at the time – into social consciousness in the radical upsurge of the sixties.

My aim has been to demonstrate how the idea of 'women's problems have been solved' (expressed as 'woman has come of age' and in other similar phrases) was constructed in a variety of postwar debates that spun themselves around what was a silence.

Women's liberation has been in part a reaction against that silence. Those sleeping but not dreamless years have influenced the contemporary women's movement, and in reacting against the past we have developed a way of talking about women's oppression that constructs its own silences too. We talk a great deal about ideology, but modern feminism has its own ideologies, its own cherished assumptions and prejudices. To what extent did these grow out of what went before?

OVERVIEW – 2

At the close of the Second World War there were fears of the return of mass unemployment. There was also a general expectation that the number of women working outside the home would sink back to its prewar level. For there was a widespread belief, encouraged by wartime propaganda, that the entry of women, and especially married women, into the labour force during the war had been an exceptional event. It was simply not related to the longer term general trend towards higher levels of female employment, for throughout the twentieth century the numbers of married women at work had been slowly growing. When the 1947 economic crisis hit Britain the call for women to return to the factories was again seen as a temporary measure and it was even hoped that working-class women would return wholesale to domestic service. At the same time there was a shortage of labour in the traditional women's 'semi-professions', especially in teaching and nursing, and an expansion of social work which also drew largely on a female labour force. The expansion of social work was part of the transformation of areas of work that had once been voluntary into forms of paid and therefore more institutionalized work.

It would be untrue, therefore, to say that there was any kind of concerted effort at the level of government policy to get women back into the home (Riley 1979). On the contrary. Yet this is one stereotype contemporary feminists have developed of what happened after the war. Women, it is said, were driven back into the home. Actually women were drawn into the labour force in growing numbers.

Because women *had* played an important part in 'war work', there was for a time a greater understanding of their heavy double burden, and of the burden that domestic work actually was. But hopes that the new and improved welfare services would assist all women in their domestic tasks faded away; it would have been just too expensive for the state to take over the roles once performed by domestic servants.

Under the Tory governments of the 1950s money wages were allowed to rise at the expense, partly, of continued investment in welfare services, and as the labour shortage continued an apparent solution for women emerged; part time work, or the 'dual role'. This did not challenge the sexual division of labour. Women remained responsible for the home, and for the children, and men still earned a 'family wage' that was redistributed within his family of dependants. The wife's earnings did, however, give her some independence. Domestic life was sweetened since she was no longer so totally dependent on the money her husband gave her, while he might retain his overtime money to spend on himself without the bitter recriminations of the prewar working-class household.

At this period many feminists no more questioned the sexual division of labour than did politicians and planners. Some feminists indeed tended to emphasize it. In a reaction against what were seen as the false sexual freedoms of the period after the first world war, and the unattractively mannish independence and aggressiveness of some women of that time, feminists, and others, now aimed to establish married women more securely within the family. For some years the call was to improve the married women's legal and financial positions, and to 'raise the status of homemaking'. Service to others and the nurturance of children seemed more attractive to many women than careerism and aggression in a threatening and possibly doomed world in which the only hope might seem precisely women's peace-loving and nurturant qualities. It also became necessary for what might have been seen as the élite of educated women to say at home; they now lacked servants to do their domestic work for them.

This emphasis on women's domestic role was reinforced by the progressive currents of thought of the period. The child care experts – John Bowlby, Donald Winnicott, and Benjamin Spock – represented not conservative or traditional thinking – which had been far more authoritarian towards children – but a radical new departure in child care, which, they suggested, should be child-centred and permissive. Their views on the upbringing of children, the importance to the child of love, stimulation, and attention, were profoundly attractive to a generation of socially progressive mothers in rebellion against the rules, clockwork, and restraint of the Truby King era, when it had been considered wrong to comfort your crying baby or to feed it on demand. Bowlby and Winnicott, psycholoanalytic theoreticians and practitioners, have become bogeymen of British feminism, but in order to understand their popularity we have to understand that their appeal was not so much in terms of the return of women to the home – however much their masculine prejudices stamp their work – but of the flowering of love for children in a war-torn world. Their work was an indictment of élitist upper-class forms of child rearing – nannies and boarding schools – and implicitly working-class warmth and spontaneity towards children were validated. Their conservative views on women were acceptable as part of this package.

The removal of one group – the young adolescent – from the work force, and the substitution of another – the married woman – created a social problem for which women were themselves in a peculiar way held responsible. Tension and ambivalence surrounded women's role and duties and led to 'moral panics' about 'latch key children' and juvenile delinquents. These were some of the outcomes of the conflicting and incompatible demands being made on women.

During the late forties and early fifties these problems could still be discussed in moral terms of duty, selfishness, patriotism. The conflict between duty and pleasure and rights and responsibilities posed a felt moral dilemma. But to flood the market with consumer goods – part of the drive to maintain full employment – was itself to undermine the puritanism of the late forties, for these goods appealed to the short term pleasures of millions of individuals. Gradually and to an extent surreptitiously ideas of pleasure, enjoyment, and self-fulfilment replaced those of duty, responsibility, and loyalty to the group (be it family, class, or nation). In some ways, the attitudes and preoccupations of the fifties and early sixties, the vulgar hedonism of those years, may be seen as a rebellion against the lingering of the puritan tradition as exemplified by the Attlee government. For whatever the generalized worries about the juvenile delinquent, the decline of the family and the materialism of our society, the country could no longer be sustained by calls to duty and service.

Instead – I am not suggesting deliberately – psychoanalytic theories were again popularized to sustain the family with the magic of pleasure rather than by the force of necessity. Both the child care literature already mentioned and the literature of marital adjustive psychotherapy have been read by contemporary feminists as a literature of punishment and the repression of women. Yet it was intended as a literature of pleasure. It set about enhancing the joys of motherhood and the intensity of the marital orgasm.

These pleasures were, however, to be held within the marriage bond. Although it was possible to separate sexuality from fertility in the literal, biological sense, this separation was not to occur at the level of legal institutions. Even when each individual sexual act could be reliably separated from its reproductive consequences, attempts continued at the ideological level to *reinforce* the connexion between sexuality and childrearing. Contraception was to enhance the sexual life of married couples. The 'double standard' was to be replaced by true monogamy. Or, to put it slightly differently, while sexuality without its reproductive consequences was to some extent accepted, the *permantly* childless married couple was not: and once reproduction *had* occurred childrearing was the clear responsibility of the married couple whose sexual act had brought the child into being. Freudians in particular were very clear that child care must not be divorced from the heterosexual married couple who had begotten and conceived.

In rebellion against this view the women's liberation movement in its early years tended to perceive monogamy and the family as one monolithic and deliberate institution for the oppression of women. This was in reaction against not only the views of the 'traditionalists' but also against those aspects at least of the new left that emphasized the male/female relationship as a primary value. Marriage in this sense was just as precious to the radicals of the new left as it was to the psychoanalytic establishment. The new left in its first phase was a left of radical humanism. In reaction against the waste years of Stalinism the new left turned to the 'young Marx' and adopted his theories of alienation, human essence and 'natural sensuous' relationships. For in the early writings of Marx the relationship between man and woman was idealized; it even became akin to the I–Thou relationship of the Existentialists:

> 'The immediate, natural, necessary relation of human being to human being is the *relationship* of *man* to *woman*. In this *natural* species-relationship the relation of man to nature is immediately his relation to man, just as his relation to man is immediately his relation to nature, his own *natural* condition. . . . It is possible to judge from this relationship the entire level of development of mankind . . . the relation of man to woman is the most *natural* relation of human being to human being. It therefore demonstrates the extent to which man's *natural* behaviour has become *human* or the extent to which his *human* essence has become a *natural* essence for him, the extent to which his *human nature* has become *nature* for him. This relationship also demonstrates the extent to which man's *needs* have become *human* needs, hence the extent to which the *other*,

as a human being, has become a need for him, the extent to which in his most individual existence he is at the same time a communal being.' (Marx 1975:347)

This passage speaks perfectly for the sentiments of the radical left in the late fifties and early sixties and expresses their sense of the relation between man and woman as the touchstone of all social relationships. This view was akin to the Lawrentian approach to sexual relationships favoured by many who abhorred the commercialized sexual representations available in the mass media. Many could share David Holbrook's (1964) view that the imagery of women daily displayed on hoardings and in comics was an imagery of hatred not of love. For him and many others the alternative was an ideal of relationships between 'whole persons' based on a psychoanalytic assessment of 'maturity' and the ability to love another human being of the opposite sex. And this ideal of the love partnership, the most sacred meeting of man and woman, as lying at the heart of life, bypassed the question of the individual woman's emancipation which could seem trivial by comparison: divisive, shrill, and petty when set against these sonorous emotions, this reconciliation of the human and the natural, this deep beating of the blood. So, in Raymond Williams' novel, *Border Country*, first published in 1960, the hero's marriage acts simply as a frame for the action, which consists of an exploration of the relationship between father and son, and in particular of the relationship between a working class militant and his educated son who fears losing his roots. Yet the dying father's words concern not politics but marriage: 'Only a small part of your life's your work. . . . Only the one trade to get into and that's a wife to love you. The only trade, sweetheart. A loving wife. The only trade to get into.' (Williams 1964:303-304) The creation of a new and positive ideal of family life came at a time when the old defensive role of the working-class family was less evident and when changes had also occurred in the middle-class family. A new, democratic and classless family – or the idea of one – could contribute towards the building of consensus, although even as it was desirable in some ways to stress the 'embourgeoisement' of the workers, so it was simultaneously desirable to emphasize the continuity of cultural patterns along class lines. But both to left and right, liberal and radical, traditionalist and progressive, the family came to mean the preservation of British, or sometimes English, values in the face of the vulgar and cheapening influence of the Americanization threatened by the mass media.

American culture, on the other hand, called to the young. It appealed to irrationalism in a quite different way from the appeal of D.H. Lawrence. That had been a development of romanticism, this was a development of decadence, of subjectivism, and even of nihilism.

The paradox of consensus in the fifties was that the very attempt to create a homogenous society seemed to bring with it its own opposition. Out of the very heart of the family that was the organizing centre of the new welfare society came the new dissidents: the young, the alienated, the mad. The counter culture of the sixties did perceive sexuality as subversive, and its youthful hedonism was a hedonism of sexuality divorced from marriage, reproduction, and childrearing. And *because* the ideology of class was weakened, the new 'revolutionary' politics had to be recreated from the margins. The new politics of the late fifties and the sixties began in part as the politics of these marginal groups.

The new politics came also out of the attempt to recreate a socialism that was neither tainted by the cruelties of Stalinism nor reduced to economic demands, that sought to go beyond the struggle for higher wages and reach towards an understanding of why the working class was seduced by the commercialized rubbish of the mass media; and having understood, to create a culture that could unite the radical intellegentsia with the working class by means of new cultural organizations that built on the strengths of what already existed. One such attempt was Centre Forty Two at the Round House, started by Arnold Wesker with some trades union support. But although the sixties saw the growth of a militant shop stewards movement and industrial action reaped rewards, there remained a gap between intellectuals and industrial militants. The peace movement, the new left, radical psychiatry, existed in what was often a tenuous and one-sided relationship with the militant seamen and the Ford workers. Only for a brief period, when Frank Cousins led the Labour Party Conference into a rejection of nuclear arms for Britain, was the new left and the labour movement in unison.

The women's liberation movement has inherited this split and attempts by some trades unionists and from sections of the left, as well as by the media and by some anti-abortion campaigners and the National Front, to brand feminism as 'middle class' testifies to this. At the same time, the women's liberation movement challenges the split and has shown more ability to bridge the gap than the movements of the sixties were able to.

The development of mass communications, the expansion of the popular press, of television, radio, and commercial advertising – which as Stuart Hall (1975) has pointed out was only the public face of a whole industry of computers, information storage, video systems, and a range of advanced technology used privately by industry and by the state for surveillance – was viewed with suspicion by both left and right. It was feared that the cultural uniformity of its products would reduce us to a nation of zombies, that life would be literally, demoralized, as cradled in passivity we would watch anything and everything on the small screen. I may have appeared to neglect this aspect of postwar British culture, but I have not been unaware of its pervasive and sinister influence, and indeed I have come to feel that its propensity to over-simplify, distort, and stereotype has had an even more destructive effect on British cultural and political life than has been recognized.

THE FEMINIST WRITERS

Nonetheless women could, even without the support of an active movement, rebel against the cultural images of themselves with which they were increasingly bombarded. There was always a steady and influential trickle of books that protested against the psychological and cultural subordination of women. The earliest of these, first Simone de Beauvoir's *The Second Sex* (published in France in 1949 and in English in 1953) and later Betty Friedan's *The Feminine Mystique* (1963) must have had a kind of underground influence on hundreds of thousands of women who read them. Both were printed all over the Western world in popular paperback editions that sold out over and over again. Which women read them, which were influenced by them and how, we cannot altogether know. But their yeast must have been working in the doughy femininity of the fifties and early sixties. And their availability, paradoxically, was also due to the mass media explosion. If it was profitable to print them, as it was profitable to print Barbara Cartland and the James Bond stories, then printed they were, no matter how subversive.

In Britain there was the work of Viola Klein, and in 1966 *The Captive Wife* by Hannah Gavron. These books were orientated towards changes in social policy, and Betty Friedan, too, placed her hope for change in education and the formation through education of a new cultural identity for women.

As the sixties began to draw to a close there came a spate of books: *Thinking about Women* by Mary Ellman (1969), *The Female Eunuch* by Germaine Greer and *Patriarchal Attitudes* by Eva Figes, both published in 1970, and *Sexual Politics* by Kate Millett and *The Dialectic of Sex* by Shulamith Firestone in 1971. One striking feature of these writers was that, like the older generation of feminist writers, they tended to retrace the same ground and rediscover the same history of oppression.

Before the war Ray Strachey (1928), Winifred Holtby (1934), and Virginia Woolf (1938) had looked to history, anthropology, and literature for evidence of women's subjection. The relationship of women to industrial capitalism had been discussed as far back as Josephine Butler (1868). D.H. Lawrence and Freud had for years been incarnations of the phallocracy for feminists. The work of Engels was appreciated and its limitations understood for decades before the re-evaluations of socialist feminists in the 1970s.

This necessity for each generation of feminists to go over the same ground, to turn back to history, to literature, and to political economy in order to rediscover women's oppression – testifies the extent to which this history of women and their oppression never has become part of a known 'cultural heritage'. Each succeeding generation of women has to make anew the effort to retrieve a past that continues to remain hidden. This may be rewarding for those women with the time and energy to spare, but is also part of the process whereby women's knowledge of their own oppression remains muffled. If you have no access to your own tradition, and no validation from knowing that other women felt and feel as you do – which seems to have been the case in the 1950s particularly – self-doubt sets in: 'there must be something wrong with me if no-one else feels like this'. For this reason alone the existence of a feminist literature is important.

The literature of the women's liberation movement in Britain came very much out of the immediate situation in the sixties in this country. Juliet Mitchell (1971) located the origins of women's liberation in the student, black power, and hippie movements, and more recently Cora Kaplan (1979) in a brilliantly witty and insightful article has pointed out the ways in which the atmosphere and radicalism of America in the sixties stamps Kate Millett's *Sexual Politics*. Because of this atmosphere, women's liberation came into being as a consciously *revolutionary* movement, and for many of its first supporters in Britain that meant that it was a revolutionary socialist movement. By the period of the late 1960s the new left in Britain was making a conscious attempt to regenerate Marxist socialism and to free it from its reformism, its cautious devotion to struggles concerning wages, and its neglect of what were thought of as the ideological issues thrown up by the racial tensions and the sexual liberalization of the period.

Feminism was seen as part of the regeneration of socialism. Of the writers I have mentioned only Simone de Beauvoir and Juliet Mitchell were writing specifically from within a Marxist and socialist tradition, but it was from within this tradition that the new revolutionary feminism sprang. This was partly because as Juliet Mitchell said (Mitchell 1966:12): 'the problem of the subordination of women and the need for their liberation was recognized by all the great socialist thinkers of the nineteenth century'. But whereas Simone de Beauvoir, the existentialist, had ended her book with an appeal to just that companionship between man and woman of which the young Marx spoke and which had become part of the socialist humanism of the British new left in the late fifties, Juliet Mitchell's Marx was the Marx of Louis Althusser, the French Marxist structuralist.

Juliet Mitchell, in what is really the first written text of the British women's liberation movement (Mitchell 1966) asked what was for her the first question for feminists: why had *socialism* betrayed feminism and come, after its promising start, to ignore or worse, reinforce, the problem of women's subordination? Her answer was that socialists had not properly analysed the family, and for her it was the concept of the family that unlocked the door to the secret garden of women's oppression.

Her 1966 essay and later her book, *Women's Estate* (1971), under-took this analysis by differentiating out the functions of the family, and its four 'key structures'; production, reproduction, sex, and socialization. In this she followed the traditional 'functionalist' sociology of the family but gave it a left interpretation by suggest-ing that the four functions were structurally related and that only a simultaneous transformation of all four could liberate women. She argued that women should demand equality in all spheres, and that the diversification of the family was required rather than the 'abolition of the family' which she criticized as a meaningless and pseudo-revolutionary demand.

Having located the absence in Marxist analysis that had pre-vented socialists from understanding women's oppression, Juliet Mitchell suggested that: 'the Women's Liberation Movement must have a complex reaction to the nuclear family. It must concentrate on separating out the structures – the women's roles – which are oppressively fused into it. It must fragment its unity'. (Mitchell 1971:159).

Juliet Mitchell's earlier writings were important in helping feminists understand the contradictory nature of the modern nuclear family; how it was ideologically constructed as a unitary whole, yet socialized its members into an atomizing individual-ism, thus contributing towards its own disintegration. *Women's Estate* attempted to explain the women's liberation movement and its roots in sixties radicalism; it attempted to develop its relation-ship to socialism; and it attempted to begin to construct a theory of women's subordination in the family in part by using psychoanalytic theory. This project involved a rejection of the heritage of the earlier feminists, the suffragists and suffragettes, as bourgeois women pursuing a bourgeois class interest; and con-temporary British feminism, unlike its American counterpart, has remained relatively – although of course not entirely – untouched by this specifically feminist heritage. Recent books about the suffragettes (Rosen 1974; Raeburn 1976; Mitchell 1977) have all been written by non-feminists; and the search for the theoretical key to the oppression of women, the constant redemolition of the male supremacist theories of writers such as Lawrence, Talcott Parsons, Rousseau, and Freud, and the constant retracing of the historical, economic, and political ground has often ignored the work of earlier feminists such as Josephine Butler, Winifred Holtby, and Virginia Woolf, in mining the same seams of thought (although see Barrett (Woolf 1979) for a timely introduction to some of Woolf's feminist writings). Feminists are now beginning to redress this neglect, but it would be fair to say that the contemporary British women's movement in its first ten years was more sensitive to a tradition of women in class struggle than to these other women.

Although the importance of Juliet Mitchell's earlier work lay in having related capitalism to the family, her main influence has been in rehabilitating Freud for British feminists and Marxists. Again, this is a process that seems not to have occurred, certainly not to anything like the same extent, within North American feminism. It recalls past debates, in the thirties and again in the fifties, within the British left, as to the value or otherwise of Freudian theory and the possibility or impossibility of relating his theories to Marxism. (There were lengthy debates, for examples, in *The Modern Quarterly*, the theoretical periodical of the Communist Party of Great Britain, on this issue, centring round the work of Christopher Caudwell, who had interested himself in Freud in the 1930s).

Juliet Mitchell's examination of the structures within the family as separate led her on to the attempt to understand what it does to women to be locked within this false pseudo-unit where contradictory demands are continually made of her. (These were the contradictions of which women journalists, as we saw, wrote in the sixties – how could you be mother, seductress, housemaid, and hostess all at the same time?) This then led Juliet Mitchell further into the psychology of this oppression, and she seized on psychoanalysis as providing the only possibly adequate theory of the way in which *sexual difference* is established. For as Freud wrote:

> 'In conformity with its peculiar nature, psychoanalysis does not try to describe what a woman is – that would be a task it could scarcely perform – but sets about enquiring how she comes into being, how a woman develops out of a child with a bisexual disposition.' (Freud 1933, 1973:149)

It seemed as if Freud might explain how the ideologies 'out there' get inside your head, might explain why women do not have to be forced to submit or policed into wearing cosmetics and high heels, but on the contrary long to surrender and adore looking 'feminine'. It seemed as if psychoanalysis might fill the gap in Marxism which had never explained why oppressed and exploited masses consent in their own oppression. It seemed as if psychoanalysis might be the theory of ideology. Yet Juliet Mitchell's presentation of Freud to feminists has consistently underplayed both the theoretical gaps and inadequacies in Freud's work generally and the extent to which his work remains incompatible with a feminist perspective. Nor has she succeeded in uniting Freud and Marx. In *Psychoanalysis And Feminism* (1974) Marxism appeared as the theory for class struggle and psychoanalysis the theory for the analysis of patriarchy (Beechey 1979), and the relationship between the two was diminished to vanishing point. Although she still maintained that under capitalism family and kinship structures need no longer imprison women, the Freudian iron law of the development of sexual difference and the progress towards adult masculinity or femininity came to seem inexorable and inescapable (Kaplan 1979). More recently she has said: 'From its inception until today many feminists have argued not . . . for the end of the family but for, in whatever kin or communal form it occurs, an equality of reproduction with production; producing people should be as important as producing things' (Mitchell 1978).

As it stands there is nothing contentious about this statement, although we certainly did not need psychoanalysis to tell us that, but it should not be taken further, to justify the present sexual division of labour in Western capitalist societies. To say that child care is as important as paid work is one thing; to say that there is therefore nothing wrong with all domestic work being reserved for women is quite another.

Other feminist writers have taken Juliet Mitchell's exhortation to 'fragment the family' to such extremes that they virtually deny its existence. Instead of an institution, 'the family' we have a kind of Clapham Junction of 'discourses'. Just because sex manuals, the cohabitation ruling and other social security and tax provisions, arrangements relating to the custody of children, social rituals, and commercial advertising happen to focus on 'the family', we should not be deceived into believing that any such institution actually exists. The institution ideologically created by law, social policy, and the media is a fiction; a false unity created out of a coincidence of contradictory circumstances. None has dominance or primacy, and effectively we are in a world of accident and fragmentation which, whether this seems to matter or not, has little connexion with Marx. This school of thought, which is represented in the feminist periodical *m/f*, not content with fragmenting the family, has engaged in the same enterprise in relation to the individual as well. We end up quite close to the radical empiricism of the eighteenth-century philosopher, David Hume, who believed that the individual was nothing but a bundle of sensations or perceptions. Parveen Adams (1979), Parveen Adams and Jeff Minson (1978), and Mark Cousins (1978) have argued that the development of 'sexual difference', that is of masculinity and femininity, challenges the very notion of 'sexual division' when this means pregiven and eternal categories 'men' and 'women' antagonistically placed in the social formation. They argue that there is no such thing as a unitary 'woman'; we are all bundles of contradictory atoms and impulses. The idea of the unitary self, like the family, is a fiction. Leading on from this there is, logically, no such thing as 'women's oppression' in any unitary sense. Therefore, while the idea of the self, or the 'subject' as fragmented is extraordinarily interesting and fertile in one way, its relationship to politics seems utterly tenuous. It seems highly suggestive in deepening self understanding, and it adds great richness to explorations of subjective experience in fiction and autobiography, and to literary criticism generally. In emphasizing atomization and individual difference it seems effectively to close off politics and to come much closer to the individualism and aestheticism of a very 'bourgeois' world. We find ourselves spiralling back towards the individualism of the disintegrating self of the sixties (as illustrated in the exhibition The Obsessive Image) out of which came the attempt of the seventies to create a collective, *political* solution to this modern angst.

Juliet Mitchell's interest in psychoanalysis had its roots very much in the radical psychiatry as well as the new left of the sixties.

Sheila Rowbotham too has built on the politics of the sixties, although in a different way.

Her project, in the tradition of the radical historians of the fifties and sixties, notably E.P. Thompson, who sought to recover the hidden history of the working class, was to rediscover the history of women. She too, coming from the new left of the sixties, has *assumed* the central significance of socialism to feminism and yet has also, as has the women's liberation movement generally, been influenced by the meeting of socialist groupings with 'radical psychiatry', the drug culture and the 'underground'. This cultural tradition placed a very high value on the experience and the expression of emotion, on the irrational, and on the individual. Women's consciousness-raising groups drew in part, whether deliberately or not, on this tradition. The women novelists of the sixties, too, were part of the exploration of hitherto unacknowledged feelings, linked quite often with fears of insanity and disorder. The danger of this tradition was that it made of women's liberation a very personal experience, an individual struggle. This seemed to be what Nell Dunn and her friends felt. In a book of interviews, they explored their feelings as young women of the mid-sixties, and for them 'liberation' seemed to mean the space to explore their emotions and sexual feelings, to become 'people'. There was an awareness of women's inferior status, but you could get over it – almost as if it were part simply of growing up:

'We were talking about feeling more confident and certainly a bit clearer by now, our mid-twenties, about what one wants to do, having been through a gargantuan effort to decide and then reconcile it with being a woman. It is rather like being a Negro and having to get over the whole problem of being black before you can write about anything else. . . . If you feel, as one is brought up to feel a second class citizen, inferior to a man in every way, encouraged to think of oneself as the object of a man's pursuit and therefore with no vital life of your own. . . . But having got through that . . . I've got a foothold anyway . . . I'm a person in my own right. . . . I think when you're adolescent you keep writing off panic-stricken for the latest face cream because of dreadful things in women's magazines, making it appear that the whole point of a woman's life is the time when she's attractive to a man . . . It's not all a woman can do . . . I want to feel myself a human being first and a woman second.' (Dunn 1965:56-8)

This personal struggle was not in any way linked to anything political: 'I feel terribly ashamed of myself, I don't understand politics. I think terribly few women are interested in politics and I find them too objective. . . . I'm only interested in things that. deeply involve me' (Dunn 1965:143).

The 'new' movement was partly an attempt to inject this subjective area of feeling into politics. This is partly what made it seem so new.

Sheila Rowbotham has not been immune to the myth-making and stereotyping tendencies of the women's movement and has shared the general feminist over-emphasis on the horrors of the fifties as a period of undiluted reaction. She has also fallen in with the self-appraisal of the radical movements of the sixties, all of which saw themselves as above all *new*:

'Bewilderment and mystery surrounded the birth of women's liberation. It seemed to come out of an ideological lacuna belonging neither to previous feminism nor to Marxism. Orphan-like it had apparently sprung from nowhere in particular, unashamed by its lack of origin or kin.' (Rowbotham 1973b:ix)

This image is valid really only as an expression of how it felt at the time. But in excavating the subjective origins of a movement, there may be a risk of falling between the two stools of fidelity to feeling or to 'fact'.

In *Woman's Consciousness, Man's World*, Sheila Rowbotham tried to trace back the two strands that were so important in the genesis of women's liberation, the aspiration towards individual liberation and the search for a truly revolutionary form of socialism, one that would necessarily incorporate feminism. Her Marxist description of women's-oppression-under-capitalism used women's own accounts of what it really felt like to be an exploited woman worker and a harrassed mother, and was placed alongside an evocative description of the preconditions of women's liberation for one young woman (herself) in the sixties. The very way she wrote, therefore, and the material she used was an attempt to reflect 'the personal is political'.

This is the literature of personal experience welded to the more formal and academic, and it is the *typical* form for contemporary feminist writing. Feminist writings – not unlike the writings of prewar feminists such as Winifred Holtby and Virginia Woolf – have been a literary hybrid combining the polemical, the academic, and the experiential or subjective. But Sheila Rowbotham was a pioneer in injecting the personal so explicitly into *socialist* writing. Sheila Rowbotham's work also took over assumptions of the sixties about sexuality. For her, as for Juliet Mitchell, contraception alone could bring the separation between sexuality and fertility which was *the* touchstone for sexual liberation. (If that were 'true' in an uncomplicated way, surely it would mean that homosexual love must be the most liberated of all? Perhaps it is.) There was also the suggestion that sexuality is of itself subversive, a very 'sixties' idea: 'Hysteria so long contained in the womb leaps exultingly up from under. The female orgasm explodes and scrawls itself generously over the women's lavatory at Willesden railway station, "We are all the same, good or bad, slag or vergin" ' (Rowbotham 1973b:115).

Finally, Sheila Rowbotham's unearthing of women's history in revolutions (1973a) was in part an attempt to find heroines who had been socialist revolutionaries *and* feminists, who had managed to harness these two awkwardly matched steeds to the cart of social progress. Sylvia Pankhurst and Alexandra Kollontai were idealized because they managed to unite feminism and socialism. But to what extent *can* we assume that feminism and socialism are one?

THE MUTATIONS OF FEMINISM

This question is related to another question, one to which different generations of feminists have had different answers. How can feminism become popular politics – and should it? Feminists can claim to speak for all women, for half the population, yet by no means all women (let alone men) support a movement in the interests of women. Many women as well as men feel threatened rather than inspired by feminism. And along with this there have been persistent attempts from all sides to reduce feminism to the mouthpiece of a small élite group whose interests objectively differ from those of the mass of women.

Feminism in its fluidity has tried to achieve popular acceptance by adapting itself to various political positions. The demand for the vote could be related to the wider political spectrum. It could be understood as a demand that rights of equal citizenship be extended to women as well as to working-class men and was clearly related to the political liberalism of the day. Although, therefore, the suffragists did not of course gain universal support, they did place feminism within the broad and 'normal' spectrum of politics. Josephine Butler used the 'cultural lag' argument that liberal reformists were still relying on in the 1950s, arguing that, in an age of sharp transition, rapid industrial advances:

> 'have been unequally yoked with our national conservatism of certain customs, conventions and ideals of life and character. The great tide of our imperfect and halting civilization has rolled onward, and carried many triumphantly with it. But women have been left stranded.' (Butler 1868:xiii)

Once the vote was won, the future of feminism seemed less clear. Some feminists believed the fight was won and that women should concentrate on their status as citizens, should join the wider political battle once more, whether it was for peace, for piecemeal reform, or for socialism. The feminists who worked in the Women's Institutes and the Townswomen's Guilds (Stott 1977) excluded discussion of strongly feminist views as divisive, since their organizations were perceived as being for all women. But whatever hopes of universal sisterhood this concept held out, the result was a-politicism. These organizations were social and cultural rather than political or campaigning organizations. (Yet the feminists of the 1970s have valued that culture of women's arts and crafts more than the immediately preceding generation, and in a strange way the women's liberation movement has retrieved and adopted some of the cultural practices of the Institutes and Guilds – amateur dramatics has become political theatre, while today's feminists bring knitting, crochet, and embroidery to political meetings – and older women militants look askance, since they had rejected these badges of the a-political housewife.)

In the early postwar period feminism attempted to unite itself with Fabian and social democratic welfarist politics (or perhaps it would be more accurate to say that some feminists did this) but became imprisoned within this reformist tradition which also ingested Freudian ideas on child-care. This was the period when an ultimately conservative emphasis on women's difference from men and the special nurturant role of women took over the *progressive* ground. (Eleanor Rathbone's campaign for mothers' allowances had in part reflected this sort of political position between the wars, but the political climate was more propitious after 1945.) Hannah Gavron and Viola Klein were writing more or less from within this perspective. Significantly, the discussion of the origins of women's oppression under capitalism by Alva Myrdal and Viola Klein (1956) was indistinguishable from a Marxist account. Where it differed was in its assessment of the 'dual role' of women in the fifties as part-time worker and full-time mother and housekeeper. Caught up in the liberal illusion that this represented 'choice' for women, they presented this as a solution rather than as the problem it actually was. Hannah Gavron's book (1966) was even more interesting, for in her work a half-suppressed understanding of the deeper springs of women's oppression kept breaking through, yet was ultimately silenced or at least muffled by the reformist framework from which she could not escape.

The contemporary women's liberation movement came in the immediate sense out of a different radical and socialist tradition and has rejected 'reformism' out of hand. In this sense it has adapted itself to the dominant political tendencies of the late sixties. But what seemed like a euphoric rebirth for the left in 1968, for a new left untainted by the legacy of Stalinism, has led to the danger of a new form of imprisonment for feminism, within what has become – or perhaps always was – an often sectarian and ghettoized form of left politics.

Two contradictory and possibly incompatible socialist traditions

have always borne in, confusingly, on women's liberation. One is
the fidelity to sometimes romantic but always highly militant and
usually vanguardist notions of revolution as embodied in Trotskyism; the other is the 'libertarian' and partly anarchist emphasis on
personal liberation, prefigurative life-styles, and spontaneous,
small-scale, grass-roots activities. Women's liberation has at the
same time continued to work hard for small and sometimes incon-
spicuous reforms, and to defend rights that are under attack; yet its
rhetoric has always remained that of anti-reformism, and reforms
have often been perceived as useless or actually hindering us
rather than as being insufficient but useful or even necessary steps
on the way to liberation. Both Trotskyism and anarchism embody
utopian notions of what 'socialism' and 'after the revolution'
means. Utopianism quickly sours into fatalism and pessimism,
because the goal becomes an impossible perfection, and the actual
world by contrast an awful and hopeless conspiracy – and this
political pessimism can fatally mesh in with the feelings of depression, despair and self-doubt that *must* assail from time to time any
woman who is trying to break loose from the oppressive structures
that constrain us in so many different ways. And Trotskyism, with
its emphasis on the 'ultra-revolutionary' demand, so that political
actions are judged less in terms of their tactical wisdom than of
their revolutionary correctness, *and* anarchism, with its individualism, have both made the discussion of tactics and political alliances
difficult and frustrating for women's liberation.

Socialism has had a progressive influence on feminism in
enhancing our awareness of the importance of collective action
and in stressing collective solidarity rather than the individualism,
for example, of women who say: 'I am liberated. I don't need a
movement.' It has also made clear that there *is* a (complex) relationship between the subordination of woman and the inequalities
of capitalism. Yet it would seem to be a mistake to try to collapse
socialism and feminism together in some *new* new left, as Sheila
Rowbotham has argued (Wainwright, Rowbotham, and Segal
1979), a mixed movement in which, nonetheless, feminism has
equal importance with socialism. It seems more appropriate to
reaffirm the autonomy of feminism as a movement which while
making *alliances* with other groupings does not get enmeshed too

closely with their ideological assumptions as happened both after 1945 and in the wake of 1968. Socialist feminism is a relationship rather than either a unity of a pair of parallel lines. Yet the effect of 1968 has been such that today the idea of tactical alliances seems to many women to smack of compromise – yet that fear of being swamped, manipulated, or taken over or of losing one's ideological purity often comes out of weakness rather than out of strength.

CONCLUSION

Although I have described some of the struggles in which feminists engaged in the 1950s and 1960s, my main intention has been to describe how a particular coincidence of economic and political forces in that period created a 'culture' (for want of a better word) in which it was difficult to articulate or to know about any oppression of women. I have also, although very sketchily, suggested that although the scenario changed in the 1970s, so that feminist issues could once more be discussed in a period when politics became more confrontational, the *relationship* of feminism to the political climate did not change. Feminists *absorbed* the prevailing politics just as they had absorbed the political climate of 1945. Clearly no individuals or movements could have remained uninfluenced. In the case of feminism, however (a struggle for fundamental rights – at one level at least – which women still do not have on the same basis as men) this absorption has been unreflective. Feminist theory and feminist writings have reproduced this absorption and have struggled first and foremost to establish a relationship to Marxist theory.

1968 has now in a sense worked itself out. We live today in a bleaker political climate. Many women Marxists are acutely aware (Beechey 1979) of the limited success sustained by feminists in constructing a theory that united Marxism and feminism. At the same time some erstwhile Marxists (Hindess and Hirst 1978; Dews 1979) have swung round to anti-Marxist positions. Women's liberation could easily absorb these winds of change as well, and there is indeed a strong current amongst feminists of hostility to socialism. I am not suggesting that feminism is some pure essence that could exist apart from the specific circumstances at any given time. I am suggesting that we should have a more conscious and reflective attitude to the relationship of the women's movement to the general political scene.

Today a general sense of moral crisis in relation to women is as strong as ever. But whereas Josephine Butler felt that women had been left stranded, today many may feel that women in gaining a higher visibility are outpacing the rest of society in a time of crisis and decline, and, however incorrect, this belief has its effects in terms of tension and confusion. There is no longer any consensus as to what 'woman's place' is or should be. That women have legal and civil rights is on one level recognized and even that they have a right to work. Yet simultaneously on another level when these rights conflict with 'their' responsibilities as wives and mothers, or when women seem to be about to challenge the dominance of men in the workplace, then their emancipation is feared and attacked in case it is destructive to the family, to the affections, or to men.

Yet the present cultural and political climate is hardly one in which the problem of women will be 'disappeared' or become a silence as happened after the last war. Women could be forced out of employment, could be forced, effectively, to make good with their voluntary labour the cuts in welfare services, although it is just possible that the unemployment situation might push men towards a greater share in domestic labour (Coote 1979). But the questions that have been raised about the relationships between men and women cannot be wiped out. Unemployment may well increase rather than diminish the number of one-parent families and separations. History never does quite repeat itself and the ideological retro-chic of the new Freudians of the 1980s cannot mirror the past.

What I have written has been only an interpretation of events. In describing ideological tendencies and trends, in pointing up, that is, similarities, patterns, and even atmospheres, I have necessarily smoothed over some of the contradictions and may have given the appearance of an intentionality where none was. While aware of the subjectivity and fragmentation of the ideological I still think it makes sense to say that after the war individuals and groups in a positive sense set about creating explanations and constructions of the world that had particular effects for women. Far from suggesting a conspiratorial plan to which all were party, this creation of what we call consensus came out of the coincidence of diverse interests and beliefs. But it was not pure accident. And it caused real confusion and real suffering.

Today, things are different. For all its faults, gaps, and uncertainties the *way* in which feminism exists has changed. It exists as a political movement not restricted to a parliamentary perspective; we no longer believe that civil rights are the substance and end of the battle. And it is a movement that attempts to theorize itself. However faltering these theoretical attempts at understanding may seem they represent the first real attempt to move beyond Engels on the one hand and beyond psychological and biological theorizations on the other. We may not seem to have got very far, but today in returning to the 'founding fathers', Marx and Freud, feminists have perhaps done the spadework necessary before more comprehensive and complex theorizations of female subordination become possible.

References

Adams, Parveen (1979) A Note on Sexual Division and Sexual Differences. *m/f* **3**.

Adams, Parveen and Minson, Jeff (1978) The 'Subject' of Feminism *m/f* **2**.

Allsopp, Kenneth (1964) *The Angry Decade* London: Peter Owen.

Amis, Kingsley (1953) *Lucky Jim* London: Victor Gollancz.

—— (1955) *That Uncertain Feeling* London: Victor Gollancz.

—— (1957) *Socialism And The Intellectuals* Fabian Tract 309 London: The Fabian Society.

—— (1960 *Take A Girl Like You* Harmondsworth: Penguin.

—— (1968) *I Want It Now* London: Jonathan Cape.

Anderson, Michael (1971) *Family Structure in Nineteenth Century Lancashire* London: Cambridge University Press.

Anderson, Perry (1964) Origins of the Present Crisis. *New Left Review* **23** Jan/Feb.

Atkins, J. (1977) *Six Novelists Look at Society* London: John Calder.

Aves, Geraldine (1969) *The Voluntary Worker in the Social Services* London: Allen and Unwin.

Bailey, David (1965) *David Bailey's Box of Pin Ups* London: Weidenfeld and Nicolson.

Balbo, Laura (1980) The British Welfare State and the Organization of the Family. In L. Balbo and R. Zahar (Eds) *Interferenze: Lo Stato, La Vita Familiare, La Vita Private* Milano: Feltrinelli.

Banham, M. and Hillier, B. (Eds) (1976) *A Tonic To The Nation* London: Thames and Hudson.

Banks, J.A. and Banks, O. (1964) *Feminism and Family Planning in Victorian England* Liverpool: Liverpool University Press.

Beauvoir, Simone de (1953) *The Second Sex* London: Jonathan Cape.

Beechey, Veronica (1979) On Patriarchy. *Feminist Review* 3.

Bell, Colin (1968) *Middle Class Families* London: Routledge and Kegan Paul.

Bell, C. and Newby, H. (1971) *Community Studies* London: Allen and Unwin.

Betjeman, John (1958) *Collected Poems* London: John Murray.

Beveridge, William (1948) *Voluntary Action.* London: Allen and Unwin.

Beveridge, William (1952) *New Towns and the Case For Them.* Liverpool: Liverpool University Press.

Beyfus, Drusilla (1968) *The English Marriage*. London: Weidenfeld and Nicolson.

Birmingham Feminist History Group (1979) Feminism as Femininity? *Feminist Review* 3.

Booker, Christopher (1969) *The Neophiliacs.* London: Collins.

Bott, Elizabeth (1957) *Family and Social Network*. London: Tavistock Publications.

—— (1971) *Family and Social Network* (Second Edition) London: Tavistock Publications.

Boulton, D. (Ed.) (1964) *Voices From The Crowd* London: Peter Owen.

Bowen, Elizabeth (1945) *The Demon Lover and Other Stories* London: Jonathan Cape.

—— (1949) *The Heat of the Day* London: Jonathan Cape.

—— (1955) *A World of Love* London: Jonathan Cape.

Bowley, Ruth (1949) *Women in a Man's World* London: Bureau of Current Affairs (Carnegie Trust).

Boyers, R. and Orrill, R. (1971) *Laing and Anti-Psychiatry* Harmondsworth: Penguin.

Bradbury, Malcolm (Ed.) (1977) *The Novel Today: Contemporary Writers on Modern Fiction* London: Fontana/Collins.

Brittain, Vera (1953) *Lady Into Woman*. London: Andrew Dakers.

Brophy, Brigid (1962) *Flesh*. London: Secker and Warburg.

—— (1964) *The Snowball*. London: Secker and Warburg.

—— (1966) *Don't Never Forget: Collected Views and Reviews*. London: Jonathan Cape.

Busfield, Joan and Paddon, Michael (1977) *Thinking About Children – Sociology and Fertility in Postwar England*. London: Cambridge University Press.

Butler, Josephine (1868) *Woman's Work and Woman's Culture* London: Macmillan.

Campbell, Beatrix (1980) A Feminist Sexual Politics: Now You See It, Now You Don't. *Feminist Review* **5**.

Campbell, Olwen (Ed.) (1952) *The Feminine Point of View* London: Williams and Northgate.

Carpenter, Humphrey (1978) *The Inklings* London:Allen and Unwin.

Carré, John le (1960) *The Spy Who Came in from the Cold* London: Victor Gollancz.

Carstairs, G.M. (1963) *This Island Now* London: Hogarth Press.

Cartwright, Ann (1970) *Parents and Family Planning Services* London: Routledge and Kegan Paul.

Charles, Gerda (1966) *A Logical Girl* London: Eyre and Spottiswoode.

Chesler, Phyllis (1974) *Women and Madness* London: Allen Lane.

Chesser, Eustace (1958) *Live and Let Live* London: Heinemann.

—— (1960) *Is Chastity Outmoded?* London: Heinemann.

Christian Economic and Social Research Foundation (1957) *Young Mothers At Work* London: SCM Press.

Church of England (1966) *Putting Asunder: A Divorce Law for Contemporary Society*. London: SPCK.

Church of England Moral Welfare Council (1958) *The Family in Contemporary Society* London: SPCK.

Clark, Frederick le Gros (1963) *The Economic Rights of Women* Eleanor Rathbone Memorial Lecture Liverpool: Liverpool University Press.

Coates, K. and Silburn, R. (1968) *Poverty: The Forgotten Englishmen* Harmondsworth: Penguin.

Conway Cross, Beryl (1956) *Living Alone*. London: Odhams.

Cooper, David (1967) *Psychiatry and Anti-Psychiatry* London: Tavistock Publications.

Coote, Anna (1979) Equality: A Conflict of Interests. *New Statesman* 31 August.

Cousins, Mark (1978) Material Arguments and Feminism *m/f* **2**.

Coward, Ros (1978) Sexual Liberation and the Family. *m/f* **1**.

D'Arcy, M.C. (1945) *The Mind and the Heart of Love* (1962) London: Fontana.

Davis, Maxine (1957) *The Sexual Responsibility of Woman*. London: Heinemann.

Dawson, Jennifer (1961) *The Ha Ha*. London: Anthony Blond.

Decter, Midge (1973) *The New Chastity*. London:Wildwood House.

Delphy, Christine (1976) Continuities and Discontinuities in Marriage and Divorce. In Diana Leonard Barker and Sheila Allen (Eds) *Sexual Divisions and Society: Process and Change*. London: Tavistock Publications.

Denning, T. (1960) *The Equality of Women*. Eleanor Rathbone Memorial Lecture. Liverpool: Liverpool University Press.

Dennis, N. Henriques, F., and Slaughter, C. (1956) *Coal Is Our Life*. London: Eyre and Spottiswoode.

Devlin, Patrick (1959) *The Enforcement of Morals* London: Oxford University Press.

Dews, Peter (1979) 'The *Nouvelle Philosophie* and Foucault' *Economy And Society* Vol 8 No 2 May.

Donleavy, J.P. (1963) *The Ginger Man* London: Corgi Books.

Drabble, Margaret (1965) *The Millstone*. London: Weidenfeld and Nicolson.

Driver, C. (1964) *The Disarmers*. London: Hodder and Stoughton.

Duff, Peggy (1971) *Left, Left, Left*. London: Allison and Busby.

Duffy, Maureen (1966) *The Microcosm* London: Hutchinson.

Dunn, Nell (1965) *Talking to Women*. London: Pan Books.

Duverger, Maurice (1955) *The Political Role of Women*. Paris: UNESCO.

Eliot, T.S. (1922) *The Wasteland*. In (1951) *The Faber Book of Modern Verse* London: Faber and Faber.

—— (1944) *Four Quartets*. London: Faber and Faber.

—— (1948) *Notes Towards the Definition of Culture*. London: Faber and Faber.

Ellman, Mary (1969) *Thinking About Women* London: Macmillan: London: Virago (1979).

Erikson, E.H. (1965) *Childhood and Society*. Harmondsworth: Penguin.

Eysenck, H.J. (1954) *Uses and Abuses of Psychology* Harmondsworth: Penguin.

—— (1957) *Sense and Nonsense in Psychology* Harmondsworth: Penguin.

Family Planning Association (1963) *Family Planning in the Sixties*. Working Party Report. London: FPA.

Figes, Eva (1970) *Patriarchal Attitudes* London: Faber and Faber.

Firestone, Shulamith (1971) *The Dialectic of Sex* London: Jonathan Cape.

Fletcher, Ronald (1966) *The Family and Marriage in Britain* Harmondsworth: Penguin.

Florence, Lella (1956) *Progress Report on Birth Control* London: Heinemann.

Foucault, Michel (1976) *La Volonté De Savoir*. Paris: Editions Gallimard.

Freeman, Jo (1975) *The Politics of Women's Liberation*. London: Longmans.

French, Jean (1973) That Bloody Section's Out Again. *Red Rag* **3**.

Freud, Sigmund (1933) *New Introductory Lectures on Psychoanalysis*. (1973) Harmondsworth: Penguin.

Friedan, Betty (1963) *The Feminine Mystique* London: Victor Gollancz.

Fyvel, T.R. (1961) *The Insecure Offenders* London: Chatto and Windus.

Gail, Suzanne (1968) Housewife. In R. Fraser, (Ed.) *Work: Twenty Personal Accounts* Harmondsworth: Penguin.

Gamble, Andrew (1974) *The Conservative Nation*. London: Routledge and Kegan Paul.

Gavron, Hannah (1966) *The Captive Wife* London: Routledge and Kegan Paul.

Geiger, H.K. (1968) *The Family in Soviet Russia* Cambridge Massachussets Harvard University Press.

Gindin, J. (1962) *Postwar British Fiction: New Accents and Attitudes*. London: Cambridge University Press.

Glass, D.V. (1966) Contraception in Marriage. *Family Planning* **17** No. 3.

Glass, D.V., Rowntree, G., and Pierce, R. (1960) *Marriage Survey of the Population Investigation Committee*. London: London School of Economics.

Goldsmith, M. (1946) *Women and the Future*. London: Lindsay Drummond.

Gollancz, Victor (1947) *Our Threatened Values*. London: Victor Gollancz.

Gordon, Linda (1978) *Woman's Body, Woman's Right*. Harmondsworth: Penguin.

Gosling, Ray (1961) *Lady Albermarle's Boys*. Young Fabian Pamphlet London: The Fabian Society.

—— (1962) *Sum Total*. London: Faber and Faber.

Graves, Robert (1946) *The White Goddess*. London: Faber and Faber.

Green, Martin (1959) *A Mirror for Anglo-Saxons*. London: Longmans.

Greer, Germaine (1972) *The Female Eunuch*. London: Paladin.

Grieve, Mary (1964) *Millions Made My Story*. London: Victor Gollancz.

Hall, Stuart and Jefferson, T. (Eds) (1975) *Resistance Through Rituals: Youth Subcultures in Postwar Britain*. London:Hutchinson.

Hall, Stuart and Whannell, Paddy (1964) *The Popular Arts*. London: Hutchinson.

Hamilton, Richard (1962) An Exposition of She. In Russel, J. and Gablik, S. (1969) *Pop Art Redefined*. London: Thames and Hudson.

Harrison, Betty (1974) Minority of Millions. *Red Rag* **6**.

Hart, H.L.A. (1963) *Law Liberty and Morality*. London: Oxford University Press.

Henriques, Robert (1950) *Through the Valley*. London: Reprint Society.

Heron, A. (ed.) (1963) *A Quaker View of Sex*. London: Friends Home Service Committee.

Hewison, Robert (1977) *Under Siege: Literary Life in London 1939 – 1945*. London: Weidenfeld and Nicolson.

H.M. Government (1946) *Royal Commission on Equal Pay*. Cmd 6937. London: HMSO.

—— (1947) *Economic Survey*. Cmd 7047. London: HMSO.

—— (1949) *Royal Commission on Population*. Cmd 7695. London: HMSO.

—— (1956) *Royal Commission on Marriage and Divorce*. Cmd 9678. London: HMSO.

—— (1957a) *Royal Commission on the Law Relating to Mental Illness and Mental Deficiency*. Cmd 169. London: HMSO.

—— (1957b) *Report of the Committee on Homosexual Offences and Prostitution (The Wolfenden Report)*. London: HMSO.

—— (1959) *Report on the Central Advisory Council for Education in England (The Crowther Report)*. London: HMSO.

—— (1960a) *The Report of the Committee on the Youth Services in England and Wales (The Albemarle Report)*. Cmnd 929. London: HMSO.

—— (1960b) *The Report of the Committee on Children and Young Persons (The Ingleby Report)*. Cmnd 1191. London: HMSO.

—— (1963) *Half Our Future (The Newsom Report)*. London: HMSO.

Hindess, Barry and Hirst, Paul (1977) *Marx's Capital and Capitalism Today* London: Routledge and Kegan Paul.

Hobsbawm, E. (1978) '1968 – A Retrospect. *Marxism Today* May.

Hoggart, Richard (1958) *The Uses of Literacy*. Harmondsworth: Penguin.

Holbrook, David (1964) Magazines. In Denys Thompson (1964) *Discrimination and Popular Culture*. Harmondsworth: Penguin.

Holtby, Winifred (1934) *Women and a Changing Civilization*. London: John Lane.

Howard, Ebenezer (ed. F.J. Osborn) (1946) *Garden Cities of Tomorrow*. London.

Hubback, Eva (1947) *The Population of Britain* Harmondsworth: Penguin.

Hubback, Judith (1957) *Wives Who Went To College*. London: Heinemann.

Hunkins Hallinan, Hazel (Ed.) (1968) *In Her Own Right*. London: Harrap.

Hunt, A. (1968) *A Survey of Women's Employment*. London: Department of Employment.

ILO (1946) *The War and Women's Employment: The Experience of the UK and US*. Montreal: ILO.

Jacobs, P. and Landau, S. (1966) *The New Radicals*. Harmondsworth: Penguin.

Jameson, Storm (1950) *The Writer's Situation and Other Essays*. London: Macmillan.

Jephcott, Pearl, Seear, Nancy and Smith, J. (1962) *Married Women Working*, London: Allen and Unwin.

Kaplan, Cora (1979) Radical Feminism and Literature: Rethinking Millett's *Sexual Politics*. *Red Letters* **9**.

Kerr, Madeline (1958) *The People of Ship Street*. London: Routledge and Kegan Paul.

Kinsey, Alfred (1948) *Sexual Behaviour in the Human Male*. Philadelphia: Saunders.

—— (1953) *Sexual Behaviour in the Human Female*. Philadelphia: Saunders.

Kitzinger, Sheila (1962) *The Experience of Childbirth*. London: Victor Gollancz.

Klein, Josephine (1965) *Samples From English Cultures*. London: Routledge and Kegan Paul.

Klein, Viola (1965) *Britain's Married Women Workers*. London: Routledge and Kegan Paul.

Koestler, Arthur (1940) *Darkness At Noon*. London: Jonathan Cape.

—— (1954) *The Invisible Writing* London: Collins/Hamish Hamilton.

Kops, Bernard (1966) *The World is a Wedding*. London: Mayflower Books.

Laing, R.D. (1965) *The Divided Self*. Harmondsworth: Penguin.

—— (1967) *The Bird of Paradise and the Politics of Experience*. Harmondsworth: Penguin.

Laing, R.D. and Esterson, Aaron (1964) *Sanity, Madness and the Family*. London: Tavistock Publications.

Langford, C.M. (1976) *Birth Control Practice and Marital Fertility in Great Britain*. Population Investigation Report London: London School of Economics.

Lawrence, D.H. (1921) *Women in Love* London: Heinemann (1959) London:Ace Books.

—— (1929) *A Propos of Lady Chatterley's Lover*. London: Mandrake Press.

Leavis, F.R. (1930) *Mass Civilization and Minority Culture*. Cambridge: The Minority Press.

—— (1964) *D.H. Lawrence: Novelist*. Harmondsworth: Penguin.

Leavis, F.R. and Thompson, Denys (1933) *Culture and Environment: The Training of Critical Awareness*. London: Chatto and Windus.

Lehmann, John (1966) *The Ample Proposition*. London: Eyre and Spottiswoode.

Lehmann, Rosamund (1953) *The Echoing Grove*. London: Collins.

Lessing, Doris (1962) *The Golden Notebook*. London: Michael Joseph.

—— (1965) *A Man and Two Women*. London: Panther Books.

—— (1969) *The Four Gated City*. London: Macgibbon and Kee.

Leutkens, Charlotte (1946) *Women and a New Socity*. London: Nicolson and Watson.

Lewenhak, Sheila (1977) *Women and Trades Unions*. London: Ernest Benn.

Lewis, C.S. (1952) *Mere Christianity*. London: Fontana.

—— (1960) *The Four Loves*. London: Geoffrey Bles.

Longmate, Norman (1973) *How We Lived Then*. London: Arrow Books.

Macaulay, Mary (1957) *The Art of Marriage*. Harmondsworth: Penguin.

McCarthy, Mary (1960) *On The Contrary*. London: Heinemann.

McCrindle, Jean and Rowbotham, Sheila (1979) *Dutiful Daughters*. Harmondsworth: Penguin.

Mace, David (1948) *Marriage Counselling*. London: J and A Churchill.

McIntosh, Mary (1977) Theories of Sexuality. Unpublished Paper.

McGregor, O.R. (1957) *Divorce in England*. London: Heinemann.

MacInnes, Colin (1958) *City of Spades*. London: MacGibbon and Kee.

—— (1959) *Absolute Beginners*. London: MacGibbon and Kee.

—— (1960) *Mr Love and Justice*. London: MacGibbon and Kee.

MacKenzie, Norman (Ed.) (1958) *Conviction*. London: Macgibbon and Kee.

Mackie, Lindsay and Patullo, Polly (1977) *Women at Work*. London: Tavistock Publications.

Macrae, Norman (1963) *Sunshades in October*. London: Allen and Unwin.

Madge, Charles (1943) *Wartime Patterns of Saving and Spending*. Cambridge: Cambridge University Press.

Manning, Leah (no date) *Growing Up – Labour's Plan for Women and Children*. Labour Party Pamphlet.

Manning, Leah (1970) *A Life for Education*. London: Victor Gollancz.

Marcuse, Herbert (1955) *Eros and Civilization*. London: Sphere Books.

Markham, Violet (1953) *Return Passage*. London: Oxford University Press.

Marris, Peter (1958) *Widows and their Families*. London: Routledge and Kegan Paul.

Marx, Karl (1975) Economic and Philosophical Manuscripts. In *Early Writings* Harmondsworth; Penguin.

Maschler, Tom (ed.) (1957) *Declaration*. London: Macgibbon and Kee.

Mass Observation (1944) *The Journey Home*. London: John Murray.

—— (1945) *Britain and her Birthrate*. London:John Murray.

Masters, Williams and Johnson, Virginia (1966) *Human Sexual Response*. Boston: Little, Brown.

Melly, George (1972) *Revolt Into Style*. Harmondsworth: Penguin.

Millett, Kate (1971) *Sexual Politics*. London: Rupert Hart Davis.

Mitchell, David (1977) *Queen Christabel*. London: Macdonald and Jane's.

Mitchell, Juliet (1966) Women: The Longest Revolution. *New Left Review* **40**.

—— (1971) *Women's Estate* Harmondsworth: Penguin.

—— (1974) *Psychoanalysis and Feminism*. London: Allen Lane.

—— (1978) Erosion of the Family. *New Society*, 2 July.

Mitchison, Naomi (1979) *You May Well Ask: A Memoir 1920 – 1940*. London: Victor Gollancz.

Morgan, Robin (ed.) (1970) *Sisterhood is Powerful*. New York: Random House.

Mortimer, Penelope (1962) *The Pumpkin Eater*. London: Hutchinson.

Murdoch, Iris (1954) *Under The Net*. London:Chatto and Windus.

—— (1961) *A Severed Head*. London: Chatto and Windus.

Myrdal, Alva and Klein, Viola (1956) *Women's Two Roles*. London: Routledge and Kegan Paul.

Nairn, Tom (1964) The English Working Class. *New Left Review* **24**.

Newsom, John (1948) *The Education of Girls*. London: Faber and Faber.

—— (1964) The Education Women Need. *Observer* 6th September.

Newson, J. and Newson, E. (1963) *Patterns of Infant Care in an Urban*

Community. London: Allen and Unwin.

Northedge, F.S. (1970) *Descent From Power*. London: Allen and Unwin.

Nott, Kathleen (1953) *The Emperor's Clothes*. London: Heinemann.

Nuttall, Jeff (1970) *Bomb Culture*. London: Paladin.

O'Brien, Edna (1960) *The Country Girls*. London: Hutchinson.

—— (1962) *Girl With Green Eyes*. London: Jonathan Cape.

—— (1964) *Girls In Their Married Bliss*. London: Jonathan Cape.

—— (1965 *August Is A Wicked Month*. London: Jonathan Cape.

O'Malley, Jan (1977) *The Politics of Community Action: A Decade of Struggle in Notting Hill*. Nottingham: Spokesman Books.

Orwell, George (1949) *1984*. London: Secker and Warburg.

—— (1957) *Inside The Whale*. Harmondsworth: Penguin.

—— (1962) *The Road To Wigan Pier*. Harmondsworth: Penguin.

—— (1970) *Collected Essays and Journalism*. Volumes I to IV Harmondsworth: Penguin.

Paneth, M. (1944) *Branch Street*. London: Allen and Unwin.

Parkin, Frank (1964) *Middle Class Radicalism*. Manchester: Manchester University Press.

Parsons, Talcott (1964) *Essays in Sociological Theory*. revised edition New York: Free Press.

Partington, G. (1976) *Women Teachers In The Twentieth Century*. Windsor: NFER Publishing Company.

Pearse, Innes and Crocker, Lucy (1943) *The Peckham Experiment*. London: Allen and Unwin.

Petersen, William (1968) The Ideological Origins of Britain's New Towns. *Journal of the American Institute of Planners*, Volume XXXIV: **3** May.

Phillips, M. (1978) Family Policy: The Long Years of Neglect. *New Society* 8 June.

Pierce, Rachel (1961) The Extent of Family Planning in Britain. *Family Planning*, Volume X.

Pierotti, A.M. (1963) *The Story of the National Union of Women Teachers* Richmond, Surrey: NUT.

Pincus, Lily (1961) *Marriage: Studies in Emotional Conflict and Growth*. London: Tavistock Publications.

Plath, Sylvia (1965) *Ariel*. London: Faber and Faber.

—— (1975) *Letters Home*. London: Faber and Faber.

Platt, Anthony (1969) *The Child Savers: The Invention of Delinquency*. Chicago/London: Chicago University Press.

Platt, Jennifer (1971) *Social Research in Bethnal Green*. London: Macmillan.

Potter, Dennis (1960) *The Glittering Coffin*. London: Victor Gollancz.

Powell, Anthony (1971) *Books Do Furnish A Room*. London: Heinemann.

Public Records Office (1941-46) Formation of a National Corps of Domestic Orderlies: MH/55/822 File 93208/5/8.

Raeburn, Antonia (1973) *The Militant Suffragettes*. London: Michael Joseph.

Riley, Denise (1979) War in the Nursery. *Feminist Review* **2**.

Robinson, John (1963) *Honest To God*. London: SCM Press.

Robinson, Marie (1960) *The Power of Sexual Surrender*. London: W.H. Allen.

Robinson, Paul (1976) *The Modernization of Sex*. London: Paul Elek.

Rolph, C.H. (Ed.) (1961) *The Trial of Lady Chatterley*. Harmondsworth: Penguin.

Rosen, David (1974) *Rise Up Women!* London: Routledge and Kegan Paul.

Rougemont, Denis de (1938) *Passion and Society*. London: Faber and Faber.

Rowbotham, Sheila (1973a) *Women, Resistance and Revolution*. Harmondsworth: Penguin.

—— (1973b) *Woman's Consciousness, Man's World*. Harmondsworth: Penguin.

Russell, John, and Gablik, Suzi (1969) *Pop Art Redefined*. London: Thames and Hudson.

Sargant, William (1957) *Battle For The Mind*. London: Heinemann.

Schlesinger, R. (1949) *The Family in the USSR*. London: Routledge and Kegan Paul.

Schofield, Michael (1965) *The Sexual Behaviour of Young People*. London: Heinemann.

Scott James, Anne (1952) *In the Mink*. London: Michael Joseph.

Sedgwick, P. (1971) R.D. Laing: Self, Symptom and Society. In R. Boyers, and R. Orrill.

Seear, Nancy, Roberts, V., and Brock, J. (1964) *A Career for Women in Industry*? London: Oliver and Boyd.

Seward, Georgene (1953) *Sex and the Social Order*. Harmondsworth: Penguin.

Shils, Edward and Young, Michael (1953) The Meaning of the Coronation. *Sociological Review* (new series) **I** No. 2 December.

Sissons, Michael and French, Philip (1963) *The Age of Austerity*. Harmondsworth: Penguin.

Slater, Elliot and Woodside, Moya (1951) *Patterns of Marriage*. London: Cassell.

Snow, C.P. (1964) *The Two Cultures and a Second Look*. London: Cambridge University Press.

Sontag, Susan (1966) *Against Interpretation*. New York: Dell Publishing Company.

Spinley, Betty (1954) *The Deprived and the Privileged*. London: Routledge and Kegan Paul.

Spring Rice, M. (1939) *Working Class Wives*. Harmondsworth: Penguin.

Stacey, Margaret (1960) *Tradition and Change: A Study of Banbury*. London: Oxford University Press.

Storr, Anthony (1964) *Sexual Deviation*. Harmondsworth: Penguin.

Stott, Mary (1977) *Organization Women*. London: Heinemann.

Strachey, Ray (1936) *Our Freedom and Its Results*. London: Hogarth Press.

Summerskill, Edith (1967) *A Woman's World*. London: Heinemann.

Taylor, Elizabeth (1947) *A View of the Harbour*. Harmondsworth: Penguin.

—— (1949) *A Wreath of Roses* Harmondsworth: Penguin.

—— (1951) *A Game of Hide and Seek*. London: Peter Davies.

Thomas, Caitlin (1957) *Leftover Life to Kill*. London: Putnam.

Thompson, E.P. (1960) *Out of Apathy*. London: Stevens and Sons.

—— (1968) *The Making of the English Working Class*. Harmondsworth: Penguin.

—— (1977) *The Poverty of Theory and Other Essays*. London: The Merlin Press.

Titmuss, R.M. (1963) *Essays on the Welfare State*. London: Allen and Unwin.

Townsend, Peter (1957) *The Family Life of Old People*. London: Routledge and Kegan Paul.

Trilling, Lionel (1957) The Kinsey Report. In *The Liberal Imagination*. New York: The Viking Press.

TUC (1946–1968) Congress Reports.

Wain, John (1962) *Sprightly Running*. London: Macmillan.

Wainwright, Hilary, Rowbotham, Sheila and Segal, Lynne (1979) *Beyond The Fragments – Feminism and the Making of Socialism*. London: Newcastle Socialist Centre and Islington Community Press.

Walker, Kenneth and Whitney, Olwen (1965) *The Family and Marriage in a Changing World*. London: Victor Gollancz.

Wallis, J.H. (1968) *Marriage Guidance: A New Introduction*. London: Routledge and Kegan Paul.

Wallis, J.H. and Booker, H.S. (1958) *Marriage Counselling*. London: Routledge and Kegan Paul.

Waugh, Evelyn (1945)*Brideshead Revisited*. London: Chapman and Hall.

Weeks, Jeffrey (1977) *Coming Out*. London: Quartet Books.

Welch, Jane (1953) *Not Like This*. London: Lawrence and Wishart.

Werskey, Gary (1978) *The Visible College*. London: Allen Lane.

Westergaard, John and Resler, Henrietta (1975) *Class in a Capitalist Society*. London: Heinemann.

White, Antonia (1950) *The Lost Traveller*. London: Virago.

—— (1952) *The Sugar House*. London: Virago.

—— (1954) *Beyond The Glass*. London: Virago.

White, Cynthia (1977) *The Women's Periodical Press in Britain 1946 – 1976*. Royal Commission on the Press Working Paper number 4 London: HMSO.

Whiteman, P. (1953) *Speaking as a Woman*. London: Chapman and Hall.

Wildeblood, Peter (1955) *Against the Law*. Harmondsworth: Penguin.

Williams, Pat (1969) *Working Wonders*. London: Hodder and Stoughton.

Williams, Raymond (1961) *Culture and Society*. Harmondsworth: Penguin.

—— (1964) *Border Country*. Harmondsworth: Penguin.

—— (1967a) *Communications*. Harmondsworth: Penguin.

—— (Ed.) (1967b) *The May Day Manifesto*. Harmondsworth: Penguin.

—— (1971) *Orwell*. London: Fontana.

Williams Ellis, Amabel (no date) *Is Woman's Place in the Home?* Labour Party Discussion Series number 9.

Willoughby, G. (1951) The Social and Economic Factors Influencing the Employment of Married Women *Journal of the Royal Sanitary Institute* 3 May.

Wilson, Angus (1952) *Hemlock and After*. London: Secker and Warburg.

—— (1968) Sexual Revolution. *The Listener* 10th October.

Wilson, Colin (1956) *The Outsider*. London: Victor Gollancz.

Wilson, Elizabeth (1977) *Women and the Welfare State*. London: Tavistock Publications.

—— (1980) Beyond The Ghetto: Thoughts on *Beyond The Fragments – Feminism and the Making of Socialism* by Hilary Wainwright, Sheila Rowbotham and Lynne Segal *Feminist Review* 4.

Women's Group on Public Welfare (1962) *The Education and Training of Girls*. London: National Council of Social Service.

Women's TUC (1948–1968) *Women Workers*.

Wood, Neal (1959) *Communism and British Intellectuals*. London: Victor Gollancz.

Woolf, Virginia (1938) *Three Guineas*. London: Hogarth Press.

—— (1979) *Women Writing*. Introduced by Michele Barrett. London: The Women's Press.

Wootton, Barbara (1959) *Social Science and Social Pathology*. London: Routledge and Kegan Paul.

Wright, Helena (1947) *More About the Sex Factor in Marriage*. London: Williams and Northgate.

Wright, Helena (1968) *Sex and Society*. London: Allen and Unwin.

Young, Michael (1952) Distribution of Income Within the Family *British Journal of Sociology* **III** No. 4.

Young, Michael and Willmott, Peter (1957) *Family and Kinship in East London*. London: Routledge and Kegan Paul.

—— (1961) Review of Survey Research. *Sociological Review* (new series) **IX** No. 2.

Zweig, Ferdynand (1952) *Women's Life and Labour*. London: Victor Gollancz.

—— (1961) *The Worker in an Affluent Society*. London: Heinemann.

Name index

Subject index